THE MI

& THE FLORIDA KEYS

There are more than one hundred and fifty
Rough Guide travel, phrasebook, and music titles,
covering destinations from Amsterdam to Zimbabwe,
languages from Czech to Thai, and music from
World to Opera and Jazz

Forthcoming titles include

Alaska • Copenhagen
Ibiza & Formentera • Iceland

Rough Guides on the Internet

www.roughguides.com

Rough Guide Credits

Text editor: Mary Beth Maioli
Series editor: Mark Ellingham
Typesetting: Katie Pringle
Cartography: Melissa Flack
Proofreading: Margaret Doyle

Publishing Information

This first edition published August 2000 by
Rough Guides Ltd, 62–70 Shorts Gardens, London, WC2H 9AB

Distributed by the Penguin Group:
Penguin Books Ltd, 27 Wrights Lane, London W8 5TZ
Penguin Putnam, Inc., 375 Hudson Street, New York, NY 10014, USA
Penguin Books Australia Ltd, 487 Maroondah Highway,
PO Box 257, Ringwood, Victoria 3134, Australia
Penguin Books Canada Ltd, 10 Alcorn Avenue,
Toronto, Ontario, Canada M4V 1E4
Penguin Books (NZ) Ltd, 182–190 Wairau Road,
Auckland 10, New Zealand

Typeset in Bembo and Helvetica to an original design by Henry Iles.
Printed in Spain by Graphy Cems.

The publishers and authors have done their best to
ensure the accuracy and currency of all the information
in *The Rough Guide to Miami & the Florida Keys*;
however, they can accept no responsibility for any loss,
injury or inconvenience sustained by any traveler as a
result of information or advice contained in the guide.

THE MINI ROUGH GUIDE TO

MIAMI

& THE FLORIDA KEYS

by Loretta Chilcoat

ROUGH
GUIDES

We set out to do something different when the first Rough Guide was published in 1982. Mark Ellingham, just out of university, was traveling in Greece. He brought along the popular guides of the day, but found they were all lacking in some way. They were either strong on ruins and museums but went on for pages without mentioning a beach or taverna. Or they were so conscious of the need to save money that they lost sight of Greece's cultural and historical significance. Also, none of the books told him anything about Greece's contemporary life – its politics, its culture, its people, and how they lived.

So with no job in prospect, Mark decided to write his own guidebook, one which aimed to provide practical information that was second to none, detailing the best beaches and the hottest clubs and restaurants, while also giving hard-hitting accounts of every sight, both famous and obscure, and providing up-to-the-minute information on contemporary culture. It was a guide that encouraged independent travelers to find the best of Greece, and was a great success, getting shortlisted for the Thomas Cook travel guide award, and encouraging Mark, along with three friends, to expand the series.

The Rough Guide list grew rapidly and the letters flooded in, indicating a much broader readership than had been anticipated, but one which uniformly appreciated the Rough Guide mix of practical detail and humour, irreverence and enthusiasm. Things haven't changed. The same four friends who began the series are still the caretakers of the Rough Guide mission today: to provide the most reliable, up-to-date and entertaining information to independent-minded travelers of all ages, on all budgets.

We now publish more than 150 titles and have offices in London and New York. The travel guides are written and researched by a dedicated team of more than 100 authors, based in Britain, Europe, the USA and Australia. We have also created a unique series of phrasebooks to accompany the travel series, along with an acclaimed series of music guides, and a best-selling pocket guide to the Internet and World Wide Web. We also publish comprehensive travel information on our Web site: **www.roughguides.com**

Help Us Update

We've gone to a lot of effort to ensure that this first edition of *The Rough Guide to Miami & the Florida Keys* is as up to date and accurate as possible. However, if you feel there are places we've underrated or over-praised, or find we've missed something good or covered something which has now gone, then please write: suggestions, comments or corrections are much appreciated.

We'll credit all contributions, and send a copy of the next edition (or any other Rough Guide if you prefer) for the best letters. Please mark letters: "Rough Guide Miami Update" and send to:

Rough Guides, 62–70 Shorts Gardens, London, WC2H 9AB, or Rough Guides, 4th Floor, 345 Hudson St, New York, NY 10014.

Or send email to: mail@roughguides.co.uk
Online updates about this book can be found on
Rough Guides' Web site (see opposite)

The Author

Loretta Chilcoat has traveled throughout Europe and lived and worked in London for several years as a freelance travel writer. After a few too-close-for-comfort tube fires, riots and bomb explosions, she returned to her home in the US, and works as a writer/producer for a Baltimore TV news station. She has contributed to the Rough Guide to Florida, the Rough Guide to the USA, and the Rough Guides Web site. This is her first mini-guide.

Acknowlededgments

In Miami I would like to thank: Michelle Abram at the Greater Miami CVB for her tremendous help and info for this project, Linda Polansky and the outstanding crew at the Clay, and Jane and Chris Dodgson and staff for late-night canasta and tips on South Beach nightlife.

In the Keys: Didi Bushnell and Stuart Newman Assoc. for accommodation and info, Julie Olsen at Cheeca Lodge, the incredibly calm staff at Cocoplum for holding my hand during Hurricane Floyd, Mike Eden for accommodation and a great restaurant, Ron, John and Pam at Bananas Foster who went above and beyond the call of duty, and Les at Capt. Tony's who kept me safe during the Key West blackout.

Also hearty thank yous to the Rough Guides dynamic duo, Mary Beth Maioli and Andrew Rosenberg, for diligent and ceaseless editing, and Martin Dunford for getting this project started. And to my mom who played banker, receptionist and doctor during my numerous trips. Thanks too to Katie Pringle for typesetting, Melissa Flack for mapmaking and Margaret Doyle for proofreading.

CONTENTS

Introduction

Miami is, by a long shot, the most exciting city in Florida. Orlando may have the theme parks, and St. Augustine the longest history, but this is where the real action takes place, where worlds collide, whether that's the noisy mingling of the Americas or the intoxicating combination of beach culture and modern city living. Set on the cool waters of Biscayne Bay and bathed year-round in the sun's healing rays, Miami owns a tropical climate that helps attract large contingents of retirees and sunbathing young things alike. While its lush foliage and palm-treed plazas provide ample relief all throughout the urban grid, it's the beaches that serve as the stomping grounds for various fashionistas and the beautiful crowd, eager to show off their tanned and toned bodies – if you're not strutting your stuff on the sands of South Beach, you may well spend part of your time ogling those who do.

A long way from its modest beginnings as a nineteenth-century trading post, Miami spent much of the twentieth trying to define itself. With the extension of the railroad in 1896, the city began to lose its backwater feel; a building boom in the 1920s quickly gave shape to the distinct neighborhoods that comprise today's sprawl. Later posing variously as an idyllic retreat, a hotbed for Art Deco architectural experimentation, a cog in the military-industrial complex and a key player in international trade, the city acquired much of its current flavor in the 1950s and 1960s, when the influx of Cubans transformed it into a bilingual city and paved the way for all manner of Caribbean and Latin American groups to feel at home on American soil. Quite unlike most major US metropolises, half of the city's current population (about three million strong) is Hispanic, many of those Cubans, and they contribute greatly to the city's appeal – mostly in the form of authentic restaurants and cafés in strongly defined ethnic pockets – if occasionally some of its more apparent tensions as well.

Politics are no easy business here, and besides having to deal with the rumblings of Cuban exile groups, Miami must cope with similarly awkward tensions between ethnic divisions and social classes. Riots first erupted in black ghettos back in the late-1960s, and periodic outbursts of violence have occurred since. It's no secret that crime, too, was a heavy burden on the city in the late 1970s and through the 1980s, with Miami serving as a key port for the illicit drug trade, not to mention having what was at one point the nation's highest murder rate. Things are far better now, helped by a strong economic upswing, a number of city revitalization projects, and efforts to make streets safer; it should come as no surprise that this refreshed public face has coincided with Miami's emergence on the international scene as a backdrop for photo and film shoots and a breeding ground for new fashion movements.

For the casual visitor, Miami is not overly strong on typical sights; despite a few cultural institutions of some note, the city's attractions number more its diverse peoples, its sensual – almost Caribbean – feel, its hot nightlife, and its undeniable energy. Downtown Miami has most of the modern buildings and museums, but it pretty much shuts down when city workers go home; it also happens to be bordered by some of the most poverty-stricken enclaves of the city. Things spread from there mostly to the south, but it's the small island to the east, Miami Beach, that demands the most attention, with South Beach the noted home to white crushed coral beaches, funky Art Deco hotels, a raucous club scene and trendsetting restaurants. This is where everyone looks like a model or some type of celebrity (indeed, a number of big Hollywood names have sprawling mansions in the city's gated communities and own popular nightclubs); to get an idea of what this part of Miami's split personality truly thinks of itself, there's no better spot than Ocean Drive after dark.

If the pace of life wears you out, Florida's Keys are the perfect place to recoup – thirty miles and a world away from the big city. Spread out like a broken pearl necklace at the southern tip of the state, the string of islands contains the prototype for a laid-back lifestyle, where fishing, rather than fashion, is king; little pockets of civilization dot each quay and run down a solitary connecting road to the southernmost point of the continental US, Key West, a true beach bum's paradise.

When to visit

Miami enjoys consistently warm temperatures year round; thanks to this, many folks flock here during winter time to escape harsher US climates. December through March marks the high season for visitors, when the city is at its most expensive, though there certainly are advantages to coming at this point – the temperature hovers around a perfect 80°F, and some happening festivals occur, such as the Miami Film Festival, Coconut Grove Arts Festival, and the international Boat Show.

The rest of the year is hot, too, with June, July and August well-nigh scorching, or at least it seems that way,

.thanks to high humidity – many businesses down in the Keys, in fact, close during this time, and hotels are more willing to barter for their open room space. You may well wish to avoid the city during this time and come closer to the in-between seasons, in early spring and late fall, though then you run other risks. Hurricane season runs all the way from May to November, and even if the chances of getting caught in one are slim, a hurricane is serious business here, especially in the Keys, where bridges are shut down if the wind blows above 45 miles per hour (hurricane winds are 75mph). Recent hurricanes have forced evacuations from Key West and Miami; as only one road reaches the mainland from the Keys, such an ordeal can take up to twenty hours.

Miami's climate

	High °F	Low °F	High °C	Low °C	Rainfall (in)	Rainfall (mm)
J	75	59	24	15	2.0	51
F	76	60	24	15	2.1	53
M	79	64	26	18	2.4	61
A	82	68	28	19	2.8	72
M	85	72	30	23	6.2	158
J	88	75	31	24	9.3	237
J	89	76	32	25	5.7	145
A	89	77	32	25	7.6	192
S	88	76	31	24	7.6	194
O	84	72	30	23	5.6	143
N	80	67	27	17	2.7	67
D	77	61	24	15	1.8	46

THE GUIDE

Introducing the city

Curving along Biscayne Bay, Miami doesn't stretch far inland because of the natural barrier of the Everglades swamps to the west, but distances between the city's northern and southern reaches are considerable. While some of its districts are compact enough to explore on foot, you'll still need a car or bus to get between them.

The obvious starting point is **downtown Miami**, the small, bustling nerve center of the city. Its streets are lined by garishly decorated shops and filled with a startling cross-section of people, bringing a lively human dimension to an area seemingly dominated at first by futuristic office buildings. Around downtown are regions of marked contrast: its northern districts tend to be run-down and dangerous, known for their outbreaks of violent racial unrest, while just south, some of the city's more opulent businesses and residences line the Miami River. In fact, pretty much all points of interest in Miami radiate south and east from downtown; the northern portions of the city are not very visited at all, practically echoing the division between white and black Miami.

East of downtown, the sliver of **Miami Beach** is connected to the mainland by a series of six causeways racing over Biscayne Bay and is home to the most well-known part of the city – **South Beach**. Most visitors spend the majority of their time here, soaking up laser-hot rays during the day and showing off tan lines at sidewalk restaurants and velvet-roped clubs at night. Also connected to the city by causeway, **Key Biscayne**, further south, feels much more secluded and has few attractions apart from its breathtaking beaches.

Back on the mainland, southwest from the center of downtown, in the blocks between W Flagler Street and SW Eighth Street, **Little Havana** is the nominal fulcrum of Miami's Cuban culture, though of course Cuban influence spills well beyond the neighborhood borders.

The telephone area code for Miami is ©305.

South of Little Havana, the street grid gives way to the spacious boulevards of **Coral Gables**, whose finely rendered Mediterranean architecture is as impressive now as it was in the 1920s, when it set new standards in town planning. **Coconut Grove**, southeast of Coral Gables, vies with South Beach for label of the city's trendiest quarter; beautifully placed alongside Biscayne Bay, it boasts a plethora of neatly appointed streetside cafés as well as some fetching old shops and residences.

Moving beyond Coconut Grove and Coral Gables, **South Miami** has a few curious sights among its otherwise monotonous stretch of agricultural farmland, though to its west is the expanse of the swampy Everglades. Further south still, along Hwy-1, mini-malls, gas stations, and bumper-to-bumper traffic pave the way toward **Homestead**, though your only interaction with this section will most likely be on your way to the Keys.

For background information on the Florida Keys, including details on arrival and getting around, see Chapter 19, "Introducing the Keys."

ARRIVAL

Serviced by two major international **airports** (Miami and Fort Lauderdale) as well as by Greyhound **buses** and Amtrak **trains**, Miami is an extremely easy city to get to. However, once here, you'll find that the city's public transportation is severely lacking, basically servicing commuters and generally not too visitor-friendly. Major **US interstates** deposit car drivers smack in the middle of downtown – a great view of the Miami skyline can be seen from the approaching elevated highways.

By air

Miami International Airport – MIA – (©876-7000) is one of the busiest airports in the country and may seem a bit overwhelming at first. However, there are plenty of helpful signs to tell travelers where to go. The information center is located next to the baggage claim area, and you can make hotel and car reservations there. There are also several ATMs located throughout the airport, as well as a **currency exchange** desk on the lower level. The **Fort Lauderdale/Hollywood International Airport** (©954/359-6100), thirty miles north of the city, also services Miami and is often a lower-priced alternative to MIA, though you'll still have to navigate the remaining distance, either by shuttle bus to hop on the local Tri-Rail commuter service (©1-800/TRI-RAIL), or by rental car.

All **car rental agencies** have offices off-site from MIA and passengers must catch their firm's shuttle just outside baggage claim. Travelers should **naturally be cautious** if they arrive in Miami after dark since the character of certain neighborhoods can change dramatically within a few blocks of each other, including those surrounding the car rental agencies. Without traffic the drive from the agencies is an easy ten-minutes into downtown and the beaches.

Local buses ($1.25 each way, exact change only; 25¢ surcharge to South Beach) depart from several points along the airport concourse; take **#7** (every 40min; Mon–Fri 5.30am–8.30pm, Sat & Sun 7am–7pm) to downtown Miami (approximately a half-hour journey), or the **#J** bus (every 30min; daily 5.30am–11.30pm) to Miami Beach. More expensive, but definitely more luggage-friendly, are the **Airporter**, **SuperShuttle** and **Red Top minivans**, which run around the clock and will deliver you to your address in Miami for $8–30 per person. Look for them as you exit baggage claim. **Taxis** are in plentiful supply outside the airport building; fares are metered and cost around $18 to downtown Miami, $22 to Miami Beach.

By car

Most of the major **roads** into Miami take the form of elevated expressways which – accidents and rush hour permitting – make getting into the city simple and quick. From the north, **I-95** (also called the **North-South Expressway**) streaks over the downtown streets before bypassing the Rickenbacker Causeway and connecting with **Hwy-1** or **S Dixie Highway**, which continues through South Miami. The east-west **Hwy-41** (also called the Tamiami Trail) enters Miami along SW Eighth Street (Calle Ocho), and you'll save time by turning north along the **Florida Turnpike** (coming from the north and skirting the city's western periphery) to reach the **Dolphin Expressway** or **Hwy-836**, which meets I-95 just north of downtown Miami. **Hwy-27**, the main artery from central Florida, becomes the **Robert Frost Expressway** close to the airport and also intersects with I-95 north of the downtown area. The slower, scenic coastal route, **Hwy-A1A**,

Parking

Parking is a nightmare in most cities anyway, but it can be especially frustrating in Miami Beach, where spots are as common as winter coats. Most Art Deco hotels don't have lots because of their small size, and **valet parking**, apart from being expensive, is only available at larger hotels and chi-chi restaurants. One notable option is the budget hotel *Banana Bungalow* (see p.99), which has a small but efficient parking lot for guests. If you're staying in South Beach and aren't planning on traveling every day, put your car in one of the **overnight garages** located on Sixth, Tenth and Thirteenth streets ($4/24hrs weekdays; $6/24hrs weekends). Otherwise, **meters** operate between 9am and 6pm and are a whopping 25¢/15min. Best chances to find a spot are the meters on Meridian Avenue (behind the *Clay Hotel and International Hostel* and Flamingo Park), along the northern end of Ocean Drive, or along Washington Avenue.

joins the city at the northern tip of Miami Beach and continues south into South Beach along Collins Avenue.

By bus

Greyhound buses (✆1-800/231-2222) service practically every major city in Florida, and there is a regular service between Miami and various destinations in the Keys. There are five terminals in Miami, probably the most convenient one at 700 Biscayne Blvd in downtown Miami.

By rail

Miami is the end of the line for rail travel between major cities along the East Coast with **Amtrak** (✆835-1223 or

PARKING

7

1-800/USA-RAIL). Miami's main Amtrak **station** is downtown at 8303 NW 37th Ave and operates daily services to major Florida cities such as Fort Lauderdale (55min), Orlando (5hr 33min), and Tampa (5hr 13min) – a train from New York is an exhausting 27 hours.

GETTING AROUND

Because of its expansive layout, Miami is not a pedestrian-friendly city unless you're staying on the beaches, where the most popular modes of transportation are **bicycling**, **roller-blading**, or just **walking**. If you are planning to just stay on the beach, it's much more cost effective – and less of a hassle – to take a shuttle from the airport directly to your hotel and use your feet to get to the beach and back. Otherwise, to move between Miami Beach and surrounding neighborhoods you'll need a **car,** especially with the lack of a dependable public transit system, which is scatty at best. Traffic congestion is better than most US cities, and only becomes a problem during **rush hour** (8–10am and 4–6pm) and when searching for parking in South Beach and Coconut Grove.

....

**For information on where to find car rental see
Chapter 18, "Directory."**

....

Metrorail

The **Metrorail** runs from South Miami to the northern Miami suburb of Hialeah, though the most useful stops are fairly concentrated near the city center: Government Center (for downtown Miami), Vizcaya, Coconut Grove, Douglas Road, and University (for Coral Gables). Trains run every five to fifteen minutes between 5am and midnight. Stations tend to be awkwardly situated, thus you'll often need to use Metrorail services in conjunction with a bus. One-way **Metrorail fares** are $1.25 and can be bought from the machines at the station. **Transfers** to either Tri-Rail or Metromover are free, but cost 25¢ to the Metrobus. These can be purchased from the bus driver or a Metrorail station transfer machine.

The **Tri-Rail** commuter service (©1-800/TRI-RAIL) runs between Miami and West Palm Beach, north along Florida's east coast, and links directly with the Metrorail at the Tri-Rail stop at 1149 E 21st St. Fares range from $3.50 to $9.25 depending on which zones you are traveling in (there are six zones).

There is also a circular, elevated track in downtown Miami called the **Metromover** (25¢) that looks cool lit up at night and gives you a bird's-eye view of the city, but doesn't really take you anywhere. There are three loops: Omni, Brickell, and the Downtown/Inner loop – the latter of which will likely be of most use as it stops at the Government Center, for the downtown museums, and Bayside for the Bayside Marketplace. It runs daily, about every three minutes, between 5.30am and midnight (6am on the weekends), and transfers to the Metrorail at the Government Center stop are $1.

Buses

Metrobuses cover the entire city, most radiating out from downtown Miami, and run from 4am to 2.30am daily. The flat-rate one-way **bus fare** is $1.25, payable on board with the exact amount in change (no bills); transfers cost 25¢ – just tell the driver once you get on board. Unfortunately, buses rarely run according to schedule, stops are inconveniently located, and you can get stuck waiting for a very long while.

GETTING AROUND

Useful bus routes

From downtown Miami to:

Coconut Grove – #48	Coral Gables – #24
Key Biscayne – #B	Little Havana – #8
Miami Beach – #C, #K, #S	Miami International Airport – #7

In South Beach you'll no doubt notice the loudly painted **Electrowave** minibuses crawling along the road (Mon–Wed 8am–2am, Thurs–Sat 8am–4am, Sun & holidays 10am–2am). They provide a 25¢-ride up and down Washington Avenue, between Seventeenth and Fifth streets, and are usually patronized by folks with not much better to do than ride back and forth at a snail's pace. The buses' major selling points are that they run solely on electricity and are also air-conditioned – a nice option if the hot, southern sun gets to be too much.

Taxis

Taxis are often the only way to get around at night without a car. You won't find them as readily as you might in other large US cities – most of the time you will need to call ahead and book one – though empty cabs do occasionally cruise the streets in search of passengers. **Fares** are $1.80 per mile; from downtown Miami you'll pay around $11 to Coconut Grove and $15 to Miami Beach. Central Cab (©532-5555), Metro Taxi (©888-8888), Yellow (©444-4444), and Flamingo Taxi (©885-7000) are all fairly reliable.

Water taxis

If you're in no great hurry, one of the most interesting ways to get around the city is by **water taxi** (©467-0008). Two routes link to provide an extensive network that stretches from central Miami Beach in the north to Coconut Grove in the south. The **Shuttle Service** (daily 11am–11pm every 15–20min; $3.50 one-way, $6 round-trip, $7.50 all-day pass) runs from the Omni International Mall (north of the Venetian Causeway) to points along the Miami River (ideal for eating out at the numerous dockside restaurants). Picking up the slack at Bayside Marketplace, just east of downtown, the **Beach Service** ($7 one-way, $12 round-trip, $15 all-day pass) continues service south, with mooring points on the west shore of Miami Beach, Virginia Key (the Seaquarium), Key Biscayne (Crandon Park), Vizcaya, and Coconut Grove.

INFORMATION

Miami has few comprehensive **visitor information centers** – you'll fare better with neighborhood information booths and chambers of commerce. The **Miami Beach Chamber of Commerce**, directly across from the Holocaust Memorial on Meridian Avenue in South Beach (Mon–Fri 9am–6pm, Sat & Sun 10am–4pm; ℂ672-1270), is loaded with colorful maps, magazines, newspapers, and brochures galore. The **Art Deco Welcome Center**, 1001 Ocean Drive (daily 9am–5pm; ℂ672-2014), doubles as a Deco gift shop and information provider on South Beach's historic district, and organizes tours of the area.

In downtown, you can pick up brochures and maps from the kiosk outside Bayside Marketplace (daily 11.30am–8pm). The **Greater Miami Convention and Visitors Bureau**, 701 Brickell Ave 27th floor (Mon–Fri 8.30am–5pm; ℂ539-3000), is the official tourist information provider in the city, but caters more to the media and is somewhat awkward to reach on foot. One advantage to visiting, however, is the incredible view of the city from their floor-to-ceiling glass windows on the 27th floor.

If you're spending time in **Homestead**, or passing through on your way to the Keys, stop at the area's **Visitor Information Center**, 160 Hwy-1 (daily 8am–6pm; ☏1-800/388-9669), good for its maps and helpful details on the surrounding area.

The media

Miami's only **daily newspaper**, the reputable *Miami Herald* (weekdays 35¢, Sunday edition $1), is a good source of local and national information. Included in its Friday edition is an excellent weekend listings section, and the paper's online version, *www.herald.com*, is an easy way to check up on the weather and opening times. The most popular source for **local listings** is *The New Times* (*www.miaminewtimes.com*), a free weekly newspaper, chock-full of restaurant reviews, music gigs, club happenings, and upcoming events for the whole of metropolitan Miami and Fort Lauderdale. The free *Miami Metro Magazine* is a reliable, comprehensive city magazine with interesting editorial pieces on local events and a solid listings section for the whole of Miami. The *Fashion Spectrum* glossy (also free) reads like a supermodel brochure for South Beach – but lists lots of good nightlife.

SIGHTSEEING TOURS

If you're looking for a more structured approach to Miami than just ambling around town, you can choose from any number of **sightseeing tours**. There are some particularly good options for seeing Miami by water or air; most of the walking tours are designed around historical themes and provide fine context for the buildings you'll be spotting along the way.

Miami on the Internet

Trying to keep up with Miami's ever-changing nightlife can be a challenging endeavor; fortunately the **Internet** provides some excellent options for staying abreast of the scene.

www.miami.metroguide.net A thoroughly comprehensive listings site with extensive dining, nightlife, and local event links.

www.miamiandbeaches.com Official Miami Visitor's Bureau Web site, where a dancing "Tropicool" logo guides you to current events as well as history, accommodation, and nightlife options.

www.southbeachampm.com An entertaining Web site strictly about South Beach with lively columns like "Beauty and the Beach" and "Personality Parade," plus lists of restaurants and clubs, as well as live shots of South Beach updated every half hour.

www.miamiplaza.com A Spanish-language Web site on Miami and surrounding areas, with listings on current events, accommodation, and restaurants.

www.pieeyedego.com/queer Subtitled "The South Florida Guide for the Terminally Queer," this opinionated gay Web site mixes honest reviews with helpful links.

www.miamiclubs.net Everything you wanted to know about clubbing and nightlife in Miami Beach – there are even audio downloads of the latest music tracks storming the beach.

Walking tours

Art Deco District Tour ©672-2014. Thursday nights at 6.30pm and Saturday mornings at 10.30am. All you ever wanted to know about Art Deco, Moderne and Streamline architecture packed into a ninety-minute South Beach stroll. Tours begin at the Art Deco Welcome Center on the ocean side of Ocean Drive and Tenth Street, and are run by the fiercely protective Miami Design Preservation League (MDPL). $10.

Gallery Night ℂ461-2723. Though not exactly a structured tour, on the first Friday of every month the Coral Gables neighborhood hosts an upscale yet unstuffy celebration of the arts in the area. Free minibus limos take you from gallery to gallery, where you can snack on wine and cheese, while reviewing the local art. Casual but smart dress required.

Historical Museum of Southern Florida and Dr Paul George Walking Tours ℂ375-1621. Dr Paul George, ex-history professor at Miami-Dade Community College and current historian for the museum, conducts a delightful series of walks delving into Miami's lesser-known past. Tours run Oct–June on weekends and cost $15–45 depending on itinerary. The museum also offers overnight nature excursions to such places as Cabbage Key and the Everglades; prices start at $200.

Nature Tours ℂ662-4124. The Metro-Dade Parks and Recreation Department sponsors walking nature tours of Key Biscayne and other nature preserves in the area ($3). A variety of canoe trips through Coral Gables are also offered, some lasting up to ten hours ($20–30).

Water and air tours

Dade Helicopter Tours ℂ374-3737. An expensive but unique bird's-eye view of Miami's neighborhoods and expansive white beaches, soaring through the salty sea air.

Liftoff from Watson's Island (directly across MacArthur Causeway) – daily flights range from 10 to 30min. $55–149 per person.

Heritage of Miami II ℂ442-9697. An 85-foot topsail schooner glides through Biscayne Bay and features glittering views of downtown Miami, Brickell Avenue, Port of Miami, the sprawling Vizcaya estate, and Millionaire's Row. A jolly captain delivers the history in both English and Spanish, and even lets passengers take the wheel...briefly. One-hour tours leave from Bayside Marketplace five times daily, and early-evening cruises promise incredible sunsets over the gleaming city. Call for times ($10).

Sea Kruz ℂ538-8300. Hedonism on international waters: gambling, drinking, and whatnot in a Spring Break-like atmosphere. Cruises depart from the Miami Beach Marina, 300 Alton Rd, weekdays at 1.30 and 5.30pm, Saturdays 12.30 and 5.30pm, and Sundays 1.30pm ($15).

Downtown Miami

Downtown Miami's profusion of gleaming, metallic office buildings towering over smaller Cuban-owned businesses provides a sharp contrast between American wealth and the still being realized American dream. Within but one square mile cultures clash amidst traffic-lined streets, electronics shops, and sidewalks buzzing with wide-eyed tourists, clean-cut Americans with local government jobs, and frenzied businesspeople. It all evokes a feeling of being at the crossroads of the Americas, and if any place can lay claim to such status, this is it.

Since the early Sixties, when newly released Cuban Bay of Pigs veterans came here to spend their US Government back pay, the predominantly **Spanish-speaking businesses** of downtown have reaped the benefits of any boost in South or Central American incomes. The recipients pour into Miami airport and move downtown in droves, seeking the goods they can't find at home. In patches, only the solid US public architecture and whistle-blowing traffic cops remind you that you're not on the main drag of a busy Latin American capital.

Most of the action takes place along **Flagler Street**, running east-west from Biscayne Bay to the Palmetto Expressway. In addition to some choice bits of architecture, this strip holds a decent number of cultural offerings, which begin with the museums and performance centers that make up the **Metro-Dade Cultural Center**. The intersection of Flagler Street with **Miami Avenue** (which serves as the main north-south line) divides the city into quadrants from which all city addresses are determined. To the north of downtown lies **Liberty City** and **Overtown**, two desolate, poverty-stricken districts, which have been at the crux of Miami's racial unrest. Further north still, **Little Haiti**, a two-hundred-block area that centers on NE Second Avenue and 42nd Street, marks one of the most strongly defined ethnic areas in the city, though there is precious little to see, other than the everyday life of a community deeply rooted in their cultural history. More accessible sights loom just south of downtown, across Miami River, where **Brickell Avenue** holds an extraordinary line of swanky modern banks and spectacular apartments.

....

The area covered by this chapter is shown in detail on color map 3, at the back of the book.

....

FLAGLER STREET

Map 3, C6.

Nowhere gives a better first taste of downtown Miami than **Flagler Street**, by far the city's loudest, brightest, busiest strip, and long the area's main attraction. The street showcases quite successfully the architecture on which the modern city was built, beginning with the 1938 **Alfred Du Pont Building**, no. 169 E, which now houses the Florida National Bank. The interior is filled with fanciful wrought-iron screens and bulky brass fittings – typical of the Depression-era Moderne decorative style – along with soothing frescoes of south Floridian life, like swaying palms and depictions of the original Cuban settlers.

Gusman Center for the Performing Arts

Map 3, E6.

Near the Du Pont building, the even less restrained **Gusman Center for the Performing Arts**, at no. 174 E, was erected in the Twenties as a vaudeville theater, and it displays all the exquisitely kitsch trappings you'd expect inside a million-dollar building designed to resemble a Moorish palace. Although it was threatened with possible demolition in 1972, a result of the frantic redevelopment and loose laws on historic buildings, the turrets, towers, and intricately detailed columns remain and the center's original crescent moon still flits across the star-filled ceiling. The only way to get a look at the interior (the exterior is far less interesting) is by buying a ticket for a show: classical and contemporary music and dance are staged here from October to June.

See Chapter 13, "Performing arts and film," for details on attending a show at the Gusman Center.

Dade County Courthouse

Map 3, C6.

West along Flagler Street, at no. 73 W, four forbidding Doric columns mark the entrance to the **Dade County Courthouse**. Built in 1926, on the site of an earlier courthouse where public hangings used to take place, this was Miami's tallest building for fifty years, eclipsed by the NationsBank structure south of the river. Its evening lights show off a distinctive stepped pyramid peak – a visible warning to all potential criminals of its presence. Little inside the courthouse, however, is worth passing the security check for: the juiciest cases are tried in the New Courthouse a bit further north (see p.22).

FLAGLER STREET

METRO-DADE CULTURAL CENTER

Map 3, C6.

Downtown's contribution to the arts comes by way of the **Metro-Dade Cultural Center**, just north of Flagler Street on Second Avenue, an ambitious project of Philip Johnson to create a congenial gathering place where Miami could display its cultural side. It almost worked: superb **art and history museums** and a major **library** frame the courtyard, but Johnson forgot the power of the south Florida sun. Rather than pausing to rest and gossip, most people scamper across the open space toward the nearest shade.

Across the street from the Cultural Center, the **Metro-Dade Center** (also called **Government Center**) chiefly comprises county government offices and holds no interest to visitors except for providing useful bus and train timetables available from the Transit Service Center (daily 7am–6pm; ©770-3131), by the Metrorail entrance at the eastern side of the building. It is also a main stop for the Metromover – see Chapter 1, "Introducing the city."

Historical Museum of Southern Florida

Map 3, C6. Mon–Wed, Fri, & Sat 10am–5pm, Thurs 10am–9pm, Sun noon–5pm; $5.

Facing the piazza with its classic, Spanish tiled roof and white stucco facade, the **Historical Museum of Southern Florida**, at 101 W Flagler St, covers 10,000 years of southern Florida and Caribbean history. Murals, photographs, and artifacts cover nearly every inch of wall space, tracing episodes from pre-settled Florida to present-day Art Deco preservation in chronological order. Transitions between decades (and rooms) are represented by a series of ramps, short walls, and various props.

Though the museum space is fairly small, you'll still want to be selective with what you see. One of the better displays, located on the second floor, focuses on the indigenous Seminole people, with a strong collection of photographs and artifacts that reveals much about the Native Americans' lifestyle (the Creek Indians began arriving in what was then Spanish-ruled Florida during the eighteenth century, fleeing persecution further north). Another fine exhibit covers the trials and tribulations of early Miami settlers, tracing prominent local family names such as Tuttle, Brickell, and Flagler, which crop up in street, park, and bridge titles all over the city. Also well chronicled are the fluctuating fortunes of Miami Beach from its early days as a celebrities' vacation spot – with amusing photos of Twenties Hollywood greats – through to the renovation of the Art Deco strip. Recent history is also covered, with considerable space devoted to the impact of Cuban immigrants and refugees.

....

The Historical Museum offers an informative tour of the City of Miami Cemetery, North Miami Avenue, and NE Eighteenth Street, where some of Miami's earliest settlers are buried ($15; ℰ375-1625).

....

Miami Art Museum

Map 3, C6. Tues, Wed, & Fri 10am–5pm, Thurs 10am–9pm, Sat & Sun noon–5pm; $5, free Thurs 6–9pm.

Directly across the piazza from the historical museum, the quirky **Miami Art Museum**, 101 W Flagler St, showcases international works of art from the 1940s to the present. The museum was previously known as the Center for Fine Arts, and only displayed temporary traveling exhibits, but in 1996 the museum renamed itself and established a permanent collection with works by modern artists such as José

Bedia, Jean Dubuffet, Alfredo Jaar, and Frank Stella. To complement their permanent collection, the MAM also hosts traveling exhibits, which focus on works from the 1940s to modern experimental pieces.

Opposite the museum looms the **Main Public Library** (Mon–Sat 9am–6pm, Thurs 9am–9pm, Sun 1–5pm; closed Sun in summer), which, besides the usual lending sections, has temporary painting and photography exhibits showcasing local literary and artistic talents – the narrow focus of which typically makes them worth checking out – as well as a massive collection of Florida-related magazines and books.

GESU CHURCH, US FEDERAL COURTHOUSE, AND THE NEW COURTHOUSE

Map 3, D5–D6.

Heading further north of Flagler Street and east toward the water, the bustling sidewalks and throngs of cramped stores begin to fade, with a few parks popping up between parking garages and increasingly taller buildings. Dwarfed among these giants, a busy Hispanic procession passes in and out of the 1925 Catholic **Gesu Church**, 118 NE Second St, whose Mediterranean Revival exterior and stylishly decorated interior make a pleasing splash. Nothing else should slow you down until you reach the Neoclassical **US Federal Courthouse**, 300 NE First Ave (Mon–Fri 8.30am–5pm; free), a few minutes' walk away. Finished in 1931, the building functioned as a post office before becoming the city's judicial nucleus. Miami's negligible crime rate at the time didn't require much space, as can be assumed by the small second-floor courtroom, which is highlighted by the monumental **mural** Law Guides Florida's Progress, by Denman Fink, the designer behind much of Coral Gables (see p.53). The sweeping work is a striking

25-foot-long depiction of Florida's evolution from swampy backwoods to modern state; if the courtroom is locked, see if the security guard will grant you a peek. The interior **courtyard** too is worth a look, its medieval style given a modern wash by David Novros' colorful frescoes.

By the late Sixties, Miami's crime levels had become too much for the old courthouse to handle, and a $22 million **New Courthouse** was constructed next door (main entrance on North Miami Avenue; Mon–Fri 8.30am–5pm). Other than size, the major advantage of the new courthouse – a gruesome creation of concrete and glass – is that jurors can pass in and out unobserved: "Getting them out without getting them dead," as one judge commented rather grimly.

BAYFRONT PARK TO THE MARKETPLACE

On the edge of Biscayne Bay, just north of Miami River, **Bayfront Park**, a rare grassy patch, is dominated by the huge Bayside Amphitheater, host to numerous rock concerts and festivals throughout the year. The park is a great spot to relax after a hard day of shopping at the nearby Bayside Marketplace (see opposite), with the bay on one side and the impressive city skyline behind it; in fact, it's difficult to get to unless you've parked at the marketplace, as the Metromover stop is permanently closed.

Between the park and the marketplace, you'll find the **Torch of Friendship** – a continuously burning memorial to John F Kennedy, similar to his gravesite in Arlington National Cemetery. Lining the memorial are plaques honoring Caribbean and Central and South American countries, with Cuba conspicuously absent – making it a popular venue for anti-Cuban protests and demonstrations. The park also features a **memorial** dedicated to the crew of the space shuttle *Challenger* disaster in 1986.

Bayside Marketplace

Map 3, F5. Marketplace: Mon–Sat 10am–10pm, Sun 11am–9pm; restaurants and bars remain open later.

The 1980s saw the destruction of some decaying but much-loved buildings beside Biscayne Boulevard (part of Hwy-1) to make way for the **Bayside Marketplace**, 401 N Biscayne Blvd, a large, pink, open-air shopping mall providing pleasant waterfront views from its terraces. Enlivened by street musicians in its amphitheater and some choice international restaurants, it's not a bad place to while away some time, though the stores are mostly standard-issue chains. To top it all off (literally), a shamelessly oversized guitar rotates from the roof of the *Hard Rock Café*.

The majority of the boat cruises around the bay leave from here, as do the water taxis to Miami Beach (see p.11).

PORT OF MIAMI AND AROUND

Map 2, F5.

To the north of the Bayside Marketplace, endless lines of container trucks turning into Port Boulevard attest to the importance of the **Port of Miami** – one of the world's biggest cargo and cruise ship terminals. Crowds of friends, relatives, and spectators gather to wave bon voyage as the mammoth ships tote passengers out toward the Atlantic Ocean. The best vantage spots to view the cruise ships setting sail are along the MacArthur Causeway north of Bicentennial Park, or from the pier at South Pointe Park in South Beach (see p.36).

  Bicentennial Park, on the north side of Port Boulevard, is a run-down area that you'd do best to avoid, especially at night. Recently, the park was cut in half with the addition of the gleaming American Airlines Arena, home of the **Miami Heat** basketball team. This has done little to improve the atmosphere of the park, however.

Freedom Tower

Map 3, E4.

Just north of Bayside Marketplace across Biscayne Boulevard, the **Freedom Tower**, 600 Biscayne Blvd, orig- inally home to the now defunct *Miami Daily News*, earned its current name by housing the Cuban Refugee Center, which began operations in 1962. Between December 1965 and June 1972, ten empty planes a week left Miami to col- lect Cubans – over 250,000 in total – who were allowed to leave the island by Fidel Castro. While US propaganda hailed them as "freedom fighters," most of the arrivals were simply seeking the fruits of capitalism, and, as Castro astute- ly recognized, any that were seriously committed to over- throwing his regime would be far less troublesome outside Cuba.

   The 1925 building, modeled after the Giralda Bell tower in Seville, Spain, has unfortunately been closed for some time due to restoration efforts. There are no plans at present to re-open it; but in any case, its dramatic stature and Mediterranean embellishments are more impressive from a distance.

MIAMI RIVER AND BRICKELL AVENUE

Map 3, E8–E9.

Fifteen minutes' walk south from Flagler Street, the **Miami River** feeds into Biscayne Bay, dividing central downtown from the corporate banks and luxury apartments lining **Brickell Avenue**. Since the early 1900s, when William

Brickell opened his trading post, this area has been awash with money and the moneyed. It was in fact *the* address in early twentieth-century Miami, easily justifying its **"Millionaires' Row"** nickname with its profusion of mansions and well-heeled inhabitants. While the original grand homes have largely disappeared, money is still Brickell Avenue's most obvious asset: over the Brickell Avenue bridge begins a half-mile parade of **banks** whose imposing forms are softened by forecourts filled with sculptures, fountains, and palm trees.

Brickell Avenue's banks

Far from being places to change travelers' checks, the institutions that line Brickell Avenue are bastions of international high finance. From the late 1970s, Miami emerged as a corporate banking center, cashing in on political instability in South and Central America by offering a secure home for Latin American money. High-rise corporate headquarters like the sprawling **SunTrust**, **Colonial**, and the multicolored and multi-tiered **NationsBank**, the tallest building in Miami, have defined the area and become a familiar icon of Miami's wealth and success, while being matched by a slew of new condos to house the growing business population.

The Atlantis

The lone residential building of any architectural merit on Brickell Avenue, the **Atlantis**, no. 2025, may well be the most notable construction to come out of late twentieth-century Miami. First sketched in a Cuban dive in the mid-Seventies, it was completed in 1983, crowning several years of innovative construction by the small architectural firm **Arquitectonica**, whose style – variously termed "beach blanket Bauhaus" and "ecstatic modernism" – fused post-modern thought with a strong sense of Miami's eclectic architectural heritage. The building's focal point is a gaping square hole through its center where a palm tree, a jacuzzi, and a red-painted spiral staircase tease the eye. You won't be allowed inside unless you know someone who lives there, which might be just as well: even its designers admit the interior doesn't live up to the exuberance of the exterior, and claim the building to be "architecture for 55mph" – in other words, seen to best effect from a passing car.

AMERICAN POLICE HALL OF FAME & MUSEUM

Map 2, F4. Daily 10am–5.30pm; $6; ℂ573-0070.

Quite a bit north from downtown's center, the **American Police Hall of Fame & Museum**, 3801 Biscayne Blvd, occupies the former local FBI headquarters, some distance from any other noteworthy attractions. The first floor contains a somber memorial to slain police officers, though its serious intention is somewhat lessened by the availability of CIA baseball caps, the car from the film *Blade Runner*, and even the ability to have your photo taken in a mock electric chair or gas chamber. Upstairs you'll find a potpourri of police paraphernalia such as a heroin addict's kit, an arsenal of weapons found on highways, the chain gang leg-irons still used in Tennessee – and again some bits of levity, like the signed photo of Keith Richards, who, oddly enough, is a member of the museum's celebrity advisory board.

LIBERTY CITY AND OVERTOWN

Geographically and economically, the noticeably downtrodden areas of **Liberty City** and **Overtown**, north of central downtown, mark the racial boundaries of black and white Miami. Liberty City was created out of a need to alleviate

The Liberty City Riot

In December 1979, after a prolonged sequence of unpunished assaults by white police officers on members of the African-American community, a respected black professional, Arthur MacDuffie, was dragged off his motorbike in Liberty City and beaten to death by a group of white officers. Five months later, an all-white jury acquitted the accused, sparking off what became known as the **"Liberty City Riot."** On May 18, 1980, the night after the trial, the whole of Miami was ablaze, from Carol City in the far north to Homestead in the south. Reports of shooting, stone-throwing, and whites being dragged from their cars and attacked were rife, though often somewhat exaggerated. The violence began on Sunday, roadblocks sealed off African-American districts until Wednesday, and a citywide curfew lasted until Friday. In the final tally, eighteen were dead (mostly African-Americans killed by police and National Guardsmen), hundreds were injured, and damage to property was estimated at over $200 million.

the overcrowded and shameful conditions of what was known at the turn of the twentieth century as "Coloredtown," properly Overtown. Divided by train tracks from the white folks of downtown Miami, Overtown ("over-the-tracks") was clearly a racial dividing line for Miami, and it was only in the 1930s when jazz thrilled a multiracial audience did white residents begin to come here. Such fraternizing has largely receded since, and ethnically the areas have remained rather homogeneous, with few tourists coming this far north. Unless you plan specifically to see either of the two sights we mention below, your best bet is probably to skip the region completely.

The first of these sights, the **Black Archives History and Research Foundation of South Florida**, at 5400

THE LIBERTY CITY RIOT

NW 22nd Ave (Mon–Fri 9am–5pm; free), is dedicated solely to the African-American contribution to the community, and is a good resource for history and information on revitalization efforts in the black communities of Liberty City and Overtown – although such efforts have not yet produced the results that might attract much of a tourist trade. The foundation does arrange guided tours for a minimum of ten people through the black historical neighborhoods of downtown Miami, a very informative vehicle for learning more about this section of town. Not far away, the **African Heritage Cultural Arts Center**, at 6161 NW 22nd Ave, documents African-American struggles and achievements in the area through local art exhibits; there's also plenty of information on hand about current cultural events in the area.

LITTLE HAITI

About 170,000 Haitians live in Miami, forming one of the city's major ethnic groups – roughly a third of them live in **Little Haiti**, a two-hundred-block area that centers on NE Second Avenue, north of 42nd Street. Aside from hearing Haitian Creole spoken on the streets (almost all Miami's Haitians speak English as a third language after Creole and French), you'll encounter bright, colorful shops and exotic smells that conjure a decidedly Caribbean atmosphere. On the downside, many people consider this area a no-go at night due to high crime rates in the area; however, during the daytime it's safe enough to check out the main drag along Second Avenue.

The only real sight in Little Haiti – especially since the closing of the well-known Caribbean Marketplace – is the **Haitian Refugee Center**, 119 NE 54th St, which will give you a greater insight into why Haitians remain one of the more oppressed immigrant groups in Miami. The center serves as legal counsel to those seeking political asylum and acts as a community resource for its tightly knit residents. Small but informative displays illustrate how many locals find themselves scraping by as taxi drivers or hotel maids, hindered by poor education and English-language skills, and by the often racist attitudes of Anglos, Cubans, and other ethnic groups.

Miami Beach

T hree miles offshore from Miami, sheltering Biscayne Bay from the Atlantic Ocean, the long, slender arm of **Miami Beach** was simply an ailing fruit farm in the 1910s when its Quaker owner, John Collins, formed an unlikely partnership with a flashy northern entrepreneur named Carl Fisher. With Fisher's money, the bay was dredged and the muck raised from its murky bed provided the landfill that helped transform the island into what is now undoubtedly the city of Miami's main attraction: a sculpted landscape of palm trees, striking buildings, and irresistible crushed-coral-rock beaches.

In varying degrees, all twelve miles of Miami Beach are worth seeing, though only **South Beach**, a compact area at the southern end, will hold your attention for long. Its rows of tastefully restyled Thirties Art Deco buildings have become chic gathering places for the city's fashionable faces, not to mention the stamping ground of Miami's artists and free-spirits, like Coconut Grove on the mainland. Here, the city's most popular **art galleries** and **nightclubs** lead the way in cutting-edge Miami style.

For a detailed look at South Beach, see color map 4 at the back of the book.

North of South Beach, **Central Miami Beach** was Florida's hotspot of the 1950s, when Jackie Gleason, Desi Arnaz, Frank Sinatra, and Dean Martin made headlines performing at the **Fontainebleau Hotel**, one of Miami Beach's defining landmarks. Further north, **Collins Avenue** (which runs the length of Miami Beach) turns into Hwy-1 and runs along **North Miami Beach**, which doesn't have a lot to kindle the imagination, save a palm tree-studded wooden boardwalk that starts at 22nd Street and runs the length of the beach.

Connecting Miami Beach to the mainland are a series of six **causeways** that offer striking views of the city, especially at night when the lights of downtown buildings twinkle over Biscayne Bay's dark waters. Far and away the best route for reaching the beach is the **MacArthur Causeway**, which sweeps into South Beach from just north of downtown. The causeway parallels the Port of Miami and is in the shadows, literally, of the towering cruise ships awaiting their orders.

....

The MacArthur and Venetian causeways provide the only access to the artificial Venetian Islands, which are dotted with the homes of famous folk like Don Johnson, Madonna, and Gloria Estefan (all of whom live on Star Island).

....

SOUTH BEACH

Miami Beach's most exciting area is **South Beach**, which occupies the southernmost three miles of the island. Filled with pastel-colored Art Deco buildings, up-and-coming art galleries, and modish diners, the neighborhood attracts multinational swarms of photographers and film crews who zoom in on what has become – thanks to the visual famil-

SOUTH BEACH

iarity of *Miami Vice* and MTV's *House of Style*, *Real World*, and *Fashionably Loud* – the hottest high-style backdrop in the world.

Socially, South Beach (sometimes known as "SoBe") is unsurpassed both day and night, its streets and sands teeming with beautiful people rollerblading, soaking up rays, and checking out one another, then continuing their mutual admiration after sundown in the many clubs and bars. **Ocean Drive** is the heart and soul of the nightlife scene – chic terrace cafés spill across the slim sidewalk amid a procession of fashion models, wide-eyed tourists, and flamboyant drag queens. The paralleling streets of **Collins Avenue** and **Washington Avenue** are equally festive, minus the oceanfront view, and hold the majority of velvet-rope nightclubs and swanky-themed lounges – their nondescript, often derelict facades belying the extravagant dance floors and bars inside.

For listings of South Beach's restaurants, see p.107; for bars, p.123; and for clubs, p.131.

In addition to the beach and the nightlife, it is the **Art Deco district**, containing the world's greatest concentration of Art Deco architecture, that lures in the masses. Though there are no great buildings per se, just a great many of them – in fact hundreds in the rectangle bordered by 5th and 23rd streets, Ocean Drive, and Lennox Avenue – this profusion, which mostly occurred during the late Thirties, defined a style commonly referred to as "Miami Beach Art Deco."

Not all of South Beach is so sensuous. As you head west from Washington Avenue, the streets still bear the scars of the poverty-stricken 1970s and the arrival in 1980 of the "Marielitos," Fidel Castro's gift to the US of Cuban criminals and misfits (see box pp.48–49). **Alton Road** is diverting

Miami Beach Art Deco

Art Deco's roots go back to the Paris of 1901, though in the US it only began to take hold as a building style in the 1930s, as the nation shook off the restraints of Classical Revivalism and the gloom of the Depression. Mostly characterized by geometric patterns and sleek colorful ornamentation, along with unusual building materials, it conjured associations with technology and innovation, symbolic of a country on the move toward becoming the first modern superpower.

In the late 1930s, a small group of Miami architects built prolifically in this style, using local limestone and stucco to produce buildings, mainly hotels, that were cheap (and often cramped) but instantly fashionable. Recognizable Florida motifs, such as herons, pelicans, blooming flowers, and blazing sunsets, decorated facades and porches. Nautical themes were prevalent, too: windows resembled portholes, balconies stretched out like luxury liner sundecks, and any ungainly bulges on roofs were disguised as ships' funnels. Many of the buildings were painted stark white, reflecting the force of the Florida sun with matching intensity.

Miami Beach almost lost all of these significant structures a few decades later; they fell into decline and were sought after by property developers wishing to replace them with anonymous high-rise condos. In the mid-1970s, the **Miami Beach Art Deco Preservation League** (Art Deco Welcome Center, 1001 Ocean Drive ☏531-3484) sprung to action and through public awareness campaigns successfully saved numerous buildings. Still, little of the Art Deco district now looks quite like it did seventy years ago: the color scheme was altered dramatically in 1980 when local designer Leonard Horowitz replaced the existing palette of dark and dreary colors with the lavenders, salmon pinks, and seafoam greens ubiquitous today.

enough with its clusters of thrift stores and well-stocked record shops, but in the end is just a typical city thoroughfare, filled with fast-food restaurants and gas stations. Provided you stick to the main streets and exercise the usual caution, however, none of South Beach is unduly dangerous.

Ocean Drive and the Art Deco hotels

The Art Deco district's contemporary look should be assessed from **Ocean Drive**, where a line of revamped hotels have exploited their design heritage. You can venture into any lobby for a closer view, and you'll find many worth visiting for their bars or restaurants (see Chapter 10, "Eating," and Chapter 11, "Drinking"). Among them, the **Park Central**, no. 640, is a geometric *tour de force*, with octagonal windows, sharp vertical columns, and a wrought-iron decorated stairway leading up to the mezzanine level, where monochrome photos of Miami Beach in the 1920s are on display.

....

In Lummus Park, across the street from *Park Central*, the boat-shaped Beach Patrol Station is firmly planted in the sands, unmistakable for its vintage oversized date and temperature sign.

....

The rest of Ocean Drive's highlights are almost too numerous to detail individually; suffice to say that Art Deco details are truly everywhere, found externally in parapets, symbols, doorways, and lettering, and internally with murals, steel and glass fixtures, and mosaic flooring. The *Cardozo*, *Commodore*, *Carlyle*, and *Breakwater* hotels all manage the classic Art Deco hotel look of three floors, each level divided by dramatic stripes, balconies, and color splashes. Other elements to watch for are the nautical and geometric windows on the *Tides*, *Tiffany*, and *Park Central* hotels; the streamline stripes of the *Astor* and *Kent*; the rooftop projectiles of the *National*, *Essex*, and *Tudor* hotels; and flowery moldings of the *Beacon*, *Cavalier*, *Avalon*, and *Chesterfield* hotels. Many residential apartments follow suit with elaborate doorways, friezes, and color schemes, accented by the colorful lifeguard stations flecked along the local beaches.

Versace Mansion

Map 4, F5.

At the corner of Ocean Drive and Tenth Street, an out-of-place Mediterranean-style villa has become somewhat of a ghoulish tourist spot in recent years. The **Versace Mansion** was the home of Italian fashion designer **Gianni Versace** before he was gunned down on his front steps in July 1997, apparently in a motiveless act by noted serial killer Andrew Cunanan. You can't get any closer than the steps, now roped off due to the number of gawking passers-by, but it is interesting to note that the house is pretty much right on the drive, with no high-security trappings – an indication of Versace's comfort level with his neighborhood.

If you walk along the beach side of Ocean Drive at night, you'll not only find it devoid of the crowds but a perfect vantage point for seeing the shimmering neons of all the Art Deco hotels.

South Pointe

South of fifth Street, what was once a small and shabby area called **South Pointe** has been revamped into the shockingly bright orange **South Pointe Towers** – a 26-story luxury condominium complex that dwarfs the stucco-fronted homes surrounding it. The best route through South Pointe is the mile-long shorefront **boardwalk**, which takes you from the southern end of **Lummus Park** to the 300-foot-long jetty lined with people fishing off **First Street Beach**, the only surfing beach in Miami and alive with tanned, athletic bodies even when the waves are calm. You can swim and snorkel here, too, but bear in mind that the big cruise ships frequently pass close by and stir up the current.

South Pointe Park and Government Cut

Map 4, E9. Daily 8am–sunset.

On its inland side, the boardwalk skirts **South Pointe Park**, whose handsome lawns and tree-shaded picnic tables offer a respite from the packed beaches. The park is a good place to be on Friday evenings when its open-air stage is the venue for enjoyable free **music events** (details are posted up around South Beach).

Seats on the southern edge of the park give you a view of **Government Cut**, a waterway first dredged by Henry Flagler in the nineteenth century and now, substantially deepened, the route for large cruise ships beginning their journeys to the Bahamas and Caribbean. You might also witness an impounded drug-running vessel being towed along by the authorities, or hear the neighing of horses, as Miami Beach's police horses are stabled on the eastern side of the park.

Washington Avenue

Running through South Beach parallel to Ocean Drive is **Washington Avenue**, much of it lined with South Beach's infamous clubs, as well as small, Cuban-run supermarkets and some often overlooked restaurants. It's also jammed with outrageous clothing boutiques, perfect for scoring a leopard-print feather boa or four-inch black leather heels (see Chapter 15, "Shopping"). Two of Miami Beach's museums are located here, while a third lies just to the west.

Sanford L Ziff Jewish Museum of Florida

Map 4, E7. Tues–Sun 10am–5pm; $5, Sat free.

During the 1920s and 1930s, South Beach became a major destination for Jewish tourists escaping the harsh northeastern winters. In response, many of the hotels placed "Gentiles Only" notices at their reception desks, and the slogan "Always a view, never a Jew" appeared in hotel brochures. Nevertheless, by the 1940s South Beach had a largely Jewish population and, though today the center of the community has moved north to the area between 40th and 50th streets, a considerable number of elderly Jewish residents remain. The **Sanford L Ziff Jewish Museum of Florida**, 301 Washington Ave, bears testimony to Jewish life not only in Miami Beach but in all of Florida. Housed in an elegant 1936 Art Deco building, which served as an Orthodox synagogue for Miami Beach's first Jewish congregation, the museum documents Florida's Jewish heritage from the eighteenth century to the present day through documents, photographs, letters, and various cultural objects, like special cookware and clothing.

Wolfsonian Foundation

Map 4, F5. Tues, Fri, & Sat 11am–6pm, Thurs 11am–9pm, Sun 12–5pm; $5, free on Thurs 6–9pm.

A dizzying array of objects dedicated to the design arts are on display at the **Wolfsonian Foundation**, 1001 Washington Ave, the brainchild of local millionaire Mickey Wolfson, whose private collection makes up the exhibit. The foundation holds more than 70,000 items, including rare books, industrial design paintings, European furniture,

SOUTH BEACH

metal works, ceramics, posters, textiles, and wallpaper, with works by notable artists such as William Morris and Charles Rennie Mackintosh, all paying tribute to innovative design after World War II. Exhibits explore a range of themes from the Arts and Crafts movement in Industrialist Britain to the relationship between art and science in modern times. Anyone with a passing interest in the decorative arts should find something to ogle over in the spacious galleries, which also provide a wonderfully cool haven from the shadeless avenue outside.

Just four blocks north of the Wolfsonian is perhaps the most enduring relic of the less ornate Depression Moderne style of Art Deco, the **Miami Beach Post Office**, 1300 Washington Ave (lobby Mon–Fri 6am–6pm, Sat 6am–4pm). Inside, streaming sunlight brightens the murals sweeping around a rotunda; there can be few more enjoyable places to buy a stamp.

Española Way

Completed in 1925, Española Way, between 14th and 15th streets, was grandly envisaged as an "artists' colony," but only the rumba dance craze of the Thirties – said to have started on the block, and stirred up by Cuban band leader **Desi Arnaz** – came close to fitting the bill. Following South Beach's social climb in the 1980s, a group of art galleries and art supply stores have tried to somewhat revive the original concept; they now fill the first floors, while above them, small top-floor apartments are optimistically marketed as "artists' lofts." The only building worth seeing here is the **Clay Hotel**, whose narrow balconies and striped awnings make it an excellent example of Mediterranean Revival architecture; Arnaz used to perform in the now-defunct *Village Tavern*, which was inside the hotel.

Lincoln Road Mall and around

Just north of Española Way, between 16th and 17th streets, the pedestrianized **Lincoln Road Mall** was considered the flashiest shopping precinct outside of New York during the 1950s, its jewelry and clothes stores earning it the label "Fifth Avenue of the South." Today the strip is a less pretentious rival to Ocean Drive, its landscaped median strip and gurgling fountains enticing rollerbladers, dog walkers, and wary shoppers. Restaurants and cafés spill out onto the road, often hosting live music. There is also a decent selection of affordable boutiques; see Chapter 15, "Shopping," for details.

You'll also find a number of art galleries here breathing life into what were, a few years ago, fairly seedy offices and shops. The **South Florida Art Center, Inc**, 810 Lincoln Rd, is at the forefront of the recovery, representing local and immigrant artists and acting as a general resource for the art community of South Florida. Down the road, the acclaimed **New World Symphony** performs at the Art Deco Lincoln Theater at no. 555 (see "Performing arts and film," p.146).

The first of two public buildings immediately north of Lincoln Road Mall, the 3000-seat **Jackie Gleason Theater of Performing Arts**, fronted by Pop artist Roy Lichtenstein's expressive *Mermaid* sculpture, stages Broadway shows and classical concerts throughout the year. The space is perhaps best known as the home of entertainer Jackie Gleason's timeless TV show, *The Honeymooners*.

On the far side of the theater, sunlight bounces off the white exterior of the massive **Miami Beach Convention Center**, which occupies a curious niche in US political history. At the Republican Convention held here in August 1968, Richard Nixon won the nomination that would take him to the White House. Meanwhile, as

SOUTH BEACH

Nixon counted his votes, he was oblivious to the fact that the first of Miami's Liberty City riots had erupted just across the Bay.

The Holocaust Memorial

Map 4, E1.
It's hard not to be moved by Kenneth Treister's **Holocaust Memorial**, 1933-1945 Meridian Ave, completed and dedicated to Holocaust survivor and Nobel Peace Prize winner Elie Wiesel in 1990. The sculpture depicts an arm tattooed with an Auschwitz number reaching toward the sky from the center of a lily pond. Surrounding the arm are life-sized figures attempting to climb it, and the horrific story of the Nazi genocide against the Jews is retold in a series of panels that arc around the pond.

The Bass Museum of Art

Map 4, F1. Tues–Sat 10am–5pm, Sun 1–5pm, second and last Wed 1–9pm; $5, second and last Wed 5–9pm by donation.
A little further north, within a sculpture-studded garden, is the fetching coral-rock building of the **Bass Museum of Art** at 2121 Park Ave, adjacent to the Miami Beach Public Library. The museum just underwent a major expansion, overseen by acclaimed Japanese architect Arata Isozaki, who designed LA's Museum of Contemporary Art.

The permanent collection – dominated by European paintings mostly from the fifteenth to seventeenth centuries, with excellent entries from Rubens, Rembrandt, and Durer to name a few – has more than two thousand works on display. It also boasts an impressive collection of textiles, including tapestries and vestments, as well as innumerable architectural photographs and drawings that document the history of Miami Beach.

CENTRAL MIAMI BEACH

The energy of South Beach fades dramatically as you travel north of 23rd Street to **Central Miami Beach**. **Collins Avenue** charts a five-mile course through the ritzy area, past the golf courses, country clubs, and secluded palatial homes of Miami Beach's seriously rich, and the swanky hotels around which the Miami Beach high-life once revolved.

Unlike their small Art Deco counterparts in South Beach, these establishments, such as the *Fontainebleau*, the *Shawnee*, and the *Castle Beach Club*, which all remain, were built upon the notion that bigger equalled better. The high prices reflected the type of visitor the hotels hoped to attract – film and television stars who would lend the area an air of exclusivity. Yet the good times were short-lived; cheap imitations soon sprang up, forming an ugly wall of concrete along Collins Avenue. By the 1970s, many of the hotels looked like relics from another age. Today, many of the polished-up hotels are now occupied by well-heeled Latin American tourists and gray-haired swingers for whom Miami Beach never lost its cachet.

Collins Canal and Indian Creek

The southern edge of Central Miami Beach is defined by the garbage-clogged **Collins Canal**, cut in the 1910s to speed the movement of farm produce through the mangrove trees that then lined Biscayne Bay. The canal is a dismal sight, but improves as it flows into the luxury yacht-lined **Indian Creek**, and along Collins Avenue you'll see the first of the sleek condos and hotels that characterize the area.

The Fontainebleau Hotel

Prior to Central Miami Beach becoming a celebrities' playground, the nation's rich and powerful built rambling shorefront mansions here. One of them, the winter home of tire-baron Harvey Firestone, was demolished in 1953 to make room for the **Fontainebleau Hotel**, 4441 Collins Ave, a "dreamland of kitsch and consumerism" that was emblematic of the beach's high times. Joan Crawford, Joe DiMaggio, Lana Turner, and Bing Crosby were *Fontainebleau* regulars, as was rebel crooner Frank Sinatra who, besides starting a scrambled-egg fight in the coffee shop, shot many scenes here as the private-eye hero of the 1960s film *Tony Rome*. Drop in for a look around the curving lobby, overhung by weighty chandeliers, and venture through the tree-filled grounds to a swimming pool complete with rock grottoes and waterfalls.

Even if you don't step inside you can still view one of the hotel's most striking features: the hotel's southern wall holds Richard Haas' 13,000-square-foot *trompe l'oeil* **mural**, which creates the illusion of a great hole in the wall exposing the hotel directly behind – one of the biggest driving hazards in Miami.

NORTH MIAMI BEACH

Collins Avenue continues for seven uninspiring miles through **North Miami Beach**, enriched only by a few noteworthy beaches and parks. Confusingly, due to the machinations of early property speculators, the four small communities that make up this northern section of Miami Beach lack a collective appellation, and the area officially titled "North Miami Beach" is actually inland, across Biscayne Bay.

Surfside and Bal Harbour

Untouched for years as big-money developments loomed all around, the low-rise buildings of **Surfside**, which begins at North Shore Park, retain a rather appealing old-fashioned ambiance, though the community is currently in the throes of gradual gentricification, and only the neighborhood's **beach**, between 91st and 95th streets, will make you want to stick around.

Directly north, **Bal Harbour**, with its aspirations of "Olde Worlde" elegance reflected in its anglicized name, is similar in size to Surfside but entirely different in character: an upmarket area filled with the carefully guarded homes of some of the nation's wealthiest people. The exclusive **Bal Harbour Shops**, 9700 Collins Ave, packed with outrageously expensive designer stores, is worth a look just to see how much you can pay for the name on the label.

Haulover Park Beach

A better place to spend time in North Miami Beach, especially if you can lose your inhibitions easily, is **Haulover Park Beach**, 10800 Collins Ave, which has gained some notoriety for its reputation as a nude beach. Sprawling vegetation backs onto more than a mile of pristine sand, lined on its south end with families soaking in the atmosphere, and on its north with the occasional clothing-optional volleyball game. Don't let either extreme stop you from heading to the beach's **pier** for an incredible view of the electric neon of the Miami Beach skyline.

Sunny Isles

Beyond Haulover Park, **Sunny Isles** is as lifeless as they come: a place where European travel agencies dump unsuspecting package tourists and where French Canadian tourists choose to return year after year, dominating the fast-food restaurants and tacky souvenir shops along Collins Avenue. You'll quickly get a tan on Sunny Isles' sands, but

NORTH MIAMI BEACH

everything around is geared to low-budget, package tourism and, if staying here without a car, you're likely to feel trapped. Of passing interest, however, are some architecturally excessive hotels erected during the 1950s: along Collins Avenue, watch out for the camels and sheikhs guarding the *Sahara*, no. 18335; the crescent-moon-holding maidens of the *Blue Mist*, no. 19111; and the kitschy Moorish-Polynesian-Deco trappings of the *Marco Polo*, at no. 19200.

Ancient Spanish Monastery

Mon–Sat 10am–5pm, Sun noon–5pm; $4.

By the time you reach **Golden Beach**, the northernmost community of Miami Beach, much of the traffic pounding Collins Avenue has turned inland on the 192nd Street Causeway, and the anachronistic hotels have given way to quiet shorefront homes. You may as well take the Sunny Isles Causeway (163rd Street) to "North Miami Beach," on the mainland, for its one draw, the **Ancient Spanish Monastery**, 16711 West Dixie Hwy. Publishing magnate William Randolph Hearst came across the twelfth-century monastery in Segovia, Spain in 1925, bought it for $500,000, broke it into numbered pieces, and shipped it to the US – only for it to be held by Customs, who feared that it might carry foot-and-mouth disease. Photos in the monastery's entrance room show the 11,000 boxes that contained the monastery when it came ashore – and a docker standing over them, scratching his head.

....

Built in 1141, the Ancient Spanish Monastery is the oldest building in the Western hemisphere.

....

The demands of tax officials left Hearst short of ready funds, and the monastery lingered in a New York warehouse until 1952, when the pieces were brought here and reassembled. The job took a year and a half, prolonged by incorrect repackaging of the pieces. Pacing the cloisters, as Cistercian monks did for 700 years, you can see the uneven form of the buttressed ceilings and rough, honey-colored walls. Now used as an Episcopal church, the monastery is a model of tranquility, its peacefulness enhanced by a lush garden setting.

If you're not driving, **getting to the monastery** is relatively easy but not suggested; each of the following routes leaves you with a nail-biting ten-minute walk through some very dodgy streets. You can try buses #E, #H, and #V from Sunny Isles, #3 from downtown Miami, or services from the North Miami Beach Greyhound station.

Little Havana

Very much a distinct enclave, **Little Havana**, a few miles west of downtown and centered on one bustling avenue, stakes its claim as ground zero for Miami's Cuban culture and is thus a crucial stop for any visitor interested in the city's ethnic makeup. Unquestionably the largest ethnic group in Miami, **Cubans** have had an incalculable impact on the city over the last four decades. Unlike most Hispanic immigrants to the US, who trade one form of poverty for another, Miami's first Cuban arrivals in the late Fifties had already tasted affluence in their native country. They rose quickly through Miami's social strata and today wield considerable clout in the running of the city.

These arrivals settled along the main thoroughfare of SW Eighth Street, known colloquially by its Spanish name of **Calle Ocho**. According to tourist brochures, Calle Ocho and the streets that surround it are filled with old men in *guayaberas* (billowing cotton shirts) playing dominoes and are lined with exotic restaurants whose walls vibrate to the pulsating rhythms of the homeland, but the reality is a bit more subdued. While the sights, smells, and sounds of Little Havana do remain distinctly Cuban, the prevailing mood is one of a community carrying on its daily business, and many of the people you'll pass – at least those under fifty –

are less likely to be Cuban than Nicaraguan or Colombian. In this respect Little Havana is changing, becoming more pan-Latin American. This noticeable absence of younger Cuban residents is a direct result of the wealth that earlier settlers acquired; like their US peers, those who made money after transplanting from Cuba gave up their tightly grouped urban homes for a more spacious suburban lifestyle.

The main strip holds many of the reasons you might come to see Little Havana. Tiny cups of sweet Cuban coffee are sold from street-side counters, the odors of cigars being rolled and bread being baked waft across the sidewalk, and shops sell *Santeria* (a Voodoo-like religion of African origin) ephemera beside six-foot-high models of Catholic saints; you'll even spot the only branch of *Dunkin' Donuts* to sell guava-filled doughnuts. Whatever other sights dot Little Havana – and there are not many, mainly some small parks and monuments – take a back seat to the enjoyment of just strolling along Calle Ocho and soaking in the atmosphere.

The area covered by this chapter in shown in detail on color map 5, at the back of the book.

BRIGADE 2506 MEMORIAL AND MAXIMO LOPEZ DOMINO PARK

Map 5, C5–D5.

The most pertinent introduction to Little Havana is the **Brigade 2506 Memorial**, between Twelfth and Thirteenth avenues on Calle Ocho. Inscribed with the brigade crest, topped by the Cuban flag, and ringed by sculptured bullets, this simple stone remembers those who

Cubans in Miami

Proximity to the Caribbean island has long made Florida a place of refuge for **Cuba's activists**. From Jose Marti in the 1890s to Fidel Castro in the early 1950s, the country's radicals arrived here to campaign and raise funds. Still, it was not until the second half of the twentieth century that Miami became the center of Cuban emigré life.

During the mid-1950s, opposition to Cuba's Batista dictatorship saw Cubans begin to trickle in to the predominantly Jewish section of Miami called Riverside, taking over low-rent properties vacated by the increasingly wealthy extant community. The trickle became a flood when Fidel Castro took power, and soon Cuban-run businesses began to pop up in the neighborhood, which quickly became known as Little Havana. Those who left Cuba were not peasants but the affluent middle classes with the most to lose under communism. They arrived in Little Havana with nothing, and, over the course of two decades, wheedled their way back to positions of power and influence – or so the story goes.

The second great Cuban influx into Miami was of a different social nature and racial composition: the **Mariel boatlift** brought 125,000 predominantly black islanders from the Cuban port of Mariel to Miami in May 1980. Unlike their predecessors, these arrivals were poor and uneducated, and a fifth were fresh from Cuban jails – incarcerated for criminal rather than political acts. Bluntly put, Castro had called the bluff of the US administration and dumped his misfits on Miami. Only a few of this wave wound up in Little Havana: most "Marielitos" settled in South Beach, where they proceeded to terrorize the local community, thereby becoming a source of embarrassment to Miami's longer-established and determinedly respectable Cubans.

Exile politics

However much Miami Cubans have prospered in the US, for many the "liberation" of Cuba is rarely far from their minds. Some older Cubans still consider themselves to be in exile, though few would truly think about giving up their comfortable lifestyles to return, regardless of the governing regime.

Within Cuban exile politics, there's a major rift: one school of thought resents President Kennedy's supposed selling out of Cuba during the Bay of Pigs in 1961 (in fact, in 1978 the US government's House Select Committee on Assassinations listed a Miami-based Cuban "action group," Alpha 66, as having the means and motives, plus unsubstantiated links to Lee Harvey Oswald, to have assassinated Kennedy) and favors a violent overthrow of the communist regime. A more pragmatic line runs that the only useful avenue for exiled Cubans is to use their economic clout to bring about changes.

Passions definitely run high on the subject, and violent action has been prized in the past: in Miami, Cubans even *suspected* of advocating dialogue with Castro have been killed; and one man had his legs blown off for suggesting violence on the streets was counterproductive. Recent events have further inflamed exiles, if not yet to violent extremes. In 1995 President Clinton tightened the reins on allowing future refugees from Cuba, causing an uproar. Four years later, the fate of one Elian Gonzalez, a six-year-old Cuban who survived his boat capsizing – drowning his mother and nine others – to reach US shores in November 1999, raised hackles again. The boy's father, still in Cuba, demanded his return – backed by Castro – while family members in Miami tried to lay claim to him. At the time of writing, a US Court of Appeals is deciding whether Elian should receive an asylum hearing or should be sent home to live with his father. Either outcome is sure to incite protests throughout Miami.

died at the Bay of Pigs on April 17, 1961, during the attempt by a group of US-trained Cuban exiles to invade the island and wrest control from Castro. Every anniversary, veterans clad in combat fatigues and carrying assault rifles gather here to make pledges of patriotism throughout the night. Depending on who tells the story, the outcome was the result either of ill-conceived plans, or the US's lack of commitment to Cuba, selling them out to the USSR when President Kennedy withheld air support from the invading brigade. To this day, sections of the Cuban community hate JFK only slightly less than they hate Fidel Castro.

A less emotionally charged gathering place is **Maximo Lopez Domino Park**, a few yards away on a corner of Fourteenth Avenue; access to its open-air tables is (quite illegally) restricted to men over 55, and this is one place where you really will see old men in *guayaberas* playing dominoes, just like the brochures promise.

THE LATIN QUARTER

Map 5, C3.

Besides discussing the fate of Cuba, the domino players in Maximo Lopez Park might also be passing judgment on the **Latin Quarter**, a development meant to replace a line of old buildings on the north side of Calle Ocho. Most Cuban objections to the scheme are to do with the name, which doesn't, they claim, fully represent the Cuban influence in the area – though to be sure, as more Central American immigrants infiltrate the area, the name might well be more apt. Described by city planners as an attempt to "create a world-renowned showcase of Latin American culture," the development seems destined to be a Hispanicized version of Bayside Marketplace (see "Downtown Miami," p.23), with Spanish-style ceramics, plazas, and fountains decorating pricey boutiques and eateries. There's still enough authen-

ticity remaining, however, to make for an enjoyable stroll –
and you can visit any number of locally owned shops that
sell cigars made with Cuban seeds, Cuban smock shirts, and
potent café Cubanos.

....

**For places to find authentic Cuban clothes and goods
see Chapter 15, "Shopping."**

....

WOODLAWN CEMETERY

Open daily sunset–dusk.

West of the Latin Quarter, the peaceful greenery of
Woodlawn Cemetery, between 32nd and 33rd avenues,
belies the scheming and skullduggery that some of its occu-
pants indulged in during their lifetimes. Two former Cuban
heads of state are buried here: a mausoleum holds **Gerardo
Machado**, ousted from office in 1933, while one of the
protagonists in his downfall, **Carlos Prío Socarras**, president from 1948 to 1952, lies just outside. Also interred in
the mausoleum (marked only by his initials) is **Anastasio
Somoza**, dictator of Nicaragua until overthrown by the
Sandinistas in 1979, and later killed in Paraguay.

CUBAN MUSEUM OF THE AMERICAS

Map 5, D6. Tue–Fri 10am–3pm; donation suggested. ⊘529-5400.

With nondescript, low-income housing to the north and
modest Spanish Revival bungalows to the south, there's little to detain you if you stray off Calle Ocho. One prominent exception, the **Cuban Museum of the Americas**,
1300 SW Twelfth Ave, was established by Cuban exiles to
ensure the future of the Cuban legacy in Miami. Its exhibitions of contemporary work have to be carefully chosen to
avoid inflaming local passions, as the museum suffered a

bomb attack in 1989 for displaying the work of artists living in Cuba, regarded as collaborators by extreme anti-Castro exiles. A permanent collection is in the process of being formed, but there is not yet space to display it, so you'll have to be content with whatever's on show at the moment; call ahead if you want to know in advance what you might see.

ORANGE BOWL

Map 5, C2.

There's no point in actually going to the **Orange Bowl** (except for a sports event; see Chapter 17, "Sports and outdoor activities"), but from Twelfth Avenue you can see the rising hump of the 70,000-seat stadium, about ten blocks north of Calle Ocho. Home to the University of Miami's perennially successful football team, the **Hurricanes**, the Orange Bowl may be best remembered by older Cubans as the place where, on a December night in 1962, John Kennedy took the Brigade 2056 flag and vainly promised to return it "in a free Havana."

The campus of the University of Miami is in Coral Gables; see p.61 for an account of its excellent art museum.

Coral Gables

All of Miami's constituent cities are fast to assert their individuality, but none has a greater case than **Coral Gables**. South of Little Havana and slightly northeast of Coconut Grove, it is twelve square miles of broad boulevards and leafy streets, lined by elaborate Spanish- and Italian-style architecture, which make the much more famous Art Deco district over in South Beach seem decidedly uncouth.

The heart of Coral Gables begins and ends along **Coral Way** (SW 24th Street), the main east-west thoroughfare that, where it meets Le Juene Road, marks the center of the fashionable shopping area known as the **Miracle Mile**. Intersecting with Coral Way, the north-south stretch of **Ponce de Leon Boulevard** makes for a lovely walk, taking in the Spanish architecture and canopied avenues that frame the neighborhood. In southwest Coral Gables, wealth moves very much to the forefront, seen in opulent attractions such as the dramatic **Venetian Pool** and the over-the-top **Biltmore Hotel**. Not all is so fashionable and upscale: well south of central Coral Gables, along Biscayne Bay, the landscape is dotted with some lovely parks, such as the **Matheson Hammock Park** on Old Cutler Road and the **Fairchild Tropical Garden** – the largest tropical botanical garden in the US.

For a detailed look at the area covered in this chapter,
see color map 6 at the back of the book.

Some history

Whereas Miami's other early property developers built cheap
and fast in search of a quick buck, the creator of Coral
Gables, a local named **George Merrick**, was more of an
aesthete than an entrepreneur. Taking Mediterranean Europe
as his inspiration, Merrick raided street names from a Spanish
dictionary and enlisted his uncle, accomplished artist
Denman Fink, and architect Phineas Paist, to plan the plazas,
fountains, and carefully aged stucco-fronted buildings.

On the market in 1921, Coral Gables property brought
in $150 million in its first five years, making it Miami's
wealthiest neighborhood. The layout and buildings quickly
took shape, according to Merrick's vision, often working
around potential disasters: he transformed an abandoned
quarry into the Venetian Pool and disguised the construction ditches that ringed the infant Coral Gables into a network of canals and gondolas, calling them the "Miami
Riviera." The placid waterways remain today, running
between the University of Miami campus and a secluded
residential area on Biscayne Bay, just south of Coconut
Grove.

An unfortunate series of events soon ended Florida's
property boom and the visions Merrick had planned for his
exclusive community. First a devastating **hurricane** in 1926
wiped out numerous homes and destroyed the tropical
foliage for miles, and soon after the Great Depression set in,
creating an almost unrecoverable real-estate crash. Merrick
wound up as Miami's postmaster, a position he held until
his death in 1942.

The entrances of Coral Gables

Coral Gables has numerous defining architectural touches, none perhaps quite as striking as the various **entrances** that lead you into the neighborhood. Merrick had originally planned on eight entrances on the main access roads, but only four were completed (Douglas, Granada, Country Club Prado, and Commercial), three of which are well worth seeking out – all along a two-and-a-half-mile stretch of SW Eighth Street. The fourth entrance, Commercial, is at the corner of the Alhambra Circle and Douglas Road but doesn't come close to matching the others in flair or style.

The million-dollar **Douglas Entrance** (junction with Douglas Road) was the most ambitious, consisting of a gateway and tower with two expansive wings of shops, offices and artists' studios. During the Sixties it was almost bulldozed to make room for a supermarket, but survived to become a well-scrubbed business area, still upholding Merrick's Mediterranean themes. Further west, the sixty-foot-high vine-covered **Granada Entrance** (junction with Granada Boulevard) is based on the entrance to the city of Granada in Spain – a massive Renaissance gateway erected by Carlos V in the sixteenth century. The **Country Club Prado Entrance** (junction with Country Club Prado) is an elaborate recreated Italian garden, bordered by freestanding stucco and brick pillars topped by ornamental urns and gas lamps.

Despite these – and future – economic crises, Coral Gables never lost its good looks. A stroll through one of Merrick's elaborate **entrances** reveals that the area is still quite posh, its wrought-iron gated homes, immaculate landscaping, and sweeping boulevards all preserved, in part thanks to some very strict zoning laws.

THE MIRACLE MILE AND AROUND

The best way into Coral Gables from points east is along SW 24th Street, **Coral Way**, which turns into the upscale expanse known as the **Miracle Mile**, between Douglas Road (SW 37th Avenue) and Le Jeune Road (SW 42nd Avenue). This thoroughfare, conceived by Merrick as the centerpiece of his business district, remains the preferred shopping and dining strip of community-conscious locals, in spite of the profusion of bridal shops and travel agents along the way. Even if the occasional spot of splashy Art Deco makes an unusual addition to the more fanciful Mediterranean trimmings here, the blocks still continue to bear the imprint of Merrick's vision.

As you head west along Coral Way – the direction in which the shops get more pricey and exclusive – be sure to take note of the stylistic flourishes on the buildings, notably the spirals and peaks of the **Colonnade Building**, 180 Aragon Ave, completed in 1926 just a few months before the property crash, to accommodate George Merrick's sales office. Now home to a smart hotel, the *Omni Colonnade* (see p.95), its ornate center fountain and surrounding spartan art galleries make for a pleasant stop-off. Otherwise, there are just a few places on and off the strip worth a look.

Actor's Playhouse

Map 6, F4.

Originally built in the 1940s, the **Actor's Playhouse**, 280 Miracle Mile, has recently undergone a dramatic renovation – though fortunately not at the cost of its authentic old-timey feel. Stylish accents like intricately etched glass in the lobby and a gleaming, metallic ticket booth embellish the otherwise rather plain Art Deco building. In addition to attracting well-known shows such as *West Side Story* and

Jesus Christ Superstar, the theater showcases plays from resident writers, theater workshops, and holds a play-reading series performed by local actors (see "Performing arts and film," p.144).

Coral Gables City Hall

Map 6, F4. Mon–Fri 8am–5pm; free.

The Miracle Mile ends with the grandly pillared **Coral Gables City Hall**, 405 Biltmore Way, whose corridors are adorned with posters from the Twenties advertising the "City Beautiful" and with newspaper clippings bearing witness to the property mania of the time. Made entirely from coral rock, the building is surrounded by twelve stately columns and topped off by a multi-tiered, Spanish-inspired **clock tower**. From the third-floor landing you can view Denman Fink's impressive blue-and-gold **mural** of the four seasons, which decorates the interior of the bell tower. Fink also designed the Spanish coat-of-arms that hangs above the entrance of the rounded colonnade. For further information about the historic buildings in the area, pop into the preservation office on the second floor.

Around the corner from City Hall, on Aragon Avenue, is one of Miami's best bookshops, Books & Books; see our review on p.159.

Coral Gables Merrick House

Map 6, C4. Tours on Wed 1–4pm or by appointment; $2; ☎460-5361.

Along a typically peaceful and tree-lined Coral Gables residential street, half a mile west from City Hall, George Merrick's childhood home, the **Coral Gables Merrick**

House, 907 Coral Way, acts as a museum charting his family's history. In 1899, when George was twelve, his family arrived here from New England to run a 160-acre fruit and vegetable farm – such a success that the house quickly grew from a wooden shack into a modestly elegant dwelling of coral rock and gabled windows (the inspiration behind the name of the city that later grew up around the family farm). The dual blows of the property crash and a citrus blight led to the gradual deterioration of the house, until a restoration effort in the Seventies stopped the decay. There's only enough inside to occupy half an hour or so, but the antique furnishings, family photographs, and paintings by Mrs Merrick herself provide some interesting background.

THE VENETIAN POOL AND SOUTH ON DESOTO BOULEVARD

Map 6, C4. June–Aug Mon–Fri 11am–7.30pm; Sept–Oct, April–May Tues–Fri 11am–5.30pm; Nov–March Tues–Sun 10am–4.30pm; year round Sat & Sun 10am–4.30pm; April–Oct adult non-residents $8, children non-residents 3–12 $4; Nov–March adults $5, children $2; ©460-5356.

Coral Gables boasts two of the best swimming holes in the country, and you'll find one of them at the **Venetian Pool**, 2701 DeSoto Blvd (see *Biltmore Hotel*, opposite, for the other). This former quarry sat lifeless until 1924, when Merrick had a vision to transform it into a sumptuous Mediterranean-style pool. Surrounded by shaded porticos, wrought-iron railings, palm-studded paths, and Venetian-style bridges, the deep-blue water winds its way through coral rock caves and spills over two waterfalls. As inviting as it looks, the 820,000-gallon pool maintains a slightly chilly temperature, fed daily with cool spring water. Despite its ornamentation, the pool was never aimed at the social elite;

admission has always been cheap and open to all, with local residents receiving a special discount. Lockers, a changing area, and even a small café (though with designer prices – sodas start at $2) are available.

Coral Gables Congregational Church

Map 6, B5. Mon–Fri 8am–4pm; free.

On land donated to the community by Merrick stands the **Coral Gables Congregational Church**, 3010 DeSoto Blvd. Built in 1925, this relatively small church is a bright Spanish Revival flurry topped by a barrel-tiled roof and enhanced by Baroque decor such as an elaborate bell tower and portal. The building's excellent acoustics make it a popular venue for the occasional jazz and classical **concert**; ask for details at the church office, just inside the entrance.

Biltmore Hotel

Map 6, B5.

Merrick's crowning achievement – aesthetically if not financially – was the **Biltmore Hotel**, 1200 Anastasia Ave, which wraps its broad wings around the southern end of DeSoto Boulevard. The 26-story tower of the hotel is visible from much of Miami, and like the Freedom Tower (see p.24) it was modeled on the **Giralda bell tower** of Seville Cathedral in Spain. The *Biltmore* was hawked as "the last word in the evolution of civilization," and everything about it was outrageous: 25-foot-high frescoed walls, vaulted ceilings, a wealth of imported marble and tile, immense fireplaces, and custom-loomed rugs. To mark the opening in January 1926, VIP guests were brought in on chartered, long-distance trains, fed on pheasant and trout, and given the run of the casino. Activities for the following day included fox-hunts, polo matches, and swimming in the

THE VENETIAN POOL AND SOUTH ON DESOTO BOULEVARD

largest hotel pool in the US – whose first swimming instructor was Johnny Weissmuller, future Olympic champion and the original screen Tarzan.

Although high-profile celebrities such as Bing Crosby, Judy Garland, and Ginger Rogers kept the *Biltmore* on their itineraries, the end of the Florida land boom and the start of the Depression meant that the hotel was never the success it might have been. In the Forties, many of the finer furnishings were lost when the hotel became a **military hospital**, and decades of decline followed. The future looked rosier in 1986, when $55 million was lavished on a restoration program, but the company involved filed for bankruptcy, and the great building remained closed. Only in 1993 did it finally re-open, after another multimillion-dollar refit; if you can't afford to stay here, at least step in to gawk or to take afternoon tea (for $15), or – better yet – join the free **historical tours** every Sunday in the lobby at 12.30, 1.30, and 2.30pm.

The neighboring **Biltmore Country Club**, also open to the public, is as stately as it sounds. You can poke your head inside for a closer look at its painstakingly renovated Beaux-Arts features, but most people turn up to knock a ball along the lush fairways of the **Biltmore Golf Course**, which, in the glory days of the hotel, hosted the highest-paying golf tournament in the world.

For listings of where to play golf in the Miami area, see Chapter 17, "Sports and outdoor activities."

THE VILLAGES

By driving (or cycling) around the less busy parts of Coral Gables south of the *Biltmore*, you'll catch glimpses of several "**Villages**," small pockets of residential architecture intended to add diversity to the area's Mediterranean look. The construction of these houses and townhouses was rumored to be Merrick's attempt at imitating Disney, not surprising considering how many styles they include: Chinese, Colonial, Dutch South African, French city, French country, French Normandy, and Italian. Seek out especially the brightly colored roofs and ornately carved balconies of the **Chinese Village**, on the "5100" block of Riviera Drive and Maggiore Street; the timber-beamed town houses of the **French Normandy Village**, on the "400" block of Vizcaya Avenue, at Le Jeune Road; and, perhaps strangest of all, the twisting chimneys and scroll-work arches of the **Dutch South African Village**, at Le Jeune Road and Riviera Avenue.

UNIVERSITY OF MIAMI: LOWE ART MUSEUM

Map 6, C9. Tues, Wed, Fri, & Sat 10am–5pm; Thurs noon–7pm; Sun noon–5pm; $5.

One of the few parts of Coral Gables where Mediterranean architecture doesn't prevail is on the campus of the **University of Miami**, about two miles south of the *Biltmore*, where dismal, box-like buildings have traditionally accommodated the relatively small student body.

The sole reason to visit the campus is the **Lowe Art Museum**, 1301 Stanford Drive, which was established in 1950 and has, thanks to a 1995 expansion, become Miami's foremost fine arts museum. The diverse permanent collection contains more than eight thousand works covering all manner of styles and periods, with some notable entries from the likes of Isenbrandt, Picasso, Monet, Lichtenstein, and Warhol. As well as plenty of Spanish "Old Masters," nineteenth-century European paintings, and a considerable number of contemporary American works, non-Western art is well represented, in varied pre-Columbian, African, and East Asian galleries, Guatemalan textiles, plus one of the finest Native American art collections in the country.

MATHESON HAMMOCK PARK AND AROUND

Map 2, D7. Daily 6am to sunset; $3.

Before becoming a public park in 1930, **Matheson Hammock Park**, 9610 Old Cutler Rd, was a coconut plantation operating on the southern edge of Coral Gables. The natural hardwood hammock creates a great backdrop for the thousands who come here on weekends to picnic and use the marina. The park also features a man-made atoll pool (a ring-shaped coral reef), filled by Biscayne Bay's tidal action, as well as a laid-back peaceful beach. The sizeable park can get crowded by the bay, but the rest of the sprawling green is often only sprinkled with people, and you can easily while away a few hours strolling around the wading pond or along the winding trails above the mangrove swamps.

Fairchild Tropical Garden

Map 2, D7. Daily 9.30am–4.30pm; $8.
Fairchild Tropical Garden, 10901 Old Cutler Rd, turns the same terrain that fills the Matheson Hammock Park into lawns, flowerbeds, and gardens, complemented by a few placid lakes. A good way to begin exploring the 83-acre site is to hitch a ride on the free **tram** (departing hourly, on the hour, from inside the garden's entrance) for a forty-minute meander along the trails.

Along the way, you'll get a feel for what the aim of the garden is. As a research institution, Fairchild works with scientists from all over the world to preserve the diversity of the tropical environment; many of the plant species here are extinct in their original environments, and part of their efforts is to transplant them to their places of origin. The tropical habitats reproduced in the garden – some more successfully than others – range from desert to rainforest, though curiously there's relatively little space devoted to fauna endemic to south Florida.

....

Hurricane Andrew in 1992 destroyed or badly damaged nearly two-thirds of Fairchild's plants.

....

MATHESON HAMMOCK PARK AND AROUND

Coconut Grove

Despite being incorporated into Miami in the late nineteenth century with the construction of S Bayshore Drive and Brickell Avenue, **Coconut Grove**, finely placed along Biscayne Bay, has always stayed very much a place apart. In its role as one of the city's more iconoclastic neighborhoods, it has gone from ethnic melting pot to bohemian and arty intellectual hangout to a present-day, fashionable place full of art galleries, chic restaurants, and towering bay-view apartments. Some bawdier traces do remain, and the area does boast some of the city's better establishments for drinking and listening to live music.

Originally separated from Miami by a dense, jungle-like wedge of tropical foliage, Coconut Grove was settled in the 1860s, more than a decade before Flagler's railroad brought the masses to settle in Miami. Its early population was an evenly balanced mix of Bahamian laborers who built most of the town, and liberal-minded Anglo settlers who spurred on its growth, creating a racially diverse community with an eclectic bohemian flair. By 1896 when Miami established itself as a city, Coconut Grove was already thriving with the first school in Dade County, a few churches, a yacht club, and a library. Intellectuals lived here. Abetted by this early independence, and by the many liberal-minded artists and leftists who have migrated here thanks to its tolerant attitudes, locals have tried at least three times to secede from the city, though never to any avail.

Laid-back atmosphere aside, the shops near **central Coconut Grove**'s intersection at Main Highway and Grand Avenue are the primary pull for visitors – just strolling along the open-air malls of **CocoWalk** and the **Streets of Mayfair** can make for quite a pleasant afternoon. To the north, the grandiose **Villa Vizcaya** estate is a top attraction as well, and a few other, minor architectural attractions, like the **Barnacle**, the minimalist home of philosopher and naturalist Ralph Middleton Munroe, round the neighborhood out.

The area covered in this chapter can be seen in detail on color map 7, at the back of the book.

VILLA VIZCAYA

Map 5, E9. Daily 9.30am–5pm, last admission 4.30pm; gardens open until 5.30pm; $10.

In 1914, farm-machinery mogul James Deering followed his brother, Charles (of Deering Estate fame, see "South Miami and Homestead," p.78), to south Florida and blew $15 million on recreating a sixteenth-century Italian villa within the belt of vegetation between Miami and Coconut Grove. A thousand-strong workforce, including ten percent of Miami's population at the time, completed his **Villa Vizcaya**, 3251 South Miami Ave, in just two years. The lasting impression of the grandiose structure is that both Deering and his designer (the crazed Paul Chalfin, hell-bent on becoming an architectural legend) had more money than taste: Deering's madly eclectic **art collection**, and the concept that the villa should appear to have been inhabited for four hundred years, resulted in a thunderous clash of Baroque, Renaissance, Rococo, and Neoclassical fixtures and furnishings. Even the landscaped **gardens** aren't spared the pretense, from the intricate great stone barge sitting a stone's throw from the villa in Biscayne Bay, the orange jasmine maze garden and mythological statues lining the walkways, to the series of cascading and gurgling fountains that dot the grounds. The gardens have become a popular backdrop for brides and young Cuban girls celebrating their fifteenth birthday – a celebration called the *quince* – hence you may see brigades of women in white beaming among the rose bushes.

The sheer spectacle of Villa Vizcaya makes it one of Miami's most popular attractions, with much to offer – electric dumbwaiters, secret doors behind towering mahogany bookshelves, a fifteenth-century Moorish rug, and wallpaper panels printed from woodblocks and hand-painted in Paris. Free guided **tours** leave hourly from the entrance loggia – which is dominated by a second-century marble **statue of Bacchus** – and provide solid background information, after which you're free to explore at leisure.

MUSEUM OF SCIENCE AND SPACE TRANSIT PLANETARIUM

Map 5, E8. Daily 10am–6pm, last admission 5pm; $9, after 4.30pm $4.50; rock music laser shows Fri & Sat nights 9pm, $6.

Across from Villa Vizcaya, the **Museum of Science and Space Transit Planetarium**, 3280 South Miami Ave, sets a decidedly more modern tone than its wacky neighbor. The museum aims to make the loftiest of scientific theories available to the average visitor, particularly those under 15, resulting in exhibits like the one that examined space travel through the use of *Star Trek* sets.

At the rear of the museum is a hands-on **wildlife refuge**, one of the permanent displays in the museum. Vultures and owls are among a number of injured birds seeing out their days here at the Falcon Batchelor Bird of Prey Center. A variety of snakes can be viewed here as well at disturbingly close quarters, and the resident tarantula is happy to be handled, if you can stomach the notion. The adjoining **planetarium** has the usual trips-around-the-cosmos shows but with an extremely amusing narrator, and hosts head-banging rock music laser shows on the weekends.

BAYSHORE DRIVE AND AROUND

Map 7, F1–F4.

You'll catch glimpses of limestone jutting through the greenery on the inland side of **Bayshore Drive**, which winds down the scenic coast of Coconut Grove. It was on this ridge, known as **Silver Bluff**, that several early settlers established their homes, later joined by the well-heeled notables of 1910s Miami. A few of their houses still stand, but all are privately owned and closed to the public. Today, the area remains a preserve of the rich, whose opulent abodes are shielded from prying eyes by carefully maintained trees.

The suggestion of major money around Silver Bluff yields to blatant statements of wealth once you draw closer to central Coconut Grove, as Bayshore Drive proceeds past expensive, high-rise condos and jogger-filled, landscaped parks. Heading down Pan American Drive, east off Bayshore Drive, you will arrive at the marina on **Dinner Key**, named for a popular picnic spot for settlers at the turn of the twentieth century and now a mooring for lines of ultra-pricey yachts.

Next door, the **Coconut Grove Exhibition Center** has a history far more exciting than its present status as a car-show venue. It was, in fact, previously known as the

Dinner Key Auditorium, where in 1969 rock legend **Jim Morrison** dropped his leather pants to expose himself during the band's first – and consequently last – Florida show.

Church of Ermita de la Curidad

Where South Miami Drive becomes Bayshore Drive, close to Mercy Hospital, the road off to the left leads to the **Church of Ermita de la Curidad** (Our Lady of Charity Shrine), a sweet Catholic church erected by Miami Cubans in the first half of the twentieth century. A mural behind the altar traces the history of Cuban immigration, and the conical-shaped church is angled to allow worshippers to look out across the bay in the direction of Cuba.

Miami City Hall

Map 7, G3.

The gigantic Coconut Grove Exhibition Center overshadows the more cheerful **Miami City Hall**, 3400 Pan American Drive, the small and unlikely seat of local government that used to be an airline terminal. In the Thirties, passengers checked into this blue-and-white-trimmed Art Deco building for the **Pan American Airways** seaplane service to Latin America, and the sight of the lumbering craft taking off used to draw thousands to the waterfront. In front of City Hall, a small plaque reminds visitors that this is where the veterans of the Bay of Pigs stepped ashore after their release from Cuba in 1962.

Walking from City Hall across the Exhibition Center's parking lot brings you to the *Havana Clipper* restaurant, whose ground floor houses a **historical collection** of photos and old radio parts from the seaplane times (which lasted until improvements to Latin American runways made sea landings unnecessary).

Peacock Park

Map 7, E5.

Peacock Park, at the end of Bayshore Drive beside MacFarlane Road, was a notorious hippie haunt at the time of Jim Morrison's misdemeanors in Coconut Grove. More recently it's been cleaned up to fit the area's sophisticated image, and now holds a few **public tennis courts** and some peculiar abstract **sculptures** sprinkled throughout. Even if you have no business or recreation to pursue here it's worth stopping off for the stunning **views** of Biscayne Bay from the back of the park. Check too to see if any of the neighborhood's numerous food and arts festivals are on while you're here; the park often plays host to them.

CENTRAL COCONUT GROVE

The intersection between Main Highway and Grand Avenue is the Coconut Grove most Miamians know: several blocks of trendy cafés, galleries, and boutiques that comprise, for lack of a better term, **central Coconut Grove**. You can eat, drink, and pose at **CocoWalk**, 3000 Grand Ave, an enjoyable collection of open-air restaurants, bars, and yet more stylish shops. For a taste of sheer exclusivity, drop into **Streets of Mayfair**, at the corner of MacFarlane Road and Grand Avenue, a designer shopping mall whose zigzagging walkways – punctuated with fountains, copper sculptures, and climbing vines – wind around three floors of pricey stores.

....

**For restaurants and bars in Coconut Grove, see
Chapter 10, "Eating," and Chapter 11, "Drinking."**

....

CENTRAL COCONUT GROVE

Coconut Grove Playhouse

Map 7, D6.

Firmly rooted in Coconut Grove's creative heritage is the beige-and-white **Coconut Grove Playhouse** at 3500 Main Hwy. Originally opened in 1927 as a movie theater, it evolved into a top playhouse, and was where Samuel Beckett's *Waiting for Godot* premiered in 1956. Today, the Playhouse is still going strong on a mixed diet of Broadway blockbusters and alternative offerings. Though you're likely to be seeing the inside only if you're going to be checking out a performance (for ticket details, see p.145), you may as well pause to examine the exterior, one of Coconut Grove's best examples of Mediterranean Revival architecture.

The Barnacle

Map 7, E6. Fri–Sun 9am–4pm; $1; tours depart at 10 & 11.30am, 1 & 2.30pm on the porch.

Nestled among a tranquil bayside garden at 3485 Main Hwy, the **Barnacle** is the century-old home of Ralph Middelton Munroe, one of Coconut Grove's earliest pioneers. Built in 1891, it reflects both Munroe's professional passion as a naval architect and his philosophical devotion to the Transcendentalist Movement. It's a self-consciously simple house, though informed by nautical innovations, such as a recessed verandah that enables windows to be open during rainstorms and skylights allowing air to be drawn through the house. Munroe also built the house completely above ground to prevent flooding and improve air-flow – helping to alleviate some of the discomfort of Miami's humidity – and in 1908, raised it further, adding a floor under the original one. Only with the guided tour can you see inside the house, where many original furnishings remain alongside some of Munroe's intriguing photos of pre-settled Coconut Grove. You are free to wander around the grounds: the front lawn extends to the shore of Biscayne Bay, while behind the house are the last remnants of the tropical hardwood hammock that once extended throughout the Miami area.

Charles Avenue

The Bahamian settlers of the late 1800s, who later provided the labor that went into building Coconut Grove and nearby areas, mostly lived along what became **Charles Avenue** (off Main Highway, close to the Coconut Grove Playhouse), in small, simple, wooden houses similar to the "conch houses" that fill Key West's Old Town. You'll find a trio of these still standing on the "3200" block, on the edge of a somewhat seedy section of town known casually, if unfortunately, as "**Black Coconut Grove**," which runs up to the borders of Coral Gables. The fact that such a derelict district exists within half a mile of one of the city's most fashionably upmarket areas provides a stark reminder of the divisions between Miami's haves and have nots.

Key Biscayne

A compact, immaculately manicured community five miles off the Miami shore, **Key Biscayne** is a great place to live if you can afford it – and you'll probably be going for much the same reason wealthy folk set up camp here. Seeking relaxation and creature comforts away from life in the fast lane, the moneyed set in Miami fills the island's upmarket homes and condos: even Richard Nixon had his presidential winter house here, and singer Sting chose one of the luxury shorefront hotels for a recuperative pamper between tour dates. For visitors, Key Biscayne offers an escape from the frenetic scene of the rest of Miami's beaches – the sparkling waters and soft white sands here set a tranquil mood that pervades the island. There are three main **beach areas**, but you can pretty much pull off the road as soon as you cross the **Rickenbacker Causeway**, and jump in the water.

Key Biscayne is roughly divided into three sections, starting with sprawling **Crandon Park**, which leads onto residential Key Biscayne, and dead-ending in a glorious state park complete with a weathered **lighthouse** – in fact the oldest structure in South Florida. Whatever else you do and see when visiting Key Biscayne, you likely won't be staying here at night time – cheap eats and lodging are in predictably short supply, as are bars and any sort of nightlife scene.

Without a private yacht, the only way onto Key Biscayne is the Rickenbacker Causeway, a four-mile-long continuation of SW 26th Road just south of downtown Miami. Soaring high above Biscayne Bay, the causeway allows ships to glide underneath and provides a breathtaking view of the Brickell Avenue skyline. There is a $1 toll for cars; otherwise you can cross the causeway by bus (#B), bike, or even on foot if you're up for the long, picturesque walk.

VIRGINIA KEY

Map 2, F6.

Immediately after crossing the Rickenbacker Causeway you'll be on the small, sparsely populated **Virginia Key**, an unavoidable, if scenic, obstacle on the way to Key Biscayne. Apart from checking out the Seaquarium, there's not much more to do here other than stretch out on **Virginia Key Beach** (daily 8am–sunset; cars $2) on the southeast side of the key. Secluded under a canopy of palms and pines, the beach is great for relaxing and sunbathing in its hidden coves, and less crowded than the other two major beach areas on Key Biscayne.

For the birds

Virginia Key borders on the edge of a mangrove swamp, where many species of wildlife are rapidly becoming endangered due to the development and depletion of their natural habitat. The **Virginia Key Critical Wildlife Area** is a 400-foot section of the mangrove, open from May to July only; here, migratory birds come and repopulate the shrinking numbers of red-eyed cormorants, black skimmers, roseate spoonbills, and egrets. If you're here in the summer, you shouldn't miss the chance to see these flight birds and wildfowl in such a calm, peaceful setting.

Miami Seaquarium

Map 2, F6. Daily 9.30am–6pm; adults $21.95, children 3–9 $16.95; parking extra.

In stark contrast to the isolated beaches on the right of the Virginia Key's main road, the **Miami Seaquarium** marine park is a bustling place where you can while away three or four hours watching the usual roster of performing seals and dolphins – particularly Lolita, the 8000-pound star of the spectacular killer-whale show. Almost as eye-catching are the inhabitants of the 750,000-gallon Main Reef Aquarium, which is stocked with bumpy loggerhead turtles, flat grouper, a kaleidoscope of tropical fish, and a glowing moray eel sure to terrify onlookers.

Many of the other exhibits focus on local sea life, especially those considered somewhat endangered. The manatee display, for instance, features animals rescued and rehabilitated in the Seaquarium's own program; you can also see a feature on the increasingly scarce mangrove swamp life. Still, much of the park's most important work – formulating breeding programs and serving as a halfway house for injured manatees and other sea creatures – goes on behind the scenes.

CRANDON PARK BEACH

Map 2, F6. Daily 8am–sunset; $3.

Not content with living in one of the best natural settings in Miami, the people of Key Biscayne also possess one of the finest landscaped beaches in the city – **Crandon Park Beach**, a mile along Crandon Boulevard. Three miles of golden beach frame Crandon Park, which is filled by the sounds of boisterous kids and hisses of sizzling barbecues on weekends; at nearly any other time the park seems disturbed only by the occasional jogger or holidaymaker straying from the private beaches of the expensive hotels nearby. It's a great place to relax beside the lapping ocean waters while keeping an eye out for manatees and dolphins, both known to swim by, but be sure to bring high-factor sunscreen and a beach umbrella – there is no shade to be found anywhere.

BILL BAGGS CAPE FLORIDA STATE RECREATION AREA

Map 2, F7. Daily 8am–sunset; cars $4, pedestrians and cyclists $1. Crandon Boulevard, the island's main road, terminates at the entrance of the **Bill Baggs Cape Florida State Recreation Area**, which covers most of the southern extremity of Key Biscayne. Named for the late Miami newspaper editor and local activist, this 400-acre oceanfront park affords fantastic views of Biscayne Bay and the Atlantic, with cruise ships cutting a smooth line across the horizon.

Stretching the park's length, a wide **boardwalk** divides the crowded picnic shelters from the soft, sandy beach. On weekends hordes of families unload their station wagons and proceed to barbecue on the numerous grills and string hammocks up between trees. Along the boardwalk, the concession stand next to the *Lighthouse Café* has rentals for bikes, rollerblades, ocean kayaks, and windsurf boards as well as stationary chairs and umbrellas; you can also bring your tackle and try your luck on one of the eight fishing platforms. The **beach** itself is dotted by natural "umbrellas" of young palm trees – planted after Hurricane Andrew ripped out their predecessors.

....

Bill Baggs Cape Florida State Recreation Area maintains a loggerhead turtle program, which enables visitors to watch the carefully orchestrated laying and hatching of eggs along the shore; call ©361-5811 for reservations.

....

Our Man in Stiltsville

Looking out from Bill Baggs park across the bay, you'll spy a strange grouping of fragile-looking houses seemingly floating above the water. These wooden dwellings, known collectively as **Stiltsville**, were built and occupied by fishermen in the 1940s and 1950s, who were attempting to avoid the jurisdiction of tax collectors – much to the dismay of local authorities. To guarantee Stiltsville's demise, a law was passed forbidding work on the ramshackle structures; they began to fall into further disrepair, a state compounded by the destruction wrought by Hurricane Andrew. Today just one house has a full-time occupant; the others are occasionally used illegally by revellers looking for a secluded spot to imbibe.

The southern portion of the boardwalk ends at the **Cape Florida Lighthouse**, built in 1845 to replace the previous one ambushed and burned by Seminole Indians in 1836. The lighthouse only remained in use until 1878, and has only served since as a well-photographed landmark. Only with the ranger-led **tour** (daily except Tues at 9am, 10.30am, 1pm, 2.30pm, & 3.30pm; $1) can you climb its 118 steps and visit the replica of the lighthouse keeper's original quarters. The journey to the top is worth it, though, for the terrific view of Biscayne Bay and the downtown skyline.

South Miami
and Homestead

Southof Coral Gables and Coconut Grove, monotonous middle-class suburbs consume almost all of **South Miami**, an expanse of cozy but dull family homes reaching to the edge of the Everglades. Hwy-1 will likely be your route through here and points south, though for the first stretch from central Miami, a better course is to take Old Cutler Road, which makes a pleasing meander from Coconut Grove through a thick belt of woodland between Biscayne Bay and the suburban sprawl. You'll still have to face Hwy-1 at some point – unless of course you're not heading down to the Keys – and there are some amusing and unusual attractions just off that primary thoroughfare. The **Parrot Jungle**, for example, is as good a place as any to view Miami's iconic pink flamingos, while the **Metrozoo** showcases the snow-white Bengal tiger, a decidedly un-Miami creature.

Meanwhile, cutting inland from Hwy-1 is unrewarding (and unthinkable without a car), since there are no stops of any major importance. A series of mini-malls, gas stations, cut-price waterbed outlets, and bumper-to-bumper traffic are the star attractions heading south toward **Homestead**, where suburbia yields to agriculture and broad, fertile fields grow fruit and vegetables for the nation's northern states. Aside from offering a taste of Florida farm life, Homestead has some budget accommodation options and cheap eating choices; you can, in fact, gather your own dinner in this area. Just keep an eye out for "**pick-your-own**" signs, where, for a few dollars, you can take to the fields and load up with peas, tomatoes, and a variety of other crops.

The one sight that might take you down this way, especially if you're not heading on to the Florida Keys, is **Biscayne National Park**, somewhat of a nature preserve with plenty of walking trails and excellent snorkeling opportunities.

PARROT JUNGLE

Map 2, C7. Daily 9.30am–6pm; adults $11.67, children 3-12 $8.47.
The **Parrot Jungle**, 11000 SW 57th Ave, is one of Miami's quirkier attractions, chock-full of squawky parrots, parakeets, and rainbow-plumed macaws. The shaded pathways of the gardens have been designed to protect both residents and visitors from the hot Florida sun; as you walk along you'll see hundreds of varieties of plants, waterfalls, twisted banyan trees, a petting zoo, and a lake with Caribbean pink flamingos. Apart from birds, the park is also home to numerous species of alligators and crocodiles, and giant tortoises, as well as an extremely entertaining primate section – far better in fact than the one on display at the Monkey Jungle (see p.83).

THE CHARLES DEERING ESTATE

Map 2, C8. Daily 10am–5pm, last admission 4pm; $5 (includes parking and tour of the hardwood hammock).
Long before modern highways scythed through the city, **Old Cutler Road** was the sole road between Coconut

Grove and Cutler, a small town that went into terminal decline in the 1910s after being bypassed by the new Flagler railroad. A wealthy industrialist and amateur botanist, **Charles Deering** (brother of James, the owner of Villa Vizcaya; see p.65), was so taken with the natural beauty of the area that he purchased all of Cutler and, with one exception, razed its buildings to make way for the **Charles Deering Estate**, 16701 SW 72nd Ave, completed in 1922. Deering maintained the *Richmond Inn*, Cutler's only hotel (now closed), as his living and dining quarters, which still stands in marked contrast to the limestone mansion he erected alongside. Step inside the Mediterranean-style house for a peek at its echoing halls, dusty chandeliers, and checkerboard marble floor. More impressive than either building are the expansive three-hundred-acre **grounds**, where signs of human habitation dating back 10,000 years have been found amid the pines and tropical hardwood hammocks. The terrain includes several hundred acres of pine rockland forests, coastal salt marshes, and mangrove forests – a perfect setting along Biscayne Bay for an afternoon picnic.

While in the area, take advantage of South Miami's excellent information center (daily 8am–6pm; ✆1-800/388-9669 or 245-9180), on Hwy-1 close to its junction with Hwy-9336 (344th Street).

METROZOO AND THE GOLD COAST RAILROAD MUSEUM

Map 2, A9. Zoo: Daily 9.30am–5.30pm; 4pm last admission; adults $8, children $4. Museum: Mon–Fri 10am–3pm, Sat & Sun 11am–4pm; $4.

The extensive wildlife display at Miami's **Metrozoo**, 12400 SW 152nd St, where moats and small hills are employed in place of cages, will likely keep the kids occupied for a few hours; however, comfort-wise it's hard to imagine that many of the animals enjoy baking in the heat and humidity any more than their audience – both factions tend to spend their time pursuing shade and a cool drink. The snow-white Bengal tigers are the prize exhibit, an extremely rare species that is found nowhere near Miami, though the simulated habitat seems to fit them well. Avoid visiting during the sweltering midday temperatures of summer and when it rains, as most of the zoo is outdoors.

Sharing the zoo's entrance, the **Gold Coast Railroad Museum** houses a small but intriguing collection of old locomotives that can be clambered upon for closer inspection. Among them is the *Ferdinand Magellan*, a luxury Pullman car that was custom-built in 1928 for future President Franklin Roosevelt and features escape hatches and steel armor plating. Subsequent presidential users have included George Bush, Ronald Reagan, Dwight Eisenhower, and Harry S Truman, who traveled 21,000 miles in it on his 1948 re-election campaign, giving three hundred speeches from the rear platform.

HOMESTEAD AND AROUND

Map 1, E6.

Closer in mood to *Little House on the Prairie* than an MTV music video, **Homestead** is South Miami's main agricultural town and the least galvanizing section of Miami. Krome Avenue, just west of Hwy-1, slices through the center, but besides a few restored early twentieth-century buildings, such as the **Old City Hall**, no. 43 N, there's little to detain you. Still, if you've made it this far, you may as well stop at the **Florida Pioneer Museum**, no. 826

Hurricane Andrew and Homestead

In the early-morning hours of August 24, 1992, Hurricane Andrew slammed into South Florida with 162mph sustained winds, completely devastating Homestead, Florida City, and surrounding towns before sliding off to the west and across the state. With damages totaling $28.5 billion, Andrew was the US's worst natural disaster since the 1906 San Francisco earthquake, and the costliest hurricane ever.

The destruction it brought was truly incredible – roofs were ripped off homes, boats were tossed around like bath toys, and 250,000 people were left homeless. Plants were as bad off as people: Andrew left a ruined path of flora and fauna in its wake. Biscayne National Park lost one-third of its coral reef, and ninety percent of South Dade's native pinelands, mangroves, and tropical hardwood hammocks disappeared. So complete was the wreckage that, nearly a decade later, some parts of South Florida are still working to return them to their pre-Andrew state.

(Mon–Fri 4.30–7.30pm; ©246-9531), where two yellow-painted train station buildings store photos and objects from Homestead's formative years – this end-of-the-line town was planned by Flagler's railroad engineers in 1904. To the rear, a 1926 **caboose** holds moderately entertaining railroad mementos.

Most sights of interest in the area are actually **around Homestead**, and can be viewed on your way down toward the Florida Keys without even stopping in the town.

The Coral Castle

Daily 9am–6pm; adults $7.75, children $5.

Off Hwy-1, **Coral Castle**, 28655 S Dixie Hwy, six miles northeast of Homestead, makes for a quirky stop, its bulky coral rock sculptures of furniture incapable of failing to catch the eye. Remarkably, these bumpy, bizarre pieces, whose delicate finish belies their imposing size, are the work of just one man – the enigmatic **Edward Leedskalnin**. Jilted in 1913 by his sixteen-year-old fiancée in Latvia, Leedskalnin spent seven years working his way across Europe, Canada, and the US before buying an acre of land just south of Homestead. Using a profound – and self-taught – knowledge of weights and balances, he somehow raised enormous hunks of coral rock from the ground, then used a workbench made from car running boards and hand-made tools fashioned from scrap to refine the blocks into chairs, tables, and beds. Though the furniture was apparently intended to woo back his errant sweetheart, the project failed – Leedskalnin died here alone in 1951.

You can wander around the slabs, sit on the hard but surprisingly comfortable granite chairs, and admire the numerous coral representations of the moon and planets that reflected Leedskalnin's interest in astronomy and astrology (like his twenty-foot-high telescope). Among the more unusual displays of mechanical precision is a nine-ton revolving gate, which you'll be shocked to find can be moved by the touch of your pinkie. What you won't be able to do is explain how the sculptures were made. No one ever saw the secretive Leedskalnin at work, or knows how, alone, he could have loaded 1100 tons of rock onto the rail-mounted truck that brought the pieces here in 1936.

The Fruit and Spice Park

Daily 10am–5pm; $1.

With some five hundred varieties of exotic, subtropical, and just plain weird fruits in bloom, it's tough not to notice the fragrant air surrounding the twenty-acre **Fruit and Spice Park**, north of Homestead at 24801 SW 187th Ave. Of these plant species, a staggering fifty are different types of bananas; if that doesn't get you hungry, a stroll through any of the rare spice gardens should help. On weekends the guided trolley tours (1pm & 3pm; $1.50) provide a decent introduction to all you're likely to want to learn about the plants here; should you require more, the park offers detailed classes, lectures, workshops, and tours on all things botanical in the region.

Monkey Jungle

Daily 9.30am–5pm, 4pm last admission; adults $11.50, children 3–12 $6.

Also to the north of Homestead, **Monkey Jungle**, at 14805 SW 216th St, is one of the few places of protection in the US for endangered primates, but rather disappoints for the lack of enthusiasm shown by both staff and animals. Caged walkways keep visitors in closer confinement than the monkeys and lead through a steamy hammock where several hundred baboons, orangutans, gorillas, and chimps move through the vegetation. Despite a fair amount of freedom, the animals don't appear a terribly happy lot, possibly because of overcrowding and hot, exposed living quarters. Most enjoyable is the ability for visitors to feed peanuts and raisins to the monkeys in an amusing way – they drop a tin cup on a chain down through the cage, and hoist it back up through the cage. Otherwise, the daily goings-on are quite boring, with most of the monkeys often not bothering to come out of hiding or just glaring at the gawking group of onlookers when they do.

BISCAYNE NATIONAL PARK

Map 1, F6. Daily 8am–sunset.

You should try to make a point of visiting the amazing coral reefs of **Biscayne National Park**, a closer alternative

Touring the coral reef

The lazy way to view Biscayne National Park's coral reef is on the three-hour **glass-bottomed boat** trip (daily at 10am; adults $16.50, children under 12 $8.50; reservations ℂ230-1100), but for an up-close encounter you should embark on a four-hour **snorkel tour** (daily starting at 1.30pm; $28 including all equipment). Gear can be rented from the visitor center (daily 8.30am–5pm; ℂ230-1100) at Convoy Point. For tours and dives, phone at least a day ahead to make reservations.

to many similar spots along the Florida Keys, set at the end of Canal Drive (328th Street), east of Hwy-1. Ninety percent of the park is beneath the clear ocean waters, where stunning formations of living coral provide a habitat for shoals of brightly colored fish and numerous other creatures too delicate to survive on their own. Back above ground, a pleasant boardwalk runs the length of **Convoy Point**, close to the park's entrance, home to the park's visitor center and a good place to orient yourself before you start your explorations.

From Convoy Point, you can take a tour boat out to the park's **barrier islands**, seven miles out. Boats leave for **Elliott Key** at 1.30pm on Sundays between December and May. Once ashore, besides calling at the **visitor center** (Sat & Sun 10am–4pm) and contemplating the hiking trails along the island's forested spine, there's nothing to do on Elliott Key except sunbathe in solitude. Adams Key, another of the barrier islands, has a quarter-mile nature loop as well.

For a more in-depth look at Florida's magnificent coral reef, see "John Pennecamp State Park," p.205.

LISTINGS

Accommodation

F inding **accommodation** is typically not a problem in Miami except during major holidays and some special events, like the Boat Show in early February. You'll have a decent number of options to choose from throughout the city, though the best range – and most popular hostelries – can be found in **South Beach**. These are the accommodations for which Miami is best known, the beach's **Art Deco hotels**, whose exteriors usually make up in looks what their quarters may lack in size and value. The towering, pricey hotels that cluster in **downtown Miami**, and parts of **Coconut Grove** and **Coral Gables**, tend to cater to expense-account travelers and convention-goers; as a result they are often more expensive and certainly less fun.

From December through April, rates are at their steepest, and you may be hard-pressed to hit a spot for under $100 per night, though bargains can always be found in several well-run **hostels** in Miami Beach. Also checking in on the less-expensive side are Miami's **guesthouses**, usually charming family-run spots that are most prevalent again around South Beach. On weekends year round, you may as well ask about **discount rates** at the business hotels; you never know when you might strike lucky.

Accommodation price codes

Accommodation prices quoted below are according to the cost of the least expensive double room. High season runs from December through April; the rest of the year, rooms are cheaper and bargaining is recommended, even encouraged. Bear in mind that all prices are quoted before taxes, which are 10 to 15 percent in Miami.

① – up to $40	② – $40–60
③ – $60–80	④ – $80–100
⑤ – $100–125	⑥ – $125–175
⑦ – $175–250	⑧ – $250+

HOTELS

South Beach's **Art Deco hotels** are traditionally small and rooms can border on the size of walk-in closets, so don't expect modern luxuries. Instead you'll discover the quirky patterns and eye-catching pastel color schemes for which this area has gained notoriety. Themed rooms – kitted up in red velvet walls, futuristic metallic objects, tropical kitsch, and even religious shrines – are one of the most visible gimmicks of the day. Many of the oceanfront hotels are pricey and you may do better at the lively, southern end of **Collins Avenue** and the quieter **Washington Avenue**. Big-name chains can be found throughout the rest of the city, while North Miami Beach and South Miami (Homestead along US-1) hold basic, moderately priced hotel options.

DOWNTOWN MIAMI

Doral Golf Resort and Spa

4400 NW 87th Ave ©592-2000 or 1-800/71-DORAL.

A luxury hotel with all the amenities – spacious rooms, some
with private patios, 18-hole golf course, Olympic swimming
pool, and a small tennis center (where professional tennis star
Mary Jo Fernandez is a visiting instructor). During low season
you can actually find rooms for under $150; however, March is
booked solid due to the Doral Ryder golf tournament. ⑥–⑧.

Everglades
Map 3, F5. 244 Biscayne Blvd off Third St ℂ379-5461 or 1-800/327-
5700.
The *Everglades* is not the best looking or most immaculate hotel
around, but it sure is convenient to all the downtown sights –
the swimming pool and low rates are added bonuses. ④–⑤.

Hotel Inter-Continental Miami
Map 3, F7. 100 Chopin Plaza ℂ1-800/327-0200.
It's an expensive chain hotel, but the view of the Miami skyline
from the pool is unbeatable. Rooms are modest and clean, and
the sleek white marble lobby sets a classy tone. ⑦.

Miami River Inn
Map 3, A7. 118 SW South River Drive ℂ325-0045.
This delightful inn is draped in New England charm, with its
brass beds, antique wooden wardrobes, and thick, fluffy bed
linens. Most of the rooms have private baths with inviting tubs;
some have stunning views of the city and there's a great pool
and lovely gardens as well. Though it's not in the most appealing of neighborhoods – the surrounding area holds largely
derelict waterfront warehouses – the security is airtight and it's
just a short walk to the center of downtown. ④–⑤.

SOUTH BEACH

Astor
Map 4, F5. 956 Washington Ave ℂ531-8081 or 1-800/270-4981.

The *Astor*'s double insulated windows are a welcome defense from Washington Avenue's noisy nightclubs, but plenty more sets this hotel apart: marble baths, rooms designed to look like oceanliner cabins, antique French furniture, and a waterfall that cascades into a lovely whirlpool. ⑥–⑦.

Avalon

Map 4, F6. 700 Ocean Drive ℗538-0133, 1-800/933-3306.
Situated right in the center of things, this classic Deco hotel manages to be hip but not over the top. All rooms have TV/VCR, ceiling fans, fridges, and big, clean bathrooms, and a decent continental breakfast is included. Passes are available to the South Beach Gym. ⑥.

Breakwater

Map 4, F5. 940 Ocean Drive ℗532-1220, 1-800/454-1220.
The soothing blue and yellow facade belies the fun, tropical prints found in every room. Try for a room with a wrap-around window, for a perfect panoramic view of the beach. It's adjacent to the raucous *All-Star* bar and restaurant, so if you don't want to be kept up at night, ask to be put on the north side. ③–⑤.

Cavalier

Map 4, F4. 1320 Ocean Drive ℗1-800/OUTPOST.
The Moorish themed lobby – complete with keyhole door arches and floor-to-ceiling palms – is usually buzzing with sun-burned guests, who are attended to by staff who occasionally break into song. Rooms are spacious, equipped with mini-bars, CD/cassette players, and a good selection of pop and Latin tunes. ⑥–⑦.

Chesterfield

Map 4, F6. 855 Collins Ave ℗531-5831, 1-800/244-6023.
The *Chesterfield* is often overlooked because it lacks ocean views, but it's an inexpensive and quality option – and still just

steps from the beach. Stylish rooms, a sweeping marble porch, and late-night bar round out the many pluses. ③–④.

Clay Hotel and International Hostel

Map 4, F4. 1438 Washington Ave ✆534-2988, 1-800/379-2529.
Perhaps the city's best inexpensive hotel (see p.99 for hostel details), the *Clay* is centrally located, with impeccably clean rooms, all with private bathrooms, televisions, phones, and fridges; some even have balconies overlooking Española Way. The hotel features an all-night bar and restaurant, laundry facilities, and good service. ①–②.

For an account of Española Way, see p.38.

Colony

Map 4, F6. 736 Ocean Drive ✆1-800/2-COLONY.
Though this beautifully refurbished Art Deco delight is the most photographed hotel in South Beach, largely for its famous neon marquee, its pricey rooms are actually quite plain. Still, the location is prime. ⑥-⑦.

Delano

Map 4, G2. 1685 Collins Ave ✆672-2000 or 1-800/555-5001.
The hyped and trendy hotel is the place to go if you want to be in the in-crowd, but you get relatively few amenities and fairly simple rooms for the (high) price. If you just want to see and be seen for a bit, check out the pool-side lounge. ⑦–⑧.

Essex House

Map 4, F5. 1001 Collins Ave ✆1-800/553-7739.
Metal scrollwork on the railings, etched glass, and ziggurat arches help lend a 1930s feel to this old nugget. A recent renovation upgraded the worn rooms with splashy pastels and soft, luxurious bed linens. There's a small pool in the back for lounging. ⑨-⑦.

HOTELS: SOUTH BEACH

Most South Beach hotels have 3pm check-in and noon check-out times.

Indian Creek Hotel
2727 Indian Creek Drive ©531-2727 or 1-800/491-2772.
The only drawback to this Art Deco gem is the location – at 27th Street it's a bit away from the scene – but some see that as a blessing. Regardless, it sits right on Indian Creek, just one block from the beach, and has a pool to boot. The style is a mixed bag, with Native American prints, loud tropical patterns, chunky furniture, and Deco accents, like streamlined staircase railings. ⑤–⑥.

Leslie
Map 4, F4. 1244 Ocean Drive ©1-800/OUTPOST.
You'll know you've arrived at the *Leslie* when you're nearly blinded by the shocking yellow facade on Ocean Drive. The smallish hotel has rooms awash in similarly bright colors and a friendly staff who will make you feel quite at home. ④–⑥.

Marlin
Map 4, F4. 1200 Collins Ave ©1-800/OUTPOST.
A favorite with musicians – such as Steven Tyler of Aerosmith – thanks to its onsite recording studio. There are eleven stunning suites decked out with Web-TV Internet access, stereo systems, stainless-steel kitchens, and spotless glass and steel bathrooms with Aveda samples. If you can't afford to stay here, at least have a drink at the futuristic bar or a jerk chicken sandwich in the ultra-cool *Marlin Bar*. ⑥–⑧.

For a review of the *Marlin Bar*, see p.125.

Park Central

Map 4, F6. 640 Ocean Drive ℗538-1611.
This large lilac and white hotel has an airy, banana republic-like lobby and bar area. If you're an Anne Rice fan, check out room 607, Vampire Lestat's quarters in *The Tale of the Body Thief*. The rooms are large and come equipped with ceiling fans and plush bathrobes. Check out the rooftop deck, too, with views of Ocean Drive and downtown. ⑥–⑦.

Pelican

Map 4, F6. 826 Ocean Drive ℗673-3373 or 1/800-7PELICAN.
Perhaps the best hotel on the strip for character and fun, its 25 rooms each quirkily themed, ranging from the bizarre dentist office replica "With Drill," to the frequently requested "Best Whorehouse," draped in red velvet and tassles. Tacky perhaps, but still should be seen to be believed. ⑥–⑦.

Shelborne

Map 4, G2. 1801 Collins Ave ℗531-1271 or 1-800/327-8757.
Towering pink and blue structure piping Dean Martin and rag-time tunes throughout. Rooms are big with comfy beds and, on oceanfront side, balconies. The large pool and the excellent hotel bar happy hour should add to your stay. ④–⑥.

Shelley

Map 4, F6. 844 Collins Ave ℗1-800/414-0612.
Owned by the same folks as the *Chesterfield*, this hotel has impeccably clean rooms, and you can wake up to pastries and juice in the lobby before stepping across the street to the beach. ②–③.

South Seas

Map 4, G2. 1751 Collins Ave ℗538-1411 or 1-800/345-2678.
Though it might look a bit worn from the outside, inside the rooms are filled with bright patterns, potted plants, and great

HOTELS: SOUTH BEACH

93

oceanfront views. The oversized pool is surrounded by tropical landscaping and a very good poolside café, as well as a private, elevated sundeck where clothing is optional. Complimentary breakfast served daily next to the pool. ④–⑥.

Tides
Map 4, F4. 1220 Ocean Drive ℗604-5000 or 1-800/688-7678.
Tides is one of the most luxurious, and correspondingly expensive, spots on the beach. The twelve-story stark white facade towers over Ocean Drive with its distinctive porthole windows and streamline designs. It used to have 100-plus rooms, now converted to 45 roomy suites, well equipped and all overlooking the ocean. There's a pool, but most people head straight for the Atlantic across the street. ⑧.

Waldorf Towers
Map 4, F6. 860 Ocean Drive ℗531-7684 or 1-800/933-2322.
An affordable Art Deco landmark, facing the ocean and right in the throng of the fashionable strip. ④–⑤.

COCONUT GROVE

Doubletree at Coconut Grove
Map 7, E2. 2649 South Bayshore Drive ℗1-800/222-8733.
Clean, comfortable rooms, some with great views of Biscayne Bay, make this a pleasing chain option. The hotel is well situated, merely a quarter of an hour's walk from the area's cafés and bars, and the staff is quite accommodating. ⑥–⑧.

Hampton Inn
Map 7, B1. 2800 SW 28th Terrace, US1 and 27th Ave ℗448-2800; fax 442-8655.
This relatively new addition to Coconut Grove is part of a fairly inexpensive but standard chain; rooms are clean and basic, and the price includes continental breakfast. ③–⑤.

Biltmore

Map 6, B5. 1200 Anastasia Ave ℗1-800/727-1926.
A landmark Mediterranean-style hotel that has endured mixed fortunes since it began pampering the rich and famous. If you can't afford to stay here, at least take a stroll through its long corridors or view the biggest hotel pool in the country. ⑧.

For a fuller account of the *Biltmore*, see p.59.

Gables Inn

Map 6, D9. 730 S Dixie Hwy ℗661-7999.
Basic but clean – with an fairly offputting color scheme – the *Gables Inn* is likely your least expensive option for the area. ③–④.

Hotel Place St Michel

Map 6, F3. 162 Alcazar Ave ℗444-1666.
Small, romantic hotel just off the Miracle Mile, covered in Laura Ashley decor and copious European antiques. Guests are pampered through and through, with massages in room, plush bedding, and even fruit baskets on arrival. A gourmet continental breakfast is included. ⑤–⑥.

Omni Colonnade

Map 6, G4. 180 Aragon Ave ℗1-800/533-1337.
Marble floors, oriental rugs, and brass lamps fill this Mediterranean Revival showpiece. Check out the historic photographs and heirlooms of Coral Gables' founding father, George Merrick, which line the walls and lobby of the hotel. There's an awesome, open-air pool on the 10th floor. ⑦–⑧.

CENTRAL AND NORTH MIAMI BEACH

Blue Mist
19111 Collins Ave ℗932-1000.
The cheapest option in Sunny Isles; rooms are basic but most face the ocean. ②–③.

Fontainebleau Hilton and Resort Towers
4441 Collins Ave ℗538-2000 or 1-800/445-8667.
A relic from the Art Deco heyday (see p.41 for details), the *Fontainebleau* is like an all-inclusive resort; you may never feel the need to leave its three buildings, two pools, seven tennis courts, four bars, shopping mall, beachside spa, and twelve restaurants. The rooms and service are as lavish as expected, with complimentary breakfast buffet and free tickets to the Latin revue show at *Club Tropigala*. ⑧.

Paradise Inn
8520 Harding Ave ℗865-6216.
Neatly tucked into Surfside's main street, this is one of the best bargains around. ②.

Thunderbird Resort
18401 Collins Ave ℗1-800/327-2044.
No frills, but handy for both Miami and Fort Lauderdale. As in most hotels around here, you can step straight out of your room into the pool or onto the beach. ③–⑤.

SOUTH MIAMI AND HOMESTEAD

Best Western Gateway to the Keys
1 Straus Blvd, Florida City ℗246-5100.
One of the most comfortable places to stay in the area, and usefully located between the Keys, Miami, and the Everglades. ④–⑤.

Coral Roc

1100 N Krome Ave ℭ247-4010.
An unexciting but fully functional motel with worn but clean
rooms. ②–③.

Deluxe Inn Motel

28475 S Dixie Hwy ℭ248-5622.
Maybe not "deluxe," as the name suggests, but you'll still find
good, clean rooms at a fair price. ①–②.

Everglades Motel

605 S Krome Ave ℭ247-4117.
A slightly run-down exterior, but the rooms are okay and
there's a coin-operated laundry for guests. ①–②.

Super 8

1202 N Krome Ave ℭ1-800/800-8000.
Branch of a plain but cheap motel chain, with clean and reasonably priced rooms. ①–②.

GUESTHOUSES

Miami's guesthouses, similar in many ways to bed and
breakfasts, can be pleasant alternatives for those tired of the
Art Deco entries and the faceless business hotels. Most feature comfortable and spacious rooms, homemade breakfasts,
and a common room in which visitors lounge about and
swap stories.

Brigham Gardens Guesthouse

Map 4, F4. 1411 Collins Ave, South Beach ℭ531-1331; fax 538-
9898.
You can follow the sounds of squawking tropical birds to find
this laid-back Collins Avenue lodging. Spacious rooms come
with microwaves, TVs, and coffee makers, and a lush garden

completes the serene setting. Popular spot, especially with gay and lesbian travelers, so book in advance. ④–⑤.

For listings of gay and lesbian friendly accommodations, see Chapter 14, "Gay and lesbian Miami."

Coconut Bed and Breakfast

4286 Douglas Rd, Coconut Grove ℗665-2274.
This is the Grove's hidden gem, literally, as there are no signs to announce its location, in the midst of a residential neighborhood. Special attention to detail, like marble baths and handmade tiles surrounding the fireplace, along with terrific breakfasts, make this a great alternative to impersonal hotel chains in the area. ④–⑥.

Katy's Place B&B

31850 SW 195th Ave, South Miami ℗247-0201.
Pleasant B&B with a pool, hot-tub, laundry facilities, and home-cooked breakfasts. ③–④.

Lily Guesthouse

Map 4, F6. 835 Collins Ave, South Beach ℗535-9900; fax 535-0077.
A quaint guesthouse tucked away from the madness of Collins Avenue. Sizeable rooms come equipped with a mini-kitchen (micro, fridge, and coffeemaker), table, and sofa; bathrooms are shower only. ④–⑤.

Mermaid Guesthouse

Map 4, F5. 909 Collins Ave, South Beach ℗538-5324.
Though the staff can be a bit disorganized, the funky, Caribbean-style rooms, with mosquito netting draping the beds, are worth checking out (though ask for a room in the back to dampen the noise). A central hallway leads to a vibrant

open-air portico, complete with a tiki bar, where Latin American musicians occasionally jam. ④–⑥.

Villa Paradiso

Map 5, F4. 1415 Collins Ave ℗532-0616; fax 667-0074.
Right next door to *Brigham Gardens Guesthouse*, the *Paradiso* offers up fully equipped studios and one-bedroom apartments with kitchens, at a price tag that compares favorably to most standard hotels. Lush landscaping and a relaxing tropical court-yard too. ③–⑤.

YOUTH HOSTELS AND BUDGET ACCOMMODATION

Banana Bungalow

Map 4, G1. 2360 Collins Ave, Miami Beach ℗538-1951 or 1-800/746-7835.
It's spring break all year round at this hotel-cum-hostel, where you can choose from bunk beds or hotel-style rooms. Movies are shown nightly, there is a ping pong table and a cheap bar (see p.124), and the proprietors organize land and water tours. ①–②.

Beachcomber

Map 4, F4. 1340 Collins Ave, Miami Beach ℗531-3755 or 1-888/305-4683.
This unassuming hotel, tucked in between larger, impersonal hotels, is an excellent bargain, and rooms can fill up quickly. There's not too much luxury here, but the atmosphere is relaxed, and a continental breakfast is served daily in their sunny lobby. ③–④.

Clay Hotel and International Hostel

Map 4, F4. 1438 Washington Ave, Miami Beach ℗534-2988 or 1-800/379-2529.

This beautiful converted monastery serves as the city's best budget hotel and youth hostel. Taking up an entire block of Española Way in South Beach, the hostel section of the *Clay* has spotless dorm rooms with bunk-bed accommodation and shared bathrooms. Kitchen and laundry facilities, message boards and lockers, as well as a friendly, multi-lingual staff make this one of the best venues in the city. ①.

Henry

Map 4, E7. 536 Washington Ave, Miami Beach ℗672-2511 or 1-800/253-5346.
Thrifty is the word when it comes to the *Henry*. Though dormitory-like, it offers basic rooms with TV, phone, private baths, and ceiling fans in a prime location a couple of blocks from the ocean. Hotel-style accommodation at a hostel price. ②–④.

James

Map 4, F2. 1680 James Ave, Miami Beach ℗531-1125.
All the rooms in this small hotel have full kitchens and come with free parking – a rare bonus for budget properties. It won't win any architectural awards but it's clean, comfortable, and reasonably priced. ④.

Kenmore

Map 4, F5. 1050 Washington Ave, Miami Beach ℗674-1930.
Rooms here are basic but large, with communal bathrooms in fun, eye-popping Deco tiles, and there's a pleasant but small pool as well. It's a good bargain on the beach and no need to worry about security – it's directly across from a police station. ④.

Ninth Street Hostel – Miami Beach

Map 4, F5. 236 9th St ℗534-0268 or 1-800/9SUN-SURF.
Centrally located and cheap, but you can probably do better elsewhere. Besides bunk-bed accommodations, a few private rooms are available. ①–③.

Eating

ou won't want for **eating** choices in Miami, whether it's roadside hot-dog stands or fancy gourmet restaurants. Much of what's out there is rather affordable, too, at least by American big-city standards, so you'll rarely need an expense account to dine out on that giant mess of stone crab claws – a regional specialty – or fresh picked lobsters. Indeed, **seafood** may well be what the city does best, not entirely surprising for a place surrounded by water. More than five hundred species of fish thrive offshore, both run-of-the-mill and exotic; basically, if you can't find it on your plate somewhere, it hasn't evolved yet.

Seafood crops up as a common feature in nearly every type of cuisine Miami has on offer. The newest of these is one that goes by a few different names, be it **New World**, **Nuevo Latino**, **Tropical Fusion**, or **Floribbean**. Whatever the chef has called it, it's an exciting mix of high-flavor/low-fat dishes – a combination quite popular in body-conscience Miami – that draws upon nouvelle cuisine cooking methods and Caribbean-inflected ingredients. You'll find meats and shellfish paired with exotic fruits (mango, lychee, coconuts, and guava), vegetables (hearts of palm, avocados, and starchy tubers known as "yucca" or

A brief Cuban food glossary

Aguacate	Avocado
Ajo	Garlic
Arepas	Flat, cornmeal circle, like a pancake but tasting like polenta
Arroz con pollo	Chicken and yellow rice
Bunuelos	Cuban doughnuts usually with a licorice-tasting syrup
Cabra/Chivo	Goat
Camarones	Shrimp, prawns
Chorizo	Spicy sausage
Churrasco	Beef tenderloin marinated and grilled
Empanada	Fried or baked turnover filled with a ground beef mixture
Escabeche	Pickled fish
Langosta	Florida (or spiny) lobster
Maduros	Ripe, fried sweet plantains
Mariscos	Seafood
Moros y Cristianos	Black beans and white rice
Paella	Classic Spanish dish with saffron rice, chicken, and/or seafood
Papa	Potato
Pargo	Red snapper
Pulpo	Octopus
Queso	Cheese
Ropa vieja	Shredded beef in a light tomato base with mixed vegetables
Sesos	Brains
Tostones	Mashed, fried plantains
Tres leches	A sickly sweet Nicaraguan sponge cake, soaked in "three milks" – fresh, evaporated, and condensed

"cassava"), and zesty spices (ginger and tongue-burning scotch bonnet peppers), in these not-yet-typical meals.

While that style has been catching on, it is the **Cuban** influence that is most obviously present throughout Miami, extending well beyond the traditional haunts along Calle Ocho in **Little Havana** and into the stylish cafés of Miami Beach, Coconut Grove, and elsewhere. At the most basic spots, you can find such standbys as black beans and rice, shredded pork, fried plantains, and thick sandwiches piled with fresh meats, for absurdly low prices. A meal at a typical family-run Cuban diner can fill you up for the entire day.

Most restaurants operate between noon and midnight, with dinner being served from 5pm on; some places can be open quite late on weekends. It can be wise to call ahead, in any case, as many restaurants close on Sundays and/or Mondays.

Complementing the Cuban eateries are plenty of other well-priced ethnic spots, such as **Haitian** restaurants, **Italian** trattorias, **Indian** venues, and **Greek** diners. You shouldn't have to look too far to find numerous Asian treats, as sushi has caught on here, making **Japanese** a popular choice for a night out; there are some tasty **Thai** places as well, though relatively few **Chinese** options. Traditional **American**, of course, is well-represented, if a bit boring; burgers and fries, sometimes served in old-fashioned diners, are always a reliable option.

In Miami, the trend factor may dictate that it's as important where you eat as what you eat. One of the more scenic backdrops against which to dine is the glittering promenade of Ocean Drive in **South Beach**, though you may be paying for the atmosphere and view as much as anything. In

EATING

any case, you can often get by on just appetizers, as many such dishes can serve as meals on their own. **Coral Gables** is probably best for upmarket **cafés** and Mediterranean restaurants, while **Coconut Grove** tends to cater to more adventurous palates, with many of the new-style hotspots popping up there.

....

Make sure to dress appropriately if you're heading out to one of the city's trendier spots.

....

Our restaurant listings have been price-coded into five categories according to per-person meals: **cheap** (under $10), **inexpensive** ($10–15), **moderate** ($15–20), **expensive** ($20–40), and **very expensive** (over $40). These quotes are based on a three-course meal, minus drinks, tax, and tip; booze, in fact, may often be the most expensive part of your night out.

DOWNTOWN AND AROUND

Big Fish Mayaimi

Map 3, E8. 55 SW Miami Ave Rd ℂ373-1770. Moderate.
If you can get past the tongue-shaped menus and the bizarre rotation of sculptures littering the courtyard, you will be treated to deliciously fresh fish dishes – the seafood chowder is a must – and a splendid view of the Miami River. Closed Sun; lunch only June–Nov.

Cisco's Café

Map 2, D4. 5911 NW 36th St ℂ871-2764. Inexpensive.
The main dishes won't necessarily turn any heads, but extraordinary appetizers come piled high on rainbow-colored plates. Try the butter guacamole and homemade corn tortillas.

Dick's Last Resort

Map 3, F5. Bayside Marketplace, 401 Biscayne Blvd ℗375-6575. Inexpensive.

Food comes in buckets – fried chicken, shrimp, and crab legs to name a few – and you can choose from over fifty beers. Though located in the lively Bayside Marketplace it's got the look of an abandoned fishing shed, with unfinished wooden furniture, rope netting, and colored buoys and traps strewn about. There's live music on occasion adding to the already laid-back atmosphere.

Edelweiss

Map 2, E4. 2655 Biscayne Blvd ℗573-4421. Inexpensive.

This restaurant is the real deal, with hearty German and Swiss food serving traditional schnitzel, bratwurst, and excellent strudel desserts – a rarity in the Miami food scene.

da Ermanno

Map 2, F3. 6927 Biscayne Blvd ℗759-9470. Moderate.

Head chef Ermanno Perrotti creates some beautiful, classic Italian dishes here; standouts lean toward the decidedly unfancy, like the lasagna and spaghetti and meatballs.

Fishbone Grille

Map 3, D8. 650 S Miami Ave ℗530-1915. Cheap-Inexpensive.

A busy but friendly restaurant that serves the finest budget seafood in Miami, including an excellent seafood chowder and tender blackened grouper. Located next to the cool R&B tunes of *Tobacco Road* (see p.140), where many of the diners eventually head on to.

Hiro

Map 2, F3. 17516 Biscayne Blvd ℗948-3687. Inexpensive

A rather small and intimate venue that serves as Miami's only late-night sushi bar, popular with the city's sushi chefs after

DOWNTOWN AND AROUND

work. Their "night owl special" offers dinner and a drink for
$7.50 from midnight through 3am. Open until 4am.

Orlando Seafood Restaurant and Fish Market
Map 2, D4. 501 NW 37th Ave ⊘642-6767. Inexpensive.
They put together mouth-watering sandwiches packed with
the freshest daily catch and sprinkled with tasty Cuban spices.
A steady flow of hungry locals also munches on treats like tasty
fish croquettes and kingfish *escabeche* (pickled fish).

Rita's Italian Restaurant
Map 2, F3. 7232 Biscayne Blvd ⊘757-9470. Inexpensive–
Moderate.
Family-run Italian diner with checkered tablecloths, hearty
portions, good prices, and a friendly owner who will happily
chat about the specials.

S & S Diner
Map 2, E4. 1757 NE Second Ave ⊘373-4291. Cheap.
Down-home counter service-only joint serving comfort food
at a very slow pace. Plate-fulls of meatloaf, turkey, stuffed cab-
bage, beef stew, and pork chops for under $6 make this a good
place to grab a filling meal. Opens early for breakfast on weekdays and Saturdays; closed Sun.

Tark's Clam House
Map 2, F3. 13750 Biscayne Blvd ⊘944-8275. Inexpensive.
A fine place for fast-and-fresh seafood. Shrimp, Alaskan snow
crab, stone crab claws, clams, and oysters are all in great supply
and at low prices.

SOUTH BEACH AND AROUND

Big Pink
Map 4, E8. 157 Collins Ave ⊘531-0888. Cheap-Inexpensive.

Big portions of comfort food like mashed potatoes, ribs, and macaroni and cheese at 1950s' prices. The old-time red velvet cake will take you back a few years.

Casa Salsa
Map 4, F7. 524 Ocean Drive ℭ674-0411. Moderate.
Latin heart-throb Ricky Martin owns this lavishly decorated restaurant, which specializes in Puerto Rican and Spanish dishes that are average at best – most people come to see other patrons shaking their "bon-bon" during the wild salsa and mambo dancing breakouts during dinner.

Casona De Carlitos
Map 4, G1. 2232 Collins Ave ℭ534-7013. Moderate.
Hearty Argentinean food, including lots of Latin-style pasta and grilled red meats, accompanied by live music.

China Grill
Map 4, E7. 404 Washington St at Fifth St ℭ534-2211. Very expensive.
Sleek Asian fusion hotspot, serving tasty, if pricey, "family style" dishes like Caesars salad (with wontons, not crutons), lobster pancakes, and Szechuan beef.

Chrysanthemum
Map 4, F5. 1256 Washington Ave ℭ531-5656. Moderate.
Superb Peking and Szechuan cooking at moderate prices; a nice change of pace in a city with few Chinese restaurants.

Cielito Lindo Mexican Restaurant
Map 4, E3. 1626 Pennsylvania Ave ℭ673-0480. Cheap-Inexpensive.
Low-cost Mexican food is served with a smile in this cozy restaurant, handily placed just off Lincoln Road.

SOUTH BEACH AND AROUND

Local flavor

Forget *Starbucks* and *Dunkin' Donuts*; in Miami you should get your caffeine the way the locals do by tossing back a shot of extremely sweet, high-octane *café cubano* – more potent and always cheaper (*cafecitos* start at 25¢) than American-style coffee. The best *café con leche* – for a measly buck – is at 1462 Washington Ave, a small Cuban café known only by its address (thus no sign), which also sells pastries and fruity *batidos*. The following is a guide to the local coffee lexicon:

Café cubano/Cafecito A thimble-size shot of espresso and lots of sugar.
Café con leche Half Cuban coffee, half milk.
Colada A half cup of espresso and sugar that comes with thimble size cups to share with others; office workers usually take these to morning meetings.
Cortadito Same as a *colada* but with milk.

Eleventh Street Diner

Map 4, F5. 1065 Washington Ave ©534-6373. Cheap-Inexpensive.
All-American fare served around the clock on Fri and Sat; eat inside in cozy booths or outside on the terrace.

El Viajante Segundo

Map 4, F3. 1676 Collins Ave ©534-2101. Inexpensive.
A small restaurant tucked off of busy Collins Avenue with incredibly cheap Cuban food piled high. On weekends it's packed with hungry late-night revelers.

Joe's Stone Crabs

Map 4, D8. 227 Biscayne St ©673-0365. Expensive.
Only open mid-October through May, when Florida stone crabs are in season; expect long lines of people waiting to pay $20 for a

SOUTH BEACH AND AROUND

succulent plateful. The smart ones head next door to the takeout
(©673-4611) for speedier service and make a picnic out of it.

Larios on the Beach
Map 4, F6. 820 Ocean Drive ©532-9577. Inexpensive–Moderate.
Latin singer Gloria Estefan owns this festive eatery, specializing
in Nuevo Latino dishes. The food is both better and more
affordable than expected, and when the live band strikes up,
the place takes on a decidedly Latin nightclub feel – inspiring
many diners to dance.

da Leo Trattoria
Map 4, E2. 819 Lincoln Rd ©674-0350. Inexpensive.
Beef carpaccio and veal marsala are the best items on this trat-
toria's small but exciting menu. Extremely friendly waitstaff
that's liable to break into song, and good outdoor seating along
the Lincoln Road promenade.

Les Deux Fontaines
Map 4, F4. 1230-38 Ocean Drive ©672-7878. Moderate.
Nightly seafood specials in an oceanfront setting. On Mondays,
you can get two lobsters for $21; Tuesdays are all-you-can-eat
shrimp nights. Otherwise, try any of the fresh fish dishes with
creative sauces, and live jazz, dixieland, and swing music from
Wed to Sun.

News Café
Map 4, F6. 800 Ocean Drive ©538-6397. Inexpensive-Moderate.
Utterly fashionable sidewalk café with an extensive breakfast,
lunch, and dinner menu. Its location on Ocean Drive is prime
seating for viewing the South Beach promenade.

NOA
Map 4, D2. 801 Lincoln Rd ©925-0050. Moderate.

SOUTH BEACH AND AROUND

A fun newcomer to Lincoln Road, this hotspot attracts a beautiful crowd craving creative noodle dishes and a selection of exotic drinks with which to wash them down.

Osteria del Teatro

Map 4, F4. 1443 Washington Ave ℂ538-7850. Moderate.
One look at the mouth-watering dessert table strategically placed near the door and you'll find it hard to pass by. This Italian favorite is always packed with a stylish South Beach crowd hooked on the fresh pasta specials, extensive wine list, and, of course, the desserts.

Palace Bar & Grill

Map 4, G4. 1200 Ocean Drive ℂ531-9077. Inexpensive.
One of the few trendy places for breakfast – it actually opens at 8am. Otherwise expect a standard selection of soups and sandwiches, quite inexpensive for the area.

Pizza Rustica

Map 4, E6. 863 Washington Ave ℂ674-8244. Inexpensive.
Fashionable pizzeria with creative topping combinations – individual Sicilian slices, starting at $3.50, are huge and cut into four smaller, more manageable squares. Outdoor seating is preferable to the oven-like heat inside.

Puerto Sagua

Map 4, F6. 700 Collins Ave ℂ673-1115. Cheap–Inexpensive.
Where local Cubans meet gringos over espresso, beans, and rice. Cheap, filling breakfasts, lunches, and dinners.

Rolo's

Map 4, C4. 1439 Alton Rd ℂ535-2220. Inexpensive.

Bleach-blondes and tanned Latin surfers breakfast here before surf's up. Also open for lunch and dinner with Cuban/American fare on offer – stocks a formidable range of beers as well. See Chapter 11, "Drinking."

Happy hours

Almost every restaurant in Miami has a **happy hour**, usually on weekdays from 5 to 8pm, when drinks are cheap and come in tandem with a large pile of free food – varying from chicken wings and conch fritters to chips and popcorn. Below are some of the best spots to chow down with a few cocktails.

Coco Loco's, *Sheraton*, 495 Brickell Ave near downtown Miami ✆373-6000. No better place to finish off a day downtown; the drink prices don't come down, but for a dollar you can help yourself to a massive buffet.

Doc Dammers' Bar & Grill, *Colonnade Hotel*, 180 Aragon Ave, Coral Gables ✆441-2600. Where the young(ish) and unattached of Coral Gables mingle after work to the strains of a pianist.

Monty's Raw Bar, 2550 S Bayshore Drive, Coconut Grove ✆858-1431. Cheap drinks wash down the complimentary seafood and tropical music. All this with a bay view makes it one of the best early-evening activities around.

Shagnasty's Saloon & Eatery, 638 S Miami Ave, near downtown Miami ✆381-8970. The hip yuppie's happy hour hangout, with free appetizers and many discounted drinks.

Smith & Wollensky's, 1 Washington Ave, Miami Beach ✆673-1708. Cut-price oysters, shrimp, and drinks in a lively, congenial atmosphere.

San Loco

Map 4, F4. 235 14th St ℂ538-3009. Inexpensive.
Consistently rated the number-one spot in Miami Beach for
Mexican food. Their tacos are sloppy, packed, and cheap. The
"Guaco Loco" – a hard-shell taco wrapped in a soft tortilla and
fully loaded – is the best seller here, but don't miss their fresh
and chunky guacamole as well.

Tantra

Map 4, E2. 1445 Pennsylvania Ave ℂ672-4765. Expensive.
The sensual Indian flavors offered up here are part of the
restaurant's Tantric theme – enhanced by muted lighting and a
beautiful waitstaff.

See "Nightlife," p.130, for more about the grass dance
floor and mesmerizing belly dancers.

Tap Tap Haitian Restaurant

Map 4, D7. 819 Fifth St ℂ672-2898. Inexpensive.
The tastiest and most attractively presented Haitian food in
Miami. Wander around the restaurant to admire the Haitian
murals, and visit the upstairs gallery where exhibits on worthy
Haitian themes are held. Highly recommended.

Ted's Hideaway South

Map 4, F8. 124 Second St (no phone). Inexpensive.
Downbeat bar that proffers cheap fried chicken, steak, and red
beans and rice; see review on p.125.

Thai Toni

Map 4, E6. 890 Washington Ave ℂ538-8424. Inexpensive.
The menu doesn't stray too far from standard Thai dishes, but
it's all well done and the fashionable crowd makes it a fun place
to see and be seen.

Wolfie's

Map 4, G1. 2038 Collins Ave ©538-6626. Cheap-Inexpensive.
Long-established deli drawing an entertaining mix of New
York retirees and late-night clubbers – all served generous help-
ings by beehive-haired waitresses. Open 24 hours, and serving
$1.99 "breakfast specials" throughout the day.

....

**Be aware that many South Beach restaurants have
adopted a tricky but perfectly legal way of adding a 15
percent gratuity to bills, so check before you tip
twice.**

....

Yuca

Map 4, F2. 501 Lincoln Rd ©532-9822. Very Expensive.
Still the rave of food critics up and down the land, serving
Nuevo Latino cuisine in an upscale but relaxed setting; great
stuff, but expect to pay about $50 per person.

CENTRAL AND NORTH MIAMI BEACH

Bangkok Orchid

5563 NW 72nd Ave ©887-3000. Inexpensive.
Delicious Thai dishes along a bland stretch lacking any other
remotely exotic eateries.

Café Prima Pasta

414 71st St ©867-0106. Inexpensive.
One of the best Italian restaurants in Miami – and one of the
least expensive. The place is tiny, so either arrive early or be
prepared to wait.

Chef Allen's

19088 NE 29th Ave ©935-2900. Very Expensive.

CENTRAL AND NORTH MIAMI BEACH

Outstanding New Floridian cuisine created by Allen Susser, widely rated as one of America's greatest chefs. Dine here if money's not a problem.

Rascal House

17190 Collins Ave ℭ947-4581. Inexpensive.
Largest, loudest, and most authentic New York deli in town; huge portions and cafeteria ambiance.

LITTLE HAVANA

Casa Juancho

Map 5, A5. 2436 SW Eighth St ℭ642-2452. Moderate.
Some of the entrees border on the pricey side, but overall the prices are reasonable – tapas are good value at $6–8 – and there's a convivial mood as strolling musicians serenade the wealthy Cuban clientele.

Covadonga

6480 SW Eighth St ℭ261-2406. Moderate.
This nautical-themed restaurant lets you pick your dinner from large tanks along the wall. Delicious Cuban seafood specialties, like *escabeche*, inspire the predominantly local clientele to keep this one a secret.

El Bodegon de Castilla

Map 2, D5. 2499 SW Eighth St ℭ649-0863. Moderate–Expensive.
Iberian flavors embellish the local grouper, snapper, sole, and other seafood dishes, though you may find it a bit on the pricey side.

El Cid

Map 2, C5. 117 NW 42nd Ave ℭ642-3144. Moderate.
A gargantuan Moorish-style castle where the staff dresses as knaves and displays of freshly killed fowl greet you at the door.

As accompaniment, there's lots of drinking, singing, and eating, with affordable Spanish and Cuban delicacies; decidedly kitschy, but also pretty fun.

La Carreta

3632 SW Eighth St ⓒ444-7501. Cheap-Inexpensive.
The real sugarcane growing around the wagon wheel outside is a good sign: inside, hearty portions of home-style Cuban cooking are served at unbeatable prices. The vibe is relaxed and comforting, with a nice mix of locals and inquisitive visitors making up the crowd.

La Palacio de los Jugos

Map 2, C5. 5721 W Flagler Ave ⓒ264-1503. Inexpensive–Moderate.
A handful of tables at the back of this Cuban produce market seat those too hungry to carry the goods out of the shop. The pork sandwiches and shellfish soup are the tastiest for miles.

Las Islas Canarias

Map 2, D5. 285 NW 27th Ave ⓒ649-0440. Daily 7am–11pm. Cheap–Inexpensive.
Don't let its location, tucked away inside a drab shopping mall, fool you; this chilled-out eatery serves piles of fine, Cuban food at unbeatable prices.

Malaga

Map 5, F5. 740 SW Eighth St ⓒ858-4224. Inexpensive.
Basic Spanish and Cuban cuisine, with good daily fish specials and a lovely outdoor courtyard. A dependable choice for sitting down and soaking up the culture.

Versailles

Map 2, D5. 3555 SW Eighth St ⓒ444-0240. Inexpensive.
Coming to *Versailles* is a bit like walking into someone's over-sized dining room and being treated like a special guest of the

LITTLE HAVANA

house. Lovely decor and excellent food, though there isn't too much English spoken here, so you might want to brush up on a few Cuban terms.

CORAL GABLES

Cafe Kolibri

Map 6, E9. 6901 Red Rd ℃665-2421. Inexpensive.
Doubling as a Tuscan restaurant and a top-notch bakery, *Café Kolibri* specializes in low-fat, gourmet entrees. They also have great vegan choices and, of course, fresh warm breads to die for.

Caffe Abbracci

Map 6, F3. 318 Aragon Ave ℃441-0700. Moderate–Expensive.
Classy Italian dining that holds the attention of a fashionable crowd as they sip wine on the ivy-draped portico. Potato dumplings in a light pink gorgonzola sauce, salmon ravioli, and porcini mushroom risotto are to die for – and to cut costs a little, all pasta dishes can be ordered as appetizers.

Darbar

Map 6, F3. 276 Alhambra Circle ℃448-9691. Inexpensive-Moderate.
When the call for curry arrives in seafood-obsessed Miami, *Darbar* is a good place to seek refuge, for its full selection of spicy lamb and chicken dishes. Onion Bhaji is a good starter at $4, but save room for the creamy Shahi Chicken Kurma ($12). Closed Sun.

Doc Dammers' Bar & Grill

Map 6, F4. *Colonnade Hotel*, 180 Aragon Ave ℃569-6511. Moderate.
Dine among "Doc's" famous friends in this spacious, old-style saloon, where photos of Amelia Earhart, Babe Ruth, and Will Rogers adorn the walls. Dishes are named after them as well: Valentino's lobster ravioli and Louis Armstrong's jambalaya are a couple of standouts. There is live entertainment at its outdoor patio bar nightly.

Hofbrau Pub & Grill

Map 6, G3. 172 Giralda Ave ©442-2730. Cheap-Inexpensive.
Here you will find your usual heart-stopping bar food like buffalo wings and chicken tenders as well as juicy "brau" burgers
and the best knockwurst sandwich this side of Berlin.
Wednesday nights are a $7 all-you-can-eat fish fry. If that's not
your thing, you can check out one of the fifty beers on tap and
in bottles.

Restaurant St Michel

Map 6, G3. *Hotel Place St Michel*, 162 Alcazar Ave ©444-1666.
Expensive.
Outstanding French and Mediterranean cuisine amid a romantic setting of antiques and flowers. Entrees may seem a bit
pricey at around $20 a plate, but the ambiance and attentive
service make it a memorable treat.

Victor's Café

Map 2, D6. 2340 SW 32nd Ave ©445-1313. Moderate.
The Cuban arts and crafts and mambo musicians make this
feel like old-time Havana. Black beans and rice come with
every delicious meal – try the jumbo shrimp in champagne
sauce.

Wrapido

Map 6, G4. 2334 Ponce de Leon Blvd ©443-1884. Cheap.
Pop in for a refreshing smoothie and a quick wrap sandwich in
flavorful tortillas. You can get in and out for under $10 without
a snag.

Yoko's

Map 6, F7. 4041 Ponce de Leon Blvd ©444-6622. Inexpensive.
Intimate Japanese restaurant usually packed with students from
the neighboring University of Miami. Great vegetable tempu-
ra, as well as a fresh sushi bar and friendly service.

CORAL GABLES

Café Med
Map 7, D5. 3015 Grand Ave ✆443-1770. Moderate.
Delicious Mediterranean cuisine in an excellent people-watching location. Try the "Tropicale Carpaccio," with hearts of palm, avocado, and chunky parmesan shavings.

Café Tu Tu Tango
Map 7, D5. CocoWalk, 3015 Grand Ave ✆529-2222. Cheap.
This is an absolute must in Miami – a quirky and entertaining spot themed as an artist's garret where patrons dine in full view of painters working their canvases. Try the cajun chicken eggrolls or oriental beef skewers served in tapas-sized portions and at high speed.

Greenstreet Café
Map 7, D6. 3110 Commodore Plaza ✆567-0662. Inexpensive.
Quaint sidewalk café with eclectic assortment of foods ranging from Middle Eastern to Jamaican.

Hungry Sailor
Map 7, D5. 3064 Grand Ave ✆444-9359. Inexpensive.
Pseudo-British pub with moderately successful fish'n'chips and shepherd's pie, but does better with its conch chowder; also fine just for knocking back a few pints. Also reviewed in "Drinking," p.128, and "Nightlife," p.137.

Le Bouchon du Grove
Map 7, D6. 3430 Main Hwy ✆448-6060. Moderate.
Don't let the chi-chi name fool you. Here you'll find unpretentious French food, with fabulous Kir Royales (blackcurrant liquor and champagne) and freshly prepared desserts at reasonable prices.

Paulo Luigi's
Map 7, D4. 3324 Virginia St ©445-9000. Inexpensive.
A favorite haunt of local NBA players from the Miami Heat, this attractive Italian eatery offers up inventive (and inexpensive) pasta dishes and great pizza.

Taurus Chops
Map 7, D6. 3540 Main Hwy ©448-0633. Moderate.
A burger joint that stands out as the area's most casual local watering hole. *Taurus* serves up meat without apologies and lots and lots of suds.

KEY BISCAYNE

Bayside Hut
Map 2, F6. 3501 Rickenbacker Causeway ©361-0808. Inexpensive.
Atmospheric Tiki bar, long a favorite with hungry boaters, where you may also see a few feline friends wandering around the decks. Highlights include the fresh seafood and tasty seasoned French fries.

The Sandbar
Map 2, F6. *Silver Sands Motel & Villas*, 301 Ocean Drive ©361-5441. Inexpensive.
Tucked-away seafood restaurant offering affordable lunch or dinner a pebble's throw from crashing ocean waves. There's also a good bar scene (see "Drinking," p.129).

South Fork Grill & Bar
Map 2, F6. 3301 Rickenbacker Causeway ©365-9391. Inexpensive.
Tex-Mex specialties in a gorgeous outdoor setting on the water. It's worth it to linger over the frozen sangria and experience the amazing sunsets.

KEY BISCAYNE

Sundays on the Bay

Map 2, F6. 5420 Crandon Blvd ©361-6777. Moderate.

Marina seafood eatery catering to the boats and beer set. Their elaborate brunches are spectacular. Lunch and dinner consists of seafood dishes and seasonal veggies. Very casual.

SOUTH MIAMI AND HOMESTEAD

Akashi

Map 2, C7. 5830 S Dixie Hwy ©665-6261. Inexpensive.

Generous sushi boats and tender chicken teriyaki make this a worthwhile stop if you're out in this direction – or just in the mood for some good Japanese food.

Chifa Chinese Restaurant

Map 2, A7. 12590 N Kendall Drive ©271-3823. Inexpensive.

In all probability the only restaurant in Florida specializing in Peruvian-Cantonese cuisine. Tasty deep-fried appetizers, run-of-the-mill main courses, plus a range of Chinese and Peruvian beers are served up at budget prices.

El Toro Taco

1 S Krome Ave ©245-8182. Cheap.

Excellent family-run Mexican restaurant. A gem in the center of Homestead that makes a good place to stop en route to the Keys.

Fountain & Grill

Map 2, C7. Sunset Drugs, 5640 Sunset Drive ©667-1807. Inexpensive.

Once you've done the seafood thing to death, this large retro diner, which boasts well-executed milkshakes, grilled cheese, burgers, and meatloaf, may be just what you've been craving.

Shorty's Bar-B-Q

Map 2, B7. 9200 S Dixie Hwy ©670-7732. Cheap.

Come here to sit at a picnic table, tuck in a napkin, and graze on barbecued ribs, chicken, and corn on the cob – pausing only to check out the cowboy memorabilia on the walls.

Wagons West

Map 2, B7. 11311 S Dixie Hwy ⓒ238-9942. Cheap–Inexpensive. Maximum cholesterol breakfasts and other unhealthy fare are consumed in this always crowded, budget-priced shrine to cowboys and the Wild West. The menu is made up of hearty chili, burgers, fajitas, and other southwestern favorites.

Drinking

M iami is not a city peppered with bars or other low-key **drinking** establishments, though you'll find the occasional casual dive and British-style pub in which to hoist a few pints. Instead, much of the city's imbibing often takes place in restaurants, nightclubs, and discos, with a number of hotel bars and upscale lounges serving to bolster the overall scene. For a place in the region that has a real concentration of bars, you'd likely have to move on to **Key West**, covered in chapter 23.

For reviews of Miami restaurants, see Chapter 10; for clubs and discos, see Chapter 12.

Most places here are open from 11am or noon until midnight or 2am, with the liveliest hours between 10pm and 1am. Among the following listings, some are suited to an early evening, pre-dinner tipple, while others – especially those in **Coconut Grove** and **Miami Beach** – make prime vantage points for watching the city's poseurs come and go. The flashy hotel bars lining **Ocean Drive** offer a little bit of everything, ranging from slushy frozen drinks mixed in washing machine-style blenders to Cuban *mojitos* (rum and lime spritzers).

For a key to some of the more exotic drinks Miami specializes in, see the box on p.126.

Prices generally go according to how hard it is to get in a place; the discreet lounges and flashy clubs charge well above the average. Fortunately, enough **happy hours** at mellower establishments can cut those costs way down – and fuel you up for the evening as well; see the box on p.111 in "Eating" for details.

DOWNTOWN AND AROUND

Churchill's Hideaway
Map 2, E4. 5501 NE Second Ave ©757-1807.
Tucked into Little Haiti, this is certainly the last place one would expect a pub pouring pints of bitter while rugby and soccer games play on satellite TV. If it feels a bit like a rugged old boys' club, that could be its previous occupation as a speakeasy talking, but overall the mood is convivial, aided by the occasional live music.

Tobacco Road
Map 3, E8. 626 S Miami Ave ©374-1198.
Crusty R&B venue (see "Live Music" p.140) where plenty of serious boozing goes on in the downstairs bar. Laid-back, always crowded, and good for late-night drinking.

SOUTH BEACH

The Abbey Brewing Company
Map 4, C3.1115 16th St ©538-8110.
A small and homey spot, South Beach's only microbrewery (try the creamy Oatmeal Stout – their best and most popular brew) has a long $2-per-pint happy hour (1-7pm) on weeknights.

Banana Cabana

Map 4, G1. *Banana Bungalow Hostel*, 2360 Collins Ave
℗1-800-7-HOSTEL.

Cocktails and frozen drinks start at $2, and beers are 50¢ during happy hour, at the *Banana Bungalow's* poolside tiki bar. Although the bar is primarily for guests, it's open to anyone who wants to drink on the cheap – thus is often packed with thirsty travelers.

Delano

Map 4, F2. 1685 Collins Ave ℗672-2000 or 1-800/555-5001.

Gauzy white curtains whisk you into a surreal bar area, where $9 cocktails are not unheard of. Linger casually and spot a celebrity or two slinking around the poolside cabanas in the back.

Mac's Club Deuce

Map 4, F4. 222 Fourteenth St ℗531-6200.

Raucous neighborhood bar open until 5am, with a good jukebox, pool table, and a diverse clientele of cops, transvestites, artists, models, and anyone else in search of a nightcap.

Irish House

Map 4, C4. 1430 Alton Rd ℗534-5667.

This old neighborhood haunt, with two well-used pool tables, some TVs and a few dartboards, is the definition of laid back. Far away from the busy South Beach scene, it's very much a cherished locals' place. Beer and wine only.

Lost Weekend

Map 4, F4. 218 Española Way ℗672-1707.

An interesting mix of baseball hat-wearing fraternity types, budding literary artists, and fashion plates, all of whom skulk around pool tables and the very long, inviting bar. A plush upstairs loft lets you look down (literally) on the drinkers. Good beer selection and drink specials nearly every night.

Marlin Bar

Map 4, F4. 1200 Collins Ave ℗604-5000.

Looking every bit as hip as one would expect from Miami, this sleek and futuristic bar attracts the smart set with its dimly lit lounge and dazzling martinis – which run around $10 and up.

Rebar

Map 4, F5. 1121 Washington Ave ℗672-4788.

This is the South Beach bar for the fashionably grungy. Cheap drinks and a rowdy clientele make for fun, wild nights with few pretensions. Beers are about $3 a pop.

Ted's Hideaway South

Map 4, F8. 124 Second St (no phone).

Ted's boasts beer (in the can) for a dollar and special reductions on draught when it rains. Basic bar food is available around the clock; it will do the trick, but won't win any awards.

Zeke's Roadhouse

Map 4, E2. 625 Lincoln Rd ℗532-0087.

A small, wildly popular hangout along trendy Lincoln Road for good, cheap beers – nightly specials include three beer selections starting at $2.50 each. Over 57 varieties to choose from – and no velvet rope to wait behind.

CORAL GABLES

The Crown and Garter Pub

Map 6, F5. 270 Catalonia Ave ℗441-0204.

If you're looking for a well-poured pint of Guinness, this is the place to be, popular with resident Brits and anglophiles of all nationalities for shooting the breeze over a couple of drinks.

CORAL GABLES

Cool drinks

In a city as hot as Miami, drinks both serve to keep you cool and, in many cases, to keep you looking cool. Though beer is as popular here as anywhere, it's the eye-catching, exotic cocktails, served in flashy glassware, that remind you of the tropical climate. Lime, sugar, and lots of ice are often key ingredients, but there are a number of ways to order in the know.

Cuba Libre Fancy name for rum and coke, with a dash of lime juice.

Daiquiri Originally it was made up of rum, lime, and sugar shaken over ice and served straight up. Today it has transformed into a gooey, frozen drink with fruity additions like strawberry, mango, and papaya.

Fontainebleau Special An unusual mix of brandy, anisette, and dry vermouth.

Mambo's Dream A frozen blend of dark rum, banana liqueur, triple sec, and pineapple and lemon juices.

Margarita At its most basic, it's tequilla, triple sec, and lime juice.

Mojito With fresh mint, sugar, rum, lime juice, and soda water, this is a classic Miami drink.

Rumrunner Usually served frozen, this potent rum drink is a bit of a mix and match made from rum, either banana flavored, blackberry flavored, light, or dark, and mixed with liquors, fruit juice, or sour mix.

Schnorkel Rum, pernod (a yellowish liquor with anise flavor), lime, and sugar.

Doc Dammer's

Map 6, G4. 180 Aragon Ave, *Omni Colonnade Hotel* ℂ441-2600.
Named for a former city mayor, *Doc's* is a bit clinical in atmosphere, what with its white marble floor, but the massive happy-hour food buffets make for great bargain eating.

Duffy's Tavern

Map 6, A3. 2108 SW 57th Ave ℂ264-6580.
Pool tournaments and a large TV screen for the athletically interested drinker are the main attractions here. Most of its clientele swagger over from the University of Miami, not surprising in light of the inexpensive prices.

The Globe

Map 6, F3. 377 Alhambra Circle ℂ445-3555.
Tucked into the Lorraine Travel building, this small bar serves stiff drinks and occasionally hosts live music on its outdoor patio. The upscale bar menu (with prices to match) caters to a trendy clientele.

John Martin's

Map 6, F4. 253 Miracle Mile ℂ445-3777.
This Irish pub and restaurant occasionally has folk singers and harpists accompany the never-ending flow of imported beers. Rich oak, mahogany, and brass accents add a homey authenticity to the pub, which carries you a long way from sunny Miami.

Satchmo's

Map 6, G3. 60 Merrick Way ℂ774-1883.
Named for Louie Armstrong, *Satchmo's* is perfect for a cool, smoky evening of sultry blues and jazz tunes, with a four-hour happy hour – beginning at 3.30pm – to warm you up.

CORAL GABLES

Hungry Sailor

Map 7, D6. 3426 Main Hwy ✆444-9359.

A legendary haunt, probably more for its longevity than atmosphere, this place can be a bit of a tourist trap. Interior designs resemble a worn-out British pub with overpriced Bass and Watneys on tap. Nightly live reggae lightens things up a bit.

Iguana Cantina

Map 7, E4. Streets of Mayfair, 3rd floor ✆444-6606.

The sheer number of tropical colors in this place makes it seem like a group of parrots walked in and exploded. In any case, it's a lively enough hangout, with a slew of themed nights including free sushi on Wednesdays and 50¢ margaritas on Thursdays.

Martini Bar

Map 7, E4. Streets of Mayfair ✆444-5911.

There's nightly jazz on offer at this sleek spot filled with black-clad hipsters sipping a variety of martinis. Happy-hour specials (which alternate between 5–8pm and 9–11pm) include two-for-one deals and free champagne for the fairer sex.

Murphy's Law

Map 7, E5. 2977 McFarlane Rd ✆446-9956.

What appears to be a quaint Irish pub from the outside is really a raucous sports bar, complete with giant screen TVs, a good selection of imported British ales, and lots of shouting from the crowd. It usually fills up with stragglers from the *Hungry Sailor* or fans of soccer when games are on.

Taurus

Map 7, D6. 3540 Main Hwy ✆448-0633.

An old Coconut Grove drinking institution, with a special discounted burger grill on weekends and a nostalgic Sixties-loving crowd every day.

Tigertail Lounge
Map 7, E2. 3205 SW 27th Ave ©854-9172.
Low-key drinking establishment, where a proliferation of Budweiser and buffalo wings attests to the very lack of pretension.

KEY BISCAYNE

The Sandbar
Map 2, F6. *Silver Sands Motel & Villas*, 301 Ocean Drive ©361-5441.
The poolside bar is perfect for sipping frozen drinks while watching the ocean crash onto the shore. The crowd (if there is one) is a mix of relaxed tourists and thirsty locals.

Sunday's on the Bay
Map 2, F6. 5420 Crandon Blvd ©361-6777.
A great spot to relax and call it a day, set on the spacious deck of a waterfront restaurant overlooking Biscayne Bay (see "Eating," p.120).

Nightlife

Miami **nightlife** is pretty much centered around its **club** scene, which is one of the most happening anywhere in the world. Velvet ropes, sleek dance floors, and beautiful (if often heaving) crowds are as much a part of Miami's self-image as the beach itself – an image the city takes perhaps a bit too seriously. In fact, much of the glamour of Miami is rooted in the after-hours culture of attractive, well-dressed partyers pushing the limits of decadence and hopping between celebrity-owned places that sometimes thrive on an air of exclusivity. The trendiest spots are, unsurprisingly, secreted about Miami Beach's **South Beach**; they can be hard to ferret out, as signs are few and possibilities for smooth entry perhaps even fewer. You should definitely look to **dress up** wherever you go, as strictly enforced codes are in place, and expect to pay a hefty cover charge.

The club scene in South Beach is constantly shifting; check out the Web sites listed in Chapter 1, "Introducing the city," or the free weekly *New Times* to keep up with the changes.

A number of Miami's clubs have a Latin feel to them – with salsa and merengue blaring on the sound systems – a cultural influence that carries over into the **live music** activity here. Miami's musical heritage is very much steeped in the sounds of **Latin** musicians, and Cuban-born, Miami-bred stars like Gloria Estefan and Jon Secada helped Latin pop gain widespread acceptance in the US during the 1980s and 1990s – if not actually becoming a fixture in local music venues, due to its typically slick studio sound. More recently, though, Latin music's popularity has truly exploded in the States, with the success of singers like Enrique Iglesias and Ricky Martin and of the independent film *Buena Vista Social Club*, which documents a legendary group of Cuban musicians. The resultant interest has helped pick up the live-music landscape in Miami, with many venues beginning to supply special Latin nights. Nevertheless, **rock** music is still what's most available throughout the city, though the quality is not that of what you'd find somewhere like New York or Los Angeles. Miami fares better in terms of **reggae** – thanks to a large Jamaican community – and **jazz**, with enough **R&B** and **blues** to suit fans of those genres, and a minor **folk** scene as well.

CLUBS

Follow the snaking lines and stretch limos in South Beach to find the hottest club of the night; most actually appear to be abandoned shopfronts during the daytime, coming alive only well after the sun sets. No matter their popularity, clubs are often subject to frequent closings and openings; best to call ahead to make sure the club is still operating or hasn't changed locations. Club **hours** are usually from 11pm to 5am, and cover **costs** hover around $10–15 on average.

Amnesia

Map 4, E8. 136 Collins Ave, South Beach ©531-5535.
Thurs–Sat 11pm–5am, Sun 5pm–2am. Thurs–Sat $10, Sun $5.
Open-air, multilevel dance floor decorated with potted plants,
red marble tiles, plush tropical-printed cushions, and a three-
tiered wedding-cake fountain. Most notable for its "Foam
Parties," where thrashing dancers are doused with foam bubbles, and its "Gay Tea Parties" on Sunday evenings.

Bash

Map 4, E6. 655 Washington Ave, South Beach ©538-2274.
Mon–Sat 10pm–5am, Sun 11pm–5am. Mon–Thurs & Sun $10, Fri &
Sat $15.
In this forever "in" club, co-owned by actor Sean Penn and
Simply Red's Mick Hucknall, there's a stunning garden patio
with an intimate bar and beckoning dance floor outside, and
harder dance rhythms inside. Wednesday is "Fashion Night,"
when models, divas, and drag queens strut their stuff down a
mock runway.

Café Nostalgia

Map 5, A5. 2212 SW Eighth St, Little Havana ©541-2631.
Daily 9pm–3am. Cover varies $5–15.
The best salsa club in Miami, with fiery house band Groupo
Nostalgia making hips swing and bodies shake until the early
hours. Latin musicians pour in from earlier gigs to close out the
night here.

Club Tropigala

Map 2, G4. *Fontainebleau Hotel*, 4441 Collins Ave, Miami Beach
©538-2000.
Wed, Thurs, & Sun 7–11pm, Fri & Sat 7pm–2am. $15.
Latin-flavored supper club, staging extravagant production
numbers headed by a bevy of dancers and well-known drag
queen Candy Caramelo.

CLUBS

Groove Jet
Map 4, G1. 323 23rd St, South Beach ℂ532-2002.
Tues & Thurs–Sun 11pm–5am. $10.
This place packs in an A-list Hollywood crowd – located enough away from the rest of the club scene to seem elite. The intimate nooks and crannies throughout create a good environment for furtive people-watching.

Liquid
Map 4, F4. 1439 Washington Ave, Miami Beach ℂ532-9154.
Mon & Fri–Sun 11pm–5am. $10.
Local club gal Ingrid Casares has perhaps the hottest club on the beach. Stars galore congregate here for a wild rave-up and frequent fashion shows. Once past the seemingly impenetrable velvet ropes, dancers could care less who they're dancing next to or who may show up to observe you in the super-private VIP lounge. Monday nights have a popular funk theme; Sundays are primarily gay nights.

Living Room at the Strand
Map 4, E6. 671 Washington Ave, South Beach ℂ532-2340.
Daily 8.30pm–5am. Mon–Thurs $10, Fri & Sat $15.
Provided you get by the intimidating bouncers, an ominous red interior ushers you toward the tiny dance floor and boomerang-shaped bar. A hangout for the area's hard-at-work models, who lounge on the club's cushy couches – though you shouldn't get comfortable in one unless you're planning on buying a bottle of bubbly, the least expensive beginning at $150.

Lua
Map 4, F4. 409 Española Way, Miami Beach ℂ534-0061.
It may look like an abandoned store from the outside, but inside you'll be pleasantly surprised by an intimate dance room with plush couches, soft lighting from strategically placed

CLUBS

Comic relief

How seriously does Miami take itself? From the looks of its limited **comedy** scene – very seriously. No wonder the bouncers aren't laughing.

Improv Comedy Club, inside Streets of Mayfair, 3390 Mary St, Coconut Grove ©441-8200. Part of the nationwide chain of Improv comedy clubs and the best spot in Miami for comedy, despite the rather formal atmosphere. Reservations required.

New Theater, 65 Almeia Ave, Coral Gables ©443-5909. The last two nights of each month showcase the hilarious talents of the Laughing Gas Comedy Improv Company.

Rascals Comedy Club, 8505 Miller Drive Suite R2, South Miami ©274-5411. Also part of a national chain, this venue has played host to some impressive up-and-coming acts. $8 weekly; $10 Friday and Saturday with two-drink minimum (18 and older).

lamps, and a sampling of the beautiful people. Makes you feel like you belong to a secret club without the snobbiness and hassle of getting into one.

Penrod's

Map 4, G8. 1 Ocean Drive, South Beach ©538-1111.
Daily 11pm–5am. $10.

The extremely selective door staff is a bit tiring, but the thumping beats and slick dance floor filled with giddy beautiful people is entertaining to observe and – perhaps after a few – join. Monday night's party is the "Beehive Lounge," pulling models and music industry folks in for funk, soul, and R&B.

Salvation

Map 4, C2. 1775 West Ave, South Beach ℂ673-6508.
Fri–Sun 10pm–5am. $12–15.

Predominantly gay, this former warehouse packs in the diehard
dancers on the enormous blue and red dance floor. Gawk from
above on the surrounding balcony or squint your eyes at the
unusual art dotting the walls. The club used to be overwhelmed by club kids from LA and NY, but it now caters to a
more sophisticated (and older) set of revelers.

Shadow Lounge

Map 4, C2. 1532 Washington Ave, South Beach ℂ531-9411.
Wed–Sun 11pm–5am. $10–15.

Surprisingly enormous interior for a South Beach club; it's most
popular with a youngish crowd and hosts various parties each
night of the week: Wednesday's party, "Bitch," is gay night,
"Fashionable Friday" brings in the well-dressed, and "Shadow
Sunday" hosts top DJs from New York spinning hip hop.

Starfish

Map 4, C2.1427 West Ave, South Beach ℂ673-1717.
Daily 10pm–3am. No cover.

This is Miami's unofficial salsa headquarters, offering free lessons
on Monday and Wednesday at 7pm for the novices. Come back
on Friday, for "Strictly Salsa" night, to show off your skills.

Tantra

Map 4, E3.1445 Pennsylvania Ave, Miami Beach ℂ672-4765.
Daily 7pm–3am.

A unique spot in Miami, this Indian/Mediterranean restaurant
(see "Eating," p.112) has a grass dance floor which provides the
setting for moving to the rhythms of trance-inducing New Age
tunes. A communal hookah pipe billowing Turkish tobacco
smoke and the erotic belly dancers spinning about add to the
ambiance.

CLUBS

Warsaw Ballroom

Map 4, F4. 1450 Collins Ave, Miami Beach ℂ531-4555.

Wed–Sat 9pm–5am. $5 after 11.30pm Wed–Fri.

A glam gay club, open to everyone, with a fabulous repertoire of music, drag queens, and décor; one of the most exciting and extravagant nightspots on the beach. Don't miss the hysterically camp "Strip Night" on Wednesdays, where "dancing queens" shed their costumes. See "Gay and lesbian Miami," p.154.

LIVE MUSIC

Unlike clubs, all concentrated in South Beach, live music **venues** are spread more evenly throughout the city. Though much of the prime action takes place on weekends, you won't have a hard time finding some new band or other any day of the week. Expect to pay about $10–20 for bands you've actually heard of; for local acts admission may be free, or anywhere up to $5 or so. Most places open up at 8 or 9pm, with the main band onstage around 11pm or midnight.

The most up-to-date live show **listings** are in *New Times*, but if you can't decide where to go on a Friday night, head to South Pointe Park (see p.36), where there's entertainment ranging from city-sponsored events to the latest MTV dance party, and often lively, **free concerts**.

....

For more magazine and Web site listings, see "Introducing the city," p.13.

....

LATIN, CARIBBEAN, AND REGGAE

Bayside Hut

Map 2, F6. 3501 Rickenbacker Causeway, Key Biscayne ℂ361-0808.

Sat–Sun hours vary.

Nestled behind the old Miami Marine Stadium, this tiki-style
venue hosts mellow reggae jams on the weekends. The scene is
laid-back and lots of fun – with a good, enthusiastic crowd.

Clevelander

Map 4, F5. 1020 Ocean Drive, *Clevelander Hotel*, Miami Beach,
©531-3485.
Daily 11am–5am.
Though the first thing you see is the glowing neon of the
futuristic bar, this Art Deco hotel has a big stage behind the
bar, with plenty of space for impromptu dancing. Live
music every night beginning around 8pm – often Latino, salsa,
and Caribbean music.

Hungry Sailor

Map 2, F6. 3426 Main Hwy, Coconut Grove ©444-9359.
Daily 10am–4am.
This is the best place to catch reggae in Miami, as it always
attracts top acts and has a very loyal crowd. Wed, Fri, and Sat
are purely dedicated to reggae; other nights are a mix of local
bands and DJs of varying genres. The stage is tiny but mood
intimate; free–$3.

Mango's Tropical Café

Map 4, F5. 900 Ocean Drive, Miami Beach ©673-4422.
Daily 11am–5am.
Though the scantily clad, leopard print-wearing waitstaff instantly
raises eyebrows at this Ocean Drive noisemaker, it's hard to resist
the excellent native Brazilian and Cuban bands when they strike
up on the terrace. Usually there's no cover, and if you don't feel
like being squeezed into the madness inside, you can cheat and
listen to the bands at a safe distance across the street on the grass.

Sundays on the Bay

Map 2, F6. 5420 Crandon Blvd, Key Biscayne ©361-6777.

CHAPTER TWELVE

Fri–Sat 7pm–1am.

During the week this is a hopping waterfront restaurant where tanned boat owners tie up to the dock and sit outside on the picnic tables sipping fruity cocktails and ice-cold lemonade. On Friday and Saturday nights, reggae bands and salsa acts take to the stage and get the crowd moving to the beat. See also "Eating," p.120.

Tap Tap

Map 4, D7. 819 Fifth St, South Beach ©672-2898.
Daily 5.30pm–midnight.

Best known for its excellent restaurant (see "Eating" p.112), the *Tap Tap* hosts regular live Haitian and Caribbean music, played to a rather bohemian crowd.

ROCK, R&B, JAZZ, AND BLUES

Chili Pepper

Map 7, E4. Streets of Mayfair, Coconut Grove ©442-2228.
Daily 9pm–5am.

Formerly a hotel ballroom and presently one of the city's best spaces for loud rock shows, the *Pepper* plays host to big-name bands rolling through town. Good sight lines and a good sound system make it worth checking out. Strangely, women 18 and over can get in, but guys have to be at least 21. Cover charge starts at $5.

Churchill's Hideaway

Map 2, E4. 5501 NE Second Ave, Little Haiti ©757-1807.
Daily 11am–3am.

The only downside to this great rock club and English pub is its remote location in Little Haiti. Otherwise it's as good a place as any to hear local hopefuls, as well as watch international soccer games on television (see "Drinking," p.123). $10–15.

Big performance venues

The following characterless stadiums generally host "arena rock shows" and other giant music gigs.

American Airlines Arena, 601 Biscayne Blvd, downtown Miami ℭ577-4328.

James L Knight Center, 400 SE Second Ave, downtown Miami ℭ372-4633.

Miami Arena, 721 NW First Ave, downtown Miami ℭ374-5057.

Pro Player Stadium, 2269 NW 199th St, 16 miles northwest of downtown Miami ℭ623-6100.

Jazid
Map 4, F4. 1342 Washington Ave, Miami Beach ℭ673-9372.
Daily 9pm–3am.
A recommended, stylish venue hosting smooth jazz vocalists and swinging trio bands. Candlelit, smoky, and fairly laid-back. No cover.

John Martin's
Map 6, F4. 253 Miracle Mile, Coral Gables ℭ445-3777.
Daily 11am–3am.
Spacious Irish bar (see "Drinking," p.127) and restaurant with Irish folk music several evenings a week. An "Irish Cabaret" is performed on Saturday nights, with dancing and storytelling.

Les Deux Fontaines
Map 4, F4. 1230 Ocean Drive, Miami Beach ℭ672-7878.
Daily 7.30am–4am.
This upbeat French restaurant makes plenty of porch space for live jazz every night, including Dixieland, swing, and the occasional bit of classical jazz. Perfect accompaniment to dinner with an ocean view (see "Eating," p.109).

BIG PERFORMANCE VENUES |

Luna Star Café

Map 2, A5. 775 NE 125th St, N Miami ©892-8522.
Tues–Fri 11am–midnight, Saturday 11am–2am.
A cosmic experience awaits in this New Age hangout, where a range of local folk musicians and artists perform – "Nicholas the Storyteller" takes stage on Friday nights. It is pretty far from anything, well north of town, so you'll need to be in the mood for traditional folk music and poetry readings to make the trip worthwhile.

Scully's Tavern

Map 2, B7. 9809 Sunset Drive, South Miami ©271-7404.
Daily 11am–4am.
Expect to find rock and blues bands playing for beer-drinking, pool-playing regulars at this local joint; no cover charge.

Studio 183

Map 2, E3. 2860 NW 183 St, Overtown ©621-7295.
Daily 8pm–4am.
Heart-thumping rap, soul, jazz, and reggae blares nightly, but the club is located in one of downtown's more dangerous neighborhoods. Cover charges range from $5 to $15.

Titanic

Map 6, F4. 5813 Ponce de Leon Blvd, Coral Gables ©667-2537.
Daily 11.30am–1am.
Microbrewery and seafood bar with nightly live music ranging from swing to boogie and occasionally some Texas-blues country, which keeps the crowds packing the place.

Tobacco Road

Map 3, E8. 626 S Miami Ave, downtown Miami ©374-1198.
Mon–Fri 11.30am–5am, Sat–Sun 12pm–5am.
An institution in Miami, both for its history and rambunctious patrons. Formerly a speakeasy, today it belts out earthy R&B

LIVE MUSIC: ROCK, R&B, JAZZ, AND BLUES

on Friday and Saturday nights, and hard rocking (mostly local) bands during the rest of the week. See "Drinking," p.123. Free–$6.

Van Dyke Café

Map 4, E2. 846 Lincoln Rd, South Beach ℂ534-3600.
Mon–Thurs & Sun 8.00am–midnight, Fri–Sat 8.00am–2.00am.
One of the best people-watching spots around, *Van Dyke's* hosts good local bands playing jazz for an enthusiastic crowd, seven nights a week. Belly up at the bar for free or sit at a table, where a $5 cover will be added to your bill.

LIVE MUSIC: ROCK, R&B, JAZZ, AND BLUES

Performing arts and film

The combination of Miami's tolerant history and the Hollywood influence that pervaded the city in the 1950s has created an environment that both respects and supports the **performing arts**. Most visitors will probably be surprised by the uniformly high quality of the high culture here, as Miami is not typically regarded in the same breath as many other US cities. The New World Symphony Orchestra, one of the leading professional music programs in the country, heads up the **classical music** offerings and is certainly worth seeking out when in season (October to May). It's complemented by two other, somewhat less renowned, Miami orchestras and an adequate **opera** organization. The city doesn't have too much in the way of **dance**, though a small ballet company does its best to keep up a profile. Better is the somewhat small but highly regarded **theater** scene, which tends to side with a more cutting-edge approach to the arts, with a handful of small, independent stages throughout the city well balancing the larger venues downtown.

Despite Miami's frequent role as a backdrop in the movies and as the host of a well-respected film festival, the **cinema** choices here are largely lacking. Most are multi-screen affairs, located inside malls, with rather few arthouse screenings available.

Reviews of films set in Miami begin on p.296.

CLASSICAL MUSIC, DANCE, AND OPERA

Colony Theater
Map 4, D2. 1040 Lincoln Rd, Miami Beach ℂ673-1026.
The Ballet Flamenco La Rosa's frenetic Latin dance productions take place here, making it a great place to get acquainted with (once again) popular forms such as flamenco and tango. $18–25.

Florida Grand Opera
Map 6, G4.1200 Coral Way, Coral Gables ℂ854-1643.
This is where the greats such as Pavarotti and Placido Domingo sing, and when operas are not sung in English, subtitles are projected above the stage.

Florida Philharmonic Orchestra
Map 3, B6. 169 E Flagler St, downtown Miami ℂ930-1812 or 1-800/226-1812.
This is South Florida's resident orchestra, which performs a traditional repertoire of pops and classical programs, mixed with a few children's and contemporary shows. $15–60.

Miami Chamber Symphony Orchestra
Map 6, B9. 1314 Miller Drive, University of Miami, Coral Gables ℂ284-2438 or 284-6477.

Showcases better-known names, thus worth looking out for
top-flight soloists; performances take place at the Gusman
Concert Hall; $15–30.

Miami City Ballet
Map 4, D2. 905 Lincoln Rd ℗532-7713.
Dance companies are limited in Miami, but this one has com-
manded the city's attention with its sophisticated and challeng-
ing dance programs. You can get a taste of the finished product
by watching them rehearse in their glass-enclosed, Lincoln
Road studio – or see the real thing, usually at the Gusman
Center for Performing Arts. $17–100.

New World Symphony
Map 4, D2. 541 Lincoln Rd, Miami Beach ℗673-3330.
Founded in 1987, this Miami-based orchestra gives concert
experience to some of the finest graduate classical musicians
in the US. More than 400 alumni have gone on to positions
with professional orchestras and ensembles from here. Its
season runs from October to May with tickets ranging
upwards to $45. Most performances are at the Lincoln
Theater.

The Concert Association of Florida, 555 17th St, on
Miami Beach, brings big names in classical music and
dance to perform at the Jackie Gleason Center and the
Dade County Auditorium. Call ℗532-3491 for
information on upcoming performances.

THEATERS AND PERFORMANCE VENUES

Actor's Playhouse
Map 6, F4. 280 Miracle Mile, Coral Gables ℗444-9293.

A classic Art Deco movie house that showcases musicals and comedies and hosts a children's theater on Saturday afternoons; $25-30.

You can read more about the Actor's Playhouse in Chapter 5, "Coral Gables."

Area Stage
Map 4, D2. 645 Lincoln Rd, South Beach ©673-8002.
One of Miami's best theaters, supporting up-and-coming local talent as well as a variety of new, original dramatic pieces. The productions are usually quite well done, with a creative and independent-minded flair. $8–17.

Coconut Grove Playhouse
Map 7, D6. 3500 Main Hwy, Coconut Grove ©442-2662.
The Playhouse has two stages: the echoey 1100-seat Main Auditorium and the intimate Encore Room. Both venues mainly host plays written by local playwrights. Tickets are $22–30; $10 discount on day of performances and $10 for under-24s.

Dade County Auditorium
Map 2, D5. 2901 W Flagler St, downtown Miami ©547-5414.
Smack in the middle of downtown, this large auditorium hosts performances by the Concert Association of Florida, Miami City Ballet, and Florida Philharmonic Orchestra. $25 and up.

Edge Theater
Map 4, E3. 405 Española Way, South Beach ©531-6083.
This small theater on the third floor of a South Beach loft draws enthusiastic crowds to its alternative theatrical offerings. Big on Tennessee Williams but also throws in a variety of local unknowns. $10–15.

THEATERS AND PERFORMANCE VENUES

Florida Shakespeare Theatre

Map 6, B5.1200 Anastasia Ave, Coral Gables ℗445-1119.

They put on a good selection of classic and lesser-known Shakespeare plays, as well as a handful of Tony Award-winning shows.

Gusman Center for the Performing Arts

Map 3, E6. 25 SE Second Ave, downtown Miami ℗374-2444.

Hosts the annual Miami Film Festival, as well as performances by the New World Symphony and the Florida Philharmonic Orchestra.

Gusman Concert Hall

Map 6, B9. 1314 Miller Drive, University of Miami, Coral Gables ℗284-2438 or 284-6477.

A small performing center, on the campus of the University of Miami, that's home to the Miami Chamber Orchestra.

Jackie Gleason Center of the Performing Arts

Map 4, F2.1700 Washington Ave, Miami Beach ℗673-7300.

The center used to be the studio for the Jackie Gleason television series, *The Honeymooners*. Now it hosts the Greater Miami Broadway Series and various orchestras and acting companies. $30–50.

Lincoln Theater

Map 4, E2. 541 Lincoln Rd, Miami Beach ℗673-3331.

An Art Deco landmark, which still has its old-fashioned marquee entrance. Today it hosts the New World Symphony, Florida Philharmonic Orchestra, and Miami City Ballet.

New Theater

Map 6, G4. 65 Almeira Ave, Coral Gables ℗443-5909.

Sitting neatly between mainstream and alternative, this intimate theater (seats 70) offers creative, witty, and sharp productions of new and old material. $8–18.

FILM

Absinthe House Cinematheque
Map 6, F3. 235 Alcazar Ave, Coral Gables ℂ446-7144.
A pleasant arthouse showing mostly high-brow foreign films such as works by Fellini and Almodovar.

Alliance Cinema
Map 4, D2. 927 Lincoln Rd, Miami Beach ℂ531-8504.
What used to be a mere screening room in the Books and Books bookshop on Lincoln Road grew into a premier alternative filmhouse focusing on independent films by young up-and-coming filmmakers.

> Every February the city turns into "little Hollywood" for two star-studded weeks during the Miami Film Festival – a lavish affair teeming with bashes, premieres, and artistic films from around the globe. See Chapter 16, "Festivals and events," for details.

Astor Art Cinema
Map 6, F1. 4120 Laguna St, downtown Miami ℂ443-6777.
A cozy, arthouse theater that shows quirky, underground films as well as first-run smaller production-company films that are guaranteed not to have Bruce Willis or Steven Segal starring.

CocoWalk 16
Map 7, D5. 3015 Grand Ave, Coconut Grove ℂ466-0450.

Current-release films in a mega-mall setting. Worth mentioning for its easy location – catch a flick after some shopping or eating in one of the Grove's great restaurants.

South Beach Cinema
Map 4, D2. 1100 Lincoln Rd, Miami Beach ℗674-6766.
With over fifteen movies to choose from, it shows the latest films on screens slightly bigger than large television sets.

Gay and lesbian Miami

The cultural and economic boom that Miami has experienced over the last two decades has been in a large part due to the growth of the gay community in the city. Until the 1980s, most of Miami's gay population resided in **Coconut Grove**, taking advantage of the welcoming attitude residents had and contributing to the diverse, somewhat bohemian atmosphere that had been long established there.

Many migrated in the early 1980s to **South Beach**, and a number of gay-owned businesses, bars, and clubs were opened and began to flourish; since then, the scene has barely slowed down. In fact, these days, gay culture is the lifeblood of South Beach's high-energy daytime activities and go-go nightlife. Almost all gay-oriented **shops** are on Lincoln Road in South Beach, and **accommodation** options are sprinkled throughout the area. Most **gay bars** and **clubs** are also in South Beach, though you'll find a few in downtown, Coconut Grove, and beyond.

> Though gay life in Miami, especially South Beach, is
> fairly prominent, the city is not nearly as much of a
> magnet for gay travelers as Key West is. See Chapter
> 23 for details.

There are a few **festivals** and **special events** that cater
toward the gay community in Miami, starting with the Gay
Pride Parade in June, and including some well-known and
well-attended annual AIDS fundraisers, like the "**White
Party**" held in November among Villa Vizcaya's lavish gardens. See Chapter 17, "Festivals," for more information on
these events.

Outside of South Beach and Coconut Grove, you may
find attitudes not quite as enlightened and tolerant, though
rarely will you feel unwelcome. It should also be said that
the gay scene is very male dominated, even if a few nights
at clubs here and there are geared toward the lesbian population.

INFORMATION AND RESOURCES

Free publications that include good local bar and club
listings are *Hot Spots*, *Scoop*, *Wire*, and *The Weekly News*
(*TWN*), which is the most widely read, catering to both
gay and lesbian interests and carrying comprehensive local
news, upcoming events, and classifieds.

Lesbian-specific magazines and newspapers available
include *LIPS* and *She Times*, while *Perra* is aimed at the
Latin gay community. You shouldn't have a problem finding
any of these publications; they are usually stacked in large
piles near the entrances of various gay-oriented nightclubs,
bookstores, and shops.

If these, along with the listings we include below, don't
suffice, you may wish to purchase a copy of *The Out Pages*,

a local gay Yellow Pages packed with information from clubs to car dealers, available at any bookstore around town.

....

Listings of the best gay bookstores in Miami can be found on p.156.

....

The **South Beach Business Guild** (✆534-3336) acts as a gay and lesbian chamber of commerce, holding regular meetings to introduce local professionals to one another. Call for meeting times and location (usually held the last Thursday of the month, but at an always-changing site).

GAY ACCOMMODATION

Castle Palms
Map 4, F1. 2300 Prairie Ave, Miami Beach ✆672-2080 or 1-888/327-9118.
More like a luxurious guesthouse, this largely gay hotel is a small oasis in Miami with lush greens fronting the pool and hot tub and six immaculate rooms, some with verandas overlooking the garden, all with large, private baths. Each suite is decorated in an individual style, with warm touches like built-in bookshelves, French antique wooden furniture, and cherub statuettes. Rooms start at $195 but go down if you book at least seven nights.

....

See Chapter 9, "Accommodation," for more listings of area hotels, hostels, and the like.

....

Island House South Beach
Map 4, F4. 1428 Collins Ave, South Beach ✆865-2422 or 1-800/382-2422.

GAY ACCOMMODATION

Close to the nude Hanover beach, but a bit removed from all the action, this men-only guesthouse offers clean rooms and friendly staff. It's not too luxurious, but not too expensive either: rates run $60–130.

Jefferson House

Map 4, D5. 1018 Jefferson Ave, South Beach ©534-5247.
A lovely bed and breakfast with bright, cheery rooms surrounding the heated pool and spa. All rooms come with private bath, television, and air-conditioning. It's also within walking distance from the gay bars on Lincoln Road and Flamingo Park. Rates are $150–200 peak and $109–155 off peak.

Normandy South

Map 2, G4. 2474 Prairie Ave, Miami Beach ©674-1197.
A triumvirate of swimming options here – pool, jacuzzi, and hot tub – make up for the somewhat isolated location. Rates run $80–175.

....

For gay and lesbian friendly accommodation, call the gay-owned South Florida Hotel Network reservation service ©538-3616; the network also provides nightlife recommendations.

....

South Beach Villas

Map 4, C4.1215 West Ave, South Beach ©673-9600 or 1-800/ GAY-SOBE.
This small complex has sixteen tastefully decorated rooms ranging from studios to efficiencies, all with private bath and some with full kitchens. The large pool is clothing optional; gourmet breakfast and brunches are served poolside. *Villas* caters mostly to men though it is popular enough with women as well. Close to most of the South Beach gay bar scene. $135–195 peak and $99–150 off-peak.

GAY BARS AND CLUBS

821
Map 2, D6. 821 Lincoln Rd, South Beach ℗531-1188.
A fun bar which can get quite busy late at night, serving a
good mix of gay and lesbian drinkers. The copper bar and
plush seating areas are inviting touches. Thursday is a lesbian-
oriented "Cabaret for Women" with three hours of two-for-
one drink specials.

Amnesia
Map 4, E8. 136 Collins Ave, South Beach ℗531-5535.
For outlandish drag queen couture, *Amnesia*'s "Sunday Tea
Dances" are where to take it all in for a mere $5. See also p.132.

Cactus
Map 2, E4. 2041 Biscayne Blvd, downtown Miami ℗438-0662.
This high-energy dance club has its own pool and adjoining tiki
bar – lots of mingling, drinking, and dancing. Mainly gay men.

....
**The rest of Miami's bars and clubs can be found in
Chapter 11, "Drinking," and Chapter 12, "Nightlife."**
....

Miami Eagle
Map 6, B4. 1252 Coral Way, Coral Gables ℗860-0056.
A dimly lit bar along central Coral way, with a rather subdued
atmosphere more for picking up than partying.

O'Zone
Map 2, C6. 6620 SW 57th Ave and Red Rd, South Miami ℗667-2888.
Don't let the shopping mall location fool you – this club is one
of the rowdiest and most popular in Miami. The enormous,
warehouse-like atmosphere allows plenty of dancing and drinking; "Adorable Wednesdays" offer two-for-one drinks all night.
No cover.

Pump

Map 4, E6. 841 Washington Ave, South Beach ℗538-PUMP.
Large dance floor, two plush lounges, and two bars where you can order special "health" drinks like wheatgrass. If you still feel like partying after the other clubs shut down, come here for the "After Hours" club; doors open at 4am for more pumping music.

Salvation

Map 4, C2. 1771 West Ave, South Beach ℗673-6508.
From Friday to Sunday this giant warehouse is converted into an anything-goes club where the shirtless and rippled party to thumping techno beats until dawn. $12–15. See p.135.

Splash

Map 2, C6. 5922 S Dixie Hwy (US–1), between Coconut Grove and Coral Gables ℗662-8779.
Check out this place if you need a change of pace from the manic South Beach clubs. There's good dance space, three bars, a few pool tables, and an outdoor patio to keep you busy.

Twist

Map 4, F5. 1057 Washington Ave, South Beach ℗538-9478.
More of an intimate, comfy bar than raging nightclub, *Twist* does have high-energy techno on the small dance floor upstairs. Attracts a rather upscale crowd. No cover.

Warsaw Ballroom

Map 4, F4. 1450 Collins Ave, South Beach ℗531-4499.
While not exclusively gay (see "Nightlife," p.136), this is the busiest and biggest gay disco in town. Two floors of dancing with the downstairs dominated by an elaborately carved wooden bar. Mostly straight on Saturdays.

Westend

Map 4, E2. 942 Lincoln Rd, South Beach ℗538-WEST.

A mixed clientele of gays and lesbians frequent this casual, neighborhood-type club. Open weekdays 3pm–5am and on weekends 1pm–5am.

HEALTH AND FITNESS

Body Positive Resource Center
Map 2, E3. 175 NE 36th St, downtown Miami ©576-1111.
This is a health club for HIV-positive people, and it offers workshops in health, nutrition, and much more. There's also a small art center with works from local artists.

Club Body Center Miami
Map 2, D6. 2991 Coral Way, Coral Gables ©448-2214.
A few unusual "health club" perks at this men-only club are the frequent body contests and poolside barbeques. Open 24 hours, seven days a week.

Idol's Gym
Map 4, E2. 1000 Lincoln Rd, South Beach ©448-2214. Mostly gay male.
Day memberships are $10. If you had to pick one gym where men's muscles equal the size of the weights they're lifting, this is the place. A live DJ spins music to pump iron by on Saturday nights.

SHOPS

Gaydar
Map 4, E2. 718 Lincoln Rd, South Beach ©673-1690.
This shop doesn't leave anything to the imagination. You'll find books, body piercing, and fetish items, as well as some adventurous clothing options, t-shirts, and paraphernalia here.

HEALTH AND FITNESS, SHOPS

....

**You'll find most gay-specific shops on Lincoln Road
between Washington and Meridian avenues.**

....

GW (The Gay Emporium)

Map 4, E2. 720 Lincoln Rd, South Beach ℗534-4763.

This is the best-known gay bookstore in South Beach, with a
full selection of new and old fiction and nonfiction titles.
Magazines and gay-specific cards, postcards, and other novelty
items are also available.

Lambada Passages Bookstore

Map 2, F3. 7545 Biscayne Blvd, downtown Miami ℗754-6900.

Comfortable and well-stocked bookstore carrying fiction, nonfiction, and everything between as well as magazines, newspapers, and self-help videos and adult films.

New Concept Video

Map 4, F2. 749 Lincoln Rd, South Beach ℗674-1111.

This extensive store packs in what seems like every gay and lesbian film ever made. As well, it carries a selection of foreign,
animated, independent, and triple-X movies. VCRs can be
rented here for $9 a night with a $150 deposit.

Pink Palm Co

Map 4, E2. 737 Lincoln Rd, South Beach ℗538-8373.

Loaded with a multitude of kitsch and candles, movie posters,
quirky knickknacks (heavy on Elvis), and a grand selection of
gay greeting cards.

Whittail & Shon of Miami

Map 4, F4.1319 Washington Ave, South Beach ℗538-2606.

When the urge to raid your mother's closet comes over you,
drop by to find a brilliant selection of fun stuff like boas,
baubles, scarves, hats, and dresses.

SHOPS

Shopping

Shopping for the sake of it isn't the big deal in Miami that it is in some American cities, though it's an obvious enough pastime for a city where looking good is so prized. Pricey boutiques, quirky vintage stores, and beauty shops are scattered throughout the city. What takes the cake here, though, are the **shopping malls**, as elaborate architectural environments have been created to soften the blow of the hard-bitten commercialism of the stores that fill them. You can walk around open-air tropical landscapes, and perhaps barely even notice that you're spending your time (or more precisely, your hard-earned money) buying various high-priced goods. Prices can run high, to be sure; a mere beach towel might run you anywhere from $12 to $65, the upper end of which many will pay without batting an eyelash.

Sales tax in Miami is six percent and is not included in the marked price.

Helped in part by the influence of the late designer Gianni Versace (see p.35), **designer boutiques** have settled in **South Beach** along Washington Avenue between 7th and 8th streets – an address every designer fights to have

Shopping by categories

in Miami. Also around here, **health** and **beauty stores** act as therapy for shoppers not feeling their best. Further up Washington Avenue is an assortment of wild clothing boutiques catering to the club kids, featuring thigh-high leather boots, rubber dresses, fetish clothing, and elaborate jewelry. **Coral Gables** has a small selection of pricey clothing shops, but the better attraction here is to browse at Books & Books, one of the best **bookstores** in Miami – not that there are tons of them on the ground.

Coconut Grove's main shopping thoroughfares are the open-air CocoWalk and the slightly chi-chi Streets of Mayfair, which sounds more highbrow than it actually is. **Downtown Miami** is home mostly to dollar stores, and the quality of clothing deteriorates rapidly. For **ethnic goods**, Little Havana and northern downtown Miami are obvious focal points and make for decent souvenir shopping, especially if you'd like to purchase some smock shirts, **cigars**, or perhaps a tape of Latin **music** while you're here. Heading down through **South Miami** will run you into uninspiring mega-malls whose only upsides are their "everything-under-one-roof" motif – and perhaps some welcome air-conditioning.

BOOKS

Barnes & Noble
Map 6, F4. 152 Miracle Mile, Coral Gables ℂ446-4152.
Map 2, B6. 5701 Sunset Drive, South Miami ℂ662-4770.
Both outlets carry a solid selection of fiction and nonfiction titles. As long as it's not too obscure, you're likely to find what you're looking for here. Newsstand, comfortable chairs, and pleasant café help pass the time.

Books & Books
Map 6, F4. 296 Aragon Ave, Coral Gables ℂ442-4408.
Map 4, E2. 933 Lincoln Rd, Miami Beach ℂ532-3222.
Both branches of this excellent local bookstore have a terrific array of general titles but are especially strong on Floridian art and design, travel, and new fiction; also author signings and readings. Call ℂ444-POEM for the latest events. The Coral Gables branch has a cool rare book room on the second floor.

Borders Books and Music
Map 7, E4. Streets of Mayfair, Coconut Grove ℂ447-1655.
One of a chain of national superstores with books, CDs, and a café; good for general interest titles and finding whatever's new.

Coco Grove Antiquarian
Map 7, D4. 3318 Virginia St, Coconut Grove ℂ444-5362.
A relaxing spot in the heart of lively Coconut Grove, stocking quality used and out-of-print books, as well as some valuable first editions covering all subjects.

Cuba Art and Books
Map 6, F4. 2317 Le Jeune Rd, Coral Gables ℂ567-1640.
Small bookstore specializing in old Cuban books, prints, and paintings, mostly in Spanish. It also stocks a large selection of

BOOKS

books on Cuban politics, thus is a good place to pick up background on that very important part of Miami history and culture.

Downtown Book Center

Map 3, F6. 247 SE First St, downtown Miami ℂ377-9939.
A large selection of books and magazines can be found here, with titles ranging from the latest blockbusters to more esoteric and academic.

Kafka's Kafe

Map 5, F4. 1464 Washington Ave, Miami Beach ℂ673-9669.
A funky used bookstore with extensive domestic and foreign books and magazines, as well as gourmet coffee and Internet email access. Good place to pop in and pick up a cheap book for the beach.

The 9th Chakra

Map 4, E2. 817 Lincoln Rd ℂ538-0671.
Gifts for the soul at this New Agey store. The plethora of reading materials range from simple meditation to reiki and spiritual instruction.

CIGAR AND TOBACCO SHOPS

Cigars are big business here, not surprising considering Miami's proximity to both Cuba and the Dominican Republic, the two main centers for Caribbean cigar production. Of course **Cuban cigars** are illegal in the US, though you'll have no problem getting your hands on stogies made with Cuban tobacco seeds.

Caribbean Cigar Company

Map 4, F6. 760 Ocean Drive, Miami Beach ℂ538-6062.
Map 7, E5. 2992 McFarlane Rd, Coconut Grove ℂ445-3922.

Both branches offer a large assortment of cigars, as well as smoking bric-a-brac.

El Credito Cigars
Map 5, E5. 1106 SW Eighth St, Little Havana ©858-4162.
One of the most famous shops in Miami. Cuban *tabaqueros* (cigar rollers) who learned their technique back in the homeland roll the aromatic tobacco leaves before your eyes to create masterful cigars.

Holy Smoke
Map 4, F5.1052 Ocean Drive, Miami Beach ©674-9390.
This bustling shop does great business thanks to its proximity to the beach and its quality assortment of cigar varieties.

Smokers Road
Map 3, D8. 630 S Miami Ave, downtown Miami ©375-8178.
A "good old boys" smokers' lounge that sells a wide arrangement of quality cigars to a stogie-loving crowd.

CLOTHES

Miami does well in both the preserves of high fashion and casual dress, with plenty of thriftware for those who don't feel the need to look hyper-stylized.

DESIGNER SHOPS

Armani Exchange
Map 4, F6. 760 Collins Ave, Miami Beach ©531-5900.
High-class fashions for men and women with streamlined designs and classic styles.

Betsey Johnson
Map 4, E6. 805 Washington Ave, Miami Beach ©673-0023.

CLOTHES: DESIGNER SHOPS

Betsey's windows flourish with high-quality, breezy clothing and funky jewelry fashions for women, with a price tag to match.

Magazine

Map 4, E6. 180 Eighth St, Miami Beach ℅538-2704.
An expensive boutique showcasing the latest haute couture from names like Moschino, Galliano, Gaultier, Donna Karan, and Prada.

Nicole Miller

Map 4, F6. 656 Collins Ave, Miami Beach ℅535-2200.
Perfect tropical clothing for the perfect-figured woman.

Todd Oldham

Map 4, F6. 763 Collins Ave, Miami Beach ℅674-8090.
Stocking all of Todd's eccentric Pop Art color-schemed clothing and toys for grown boys and girls.

Versace Jeans Couture

Map 4, E6. 755 Washington Ave, Miami Beach ℅532-5993.
A one-stop shopping venue draped in lavish fabrics and ornamentation, for clothing and home decor.

VINTAGE AND THRIFT STORES

Beatnix

Map 4, F5. 1149 Washington Ave, Miami Beach ℅532-8733.
Groovy vintage clothing from polyester halter tops to animal-print catsuits and clunky platform shoes. Many clubgoers shop here before hitting the dance floors.

Coral Gables Congregational Church Thrift Shop

Map 6, B5. 3010 De Soto Blvd, Coral Gables ℅445-1721.

CLOTHES: VINTAGE AND THRIFT STORES

Next door to the well-known church is this well-stocked thrift store, where you're bound to find some cheap and interesting goods.

....

An account of the Coral Gables Congregational Church can be found on p.59.

....

Details at the Beach
Map 2, E4. 2087 NW Second Ave, downtown Miami ℂ573-8903.
Clothing with flair and innovative furnishings makes the dollars fall freely out of your pocket here. Very popular with the city's interior decorators and local designers.

Fly Boutique
Map 4, E2. 650 Lincoln Rd, Miami Beach ℂ604-8508.
Vintage clothing, though pricier than most boutiques, with funky slip dresses, patchwork jeans, and oh-so Seventies hats and accessories. When you've tired of browsing take a breather on the cushy red velvet couches.

Miami Twice
Map 2, C6. 6562 SW 40th St, Coral Gables ℂ666-0127.
A nice little shop stocked with old Florida furniture like ornate lamps and deco memorabilia, as well as good-quality vintage clothing and accessories. Don't be afraid to bargain with the owners.

One Hand Clapping
Map 2, G4. 7165 SW 47th St, Miami Beach ℂ661-6316.
Amid a wondrous assortment of antique junk, there are hats, dresses, and scarves to delight the time-warped flapper.

SoBe Thrifty
Map 4, C4. 1435 Alton Rd, Miami Beach ℂ672-7251.

CLOTHES: VINTAGE AND THRIFT STORES

Looks like walking into your grandmother's basement. Odd shoes, electrical appliances, books, sports equipment, you name it. Dig and you'll find great deals on Levi's jeans, winter coats, and the like.

CUBAN SPECIALTIES AND CRAFTS

Botanica Esperanza
Map 2, C5. 901 SW 27th Ave at SW 9th St, Little Havana ℂ642-2488.
Santeria supplies like religious candles, bead necklaces, animal skins, and milagros (silver Mexican good-luck charms). Some of these shops have a resident consultant who acts as your own personal spiritual advisor.

Coral Way Antiques
Map 2, D6. 3127 SW 22nd St, Coral Gables ℂ567-3131.
Old postcards, books, military items, and other Cuban "collectibles" are on offer in this musty, compact shop.

La Casa de las Guayaberas
Map 2, E5. 5840 SW Eighth St, Little Havana ℂ266-9683.
Here is the place to pick up one of those billowy, embroidered, short-sleeved cotton shirts called *guayaberas*, popularized by older Cuban men. A dignified fashion statement in the scorching Miami heat – *guayabera* dresses are also available for women.

La Casa de las Pinatas
Map 3, B9. 165 SW Eighth St, downtown Miami ℂ649-4711.
Homemade piñatas of paper and wood with ribbons glued to the bottoms for easy access. *Burros* (donkeys) are the most traditional, but you can get them in all shapes from Pokemon to Bugs Bunny.

DEPARTMENT STORES AND MALLS

Bal Harbour Shops
Map 2, G3. 9700 Collins Ave, Miami Beach ✆866-0311.
It's almost too expensive to buy anything here, but it's a lot of
fun to peer into the swank shops (Prada, Tiffany, Versace) in
this temple of upmarket consumerism. Thankfully, a few moderately priced stores still vie for the dollar here, though more
and more are being replaced.

Bayside Marketplace
Map 3, F5. 401 N Biscayne Blvd, near downtown Miami ✆577-3344.
This marketplace is squarely aimed at tourists, but it does at
least include a variety of diverse stores – selling everything from
Art Deco ashtrays to bubblegum, alongside some excellent
food stands.

Burdines
Map 3, D6. 22 E Flagler St, downtown Miami ✆577-2312.
In the grand tradition of Macy's or Bloomingdale's, Miami's
oldest department store remains the powerhouse clotheshorse
in downtown. You may not spot anything too special, just the
typical designer names and domestic appliances, but it's an
entertaining place to browse and observe a slice of city life.

CocoWalk
Map 7, D5. 3015 Grand Ave, Coconut Grove ✆444-0777.
In the heart of Coconut Grove, this horseshoe–shaped complex
has an interesting smattering of craft and jewelry carts mixed
among clothing boutiques, as well as a great selection of eateries and open-air bars, and a decent multiplex cinema.

Dadeland Mall
Map 2, C7. 7535 N Kendall Drive, South Miami ✆665-6226.

More top-class department stores and specialty shops in a total-ly enclosed, air-conditioned environment conducive to spending too much money.

The Falls
Map 2, B7. Hwy-1 and SW 136th St, South Miami ℂ255-4570.
Sit inside a gazebo and contemplate the waterfalls and the rain-forest that spruce up the otherwise rote selection of upscale chains like Crate and Barrel, Pottery Barn, J Crew, and Victoria's Secret.

Lincoln Road Mall
Map 4, E2. Lincoln Rd, South Beach ℂ673-7010.
Between Washington Avenue and Alton Road, this strip becomes a pedestrian-only shopping zone lined with lush plants and water fountains. There's a range of trendy clothing stores, bric-a-brac shops, and day-spas, as well as art galleries and many excellent sidewalk cafés and restaurants. A popular place for rollerbladers and their dogs, so be on the lookout.

The Lincoln Road Mall holds a string of specialty gay and lesbian shops; see Chapter 14, "Gay and lesbian Miami," for listings.

Prime Outlets at Florida City
Map 2, A9. 250 E Palm Drive, Florida City/Homestead ℂ248-4727.
Located where the Florida Turnpike meets Hwy-1, convenient for folks traveling to the Keys or Everglades; dedicated shoppers will find lots of bargains on name brands like Nike, Bass, Levis, Bugle Boy, Izod.

Streets of Mayfair
Map 7, E4. 2911 Grand Ave, Coconut Grove ℂ448-1700.

The expensive stores take second place to the landscaped tropical foliage and the discreetly placed classical sculptures. Still, there are a few small jewelry and handmade craft shops worth browsing, as well as the unavoidable assortment of chains like The Gap and Express.

FOOD AND DRINK

It's unlikely you'll be doing too much buying of food and drink supplies while in Miami, unless you're on a tight budget, though if you are looking to cook a meal or plan a picnic, any number of the stores below should more than aid you.

Apple a Day Natural Food Market
Map 4, C3. 1534 Alton Rd, South Beach ℂ538-4569.
For the health-conscious, a grocery store stocked with nuts and berries and the usual assortment of tofu, sprouts, beans, and other wholesome foods.

Epicure Market
Map 5, C3. 1656 Alton Rd, Miami Beach ℂ672-1861.
An expensive grocery stocked with exotic mushrooms, imported plum tomatoes and mustards, hard-to-find Chardonnay, and Jewish deli foodstuffs. Gourmet palates will appreciate their mouth-watering array of baked goods and hot foods.

Estate Wines and Gourmet Foods
Map 6, G4. 92 Miracle Mile, Coral Gables ℂ442-9915.
Alongside the fine foods an exquisite selection of wines has been chosen with the connoisseur in mind. Small but friendly, with a knowledgeable staff who aren't snobbish.

Joe's Stone Crab Takeaway
Map 4, D8. 227 Biscayne St, South Beach ℂ673-0365 or 1-800/780-2722.

FOOD AND DRINK

For those who can't control their cravings for stone crab claws, you can take them with you or have them shipped to your home (see "Eating," p.109).

Kingston Miami Trading Company

Map 3, E6. 280 NE 2nd St, downtown Miami ℭ372-9547.

A mixed jumble of spices, canned goods, and Jamaican specialties like fiery scotch bonnets and jerk seasonings. Also boasts odd drinks like Ting, Irish moss, and young coconut juices, all of which you'll have to taste rather than have described to you.

Lyon & Lyon

Map 5, C4. 1439 Alton Rd, South Beach ℭ534-0600.

A small French take-out market with frothy cappuccinos and home-baked pastries.

Stephan's Gourmet Market & Café

Map 4, F4. 1430 Washington Ave, South Beach ℭ674-1760.

Gourmet Italian deli with an endless selection of imported cheeses, wines, candies, and nuts arranged in pretty, pricey baskets. Also has a café on the second floor.

HEALTH AND BEAUTY

Agua

Map 4, F2. *Delano Hotel*, 1685 Collins Ave, South Beach ℭ672-2000.

This exclusive spa prides itself on its privacy so much that the layperson may find it hard to get into. However, once past the doors, you enter an indulgent excercise of pampering massages and facials on sheltered tables directly on the beach. There's also a rooftop solarium which shelters patrons who'd like to get a full-body tan.

Brownes & Co Apothecary
Map 4, E2. 841 Lincoln Rd, South Beach ℂ538-7544.
Their "Some Like it Hot" day spa features packages that
include rose petal foot soaks and vanilla body loofah scrubs.
The actual shop contains a yummy assortment of creamy
body lotions, shampoos, and makeup including Kiehls,
Aveda, Philosophy, MAC, and L'Occitane. Definitely ask for
samples.

Massage by design
Map 4, E3. 1630 Pennsylvania Ave, South Beach ℂ532-3112.
Those in the know claim the best massages are found here –
even at $50 per half-hour. Clients fill out questionnaires before
succumbing to warm, candle-lit rooms with piped-in New
Age music.

Sephora
Map 4, F6. Collins Ave, South Beach ℂ448-3003.
A colorful supermarket of makeup, designer fragrances, and
hard-to-find lotions and hair care products. Fun to browse or
create your own fragrance.

White
Map 4, F5. 900 Collins Ave, South Beach ℂ538-0604.
Step through the white doors of this unassuming house on the
corner to get a luxurious massage or facial. Other services
include waxing, manicures, and pedicures.

MUSIC

Lily's Records
Map 5, D5. 1260 SW Eighth St, Little Havana ℂ856-0536.
Unsurpassed stock of salsa, merengue, and other Latin sounds,
to keep you moving and up-to-date.

MUSIC

Revolution Records & CDs

Map 4, D3. 1620 Alton Rd, South Beach ℗673-6464.

A tiny shop with a friendly staff, boasting an impressive number of Cuban records, as well as classic and modern rock.

Spec's Music

Map 4, E7. 501 Collins Ave ℗534-3667.
Map 5, F3. 1655 Washington Ave ℗532-6455.

Spec's two locations have a decent mix of contemporary and hard-to-find music.

Uncle Sam's Musicafe

Map 4, F5. 1141 Washington Ave, South Beach ℗532-0973.

Pick up the latest in underground vinyl records and mainstream CDs, along with a hodgepodge of music paraphernalia like posters, books, and bumper stickers. There are a good number of free music listing magazines and newspapers located inside the entranceway.

Yesterday & Today Dance Music

Map 4, C3. 1614 Alton Rd, South Beach ℗534-8704.

Dusty piles of blues, jazz, R&B, and Sixties indie rarities; their contents span everything from doo-wop rarities to the smoothest salsa hits.

Festivals and events

With the tropical climate Miami enjoys, year-round outdoor **festivals** and **events** are in no short supply in the city. You're almost guaranteed to overlap with some major happening no matter when you come; if you're lucky, the celebration will be one that honors some part of the city's ethnic diversity, as these tend to be the most raucous and enjoyable, especially the Cuban-oriented festivals in early March and the month-long celebration of Hispanic culture in October. Other big doings include a few thrilling sporting events, most notably college football's Orange Bowl, on or right after New Year's Day, and accompanied by a citywide parade.

See Chapter 17, "Sports and outdoor activities," for more on local sporting events.

Unlike in most American cities, the summer months here tend to hold the fewest events. Whenever they might occur, the majority are free, though if necessary tickets can be

obtained by calling the numbers listed or by contacting the
Greater Miami Convention and Visitors Bureau, 701
Brickell Ave (Mon–Fri 8.30am–5pm; ☎539-3000).

We've listed a calendar of the city's top event offerings,
though it is by no means totally comprehensive; you may
want to consult local listings papers for complete lists, or
again, contact the CVB ahead of your trip.

JANUARY

Orange Bowl Festival
January 1. The Orange Bowl Festival centers on a big college
football game in Miami, one that sometimes features the national
champion. Make sure to get to Biscayne Boulevard early to stake
your claim along the parade route and enjoy the vibrant floats,
marching bands, and the crowning of the Orange Bowl Queen
at the Pro Player Stadium festivities. Otherwise you'll have to
pay for bleacher seats from $12 to $25 (☎371-4600).

Three Kings Day Parade
Early January. One of the top Hispanic-related events in the
country, with crowds reaching around 500,000, this parade celebrates the legend of the Three Wise Men with festivities
marching down Calle Ocho between Fourth and 27th avenues
(☎445-4020).

Art Deco Weekend
Mid-January. A wild weekend in South Beach along Ocean
Drive celebrating the signature architecture of the area with
live bands, tours, and street theater (☎672-2014).

Art Miami
Mid-January. During the second week of the month, local
galleries gather their most promising artists' creations for display at the Miami Beach Convention Center.

Martin Luther King Parade

January 16. Remembering the civil rights leader with a march through Liberty City (✆636-1920).

Taste of the Grove

Late January. Every restaurateur in Coconut Grove opens up a booth as visitors are treated to the varied culinary menus of the area. Sample an assortment of foods ranging from Cuban to Mediterranean while bopping around to the free live music being played in Coconut Grove's Peacock Park (✆444-7270).

Key Biscayne Art Festival

Late January. A low-key but entertaining festival with music, arts and crafts, and fresh seafood stands along Crandon Boulevard on Key Biscayne (✆361-0049).

FEBRUARY

Miami Film Festival

First two weeks. A highly entertaining selection of the latest US and overseas films, emphasizing Cuban and Latin works. Films are premiered in downtown Miami's Gusman Center for the Performing Arts – call for openings and times (✆662-6960).

Miami International Boat Show

February 15–20. Not the most exciting show if you're not into boats, but worth knowing about because of its impact on accommodation (reserve early if you're coming around this time). Sailing aficionados from around the world converge on South Beach (✆531-8410).

Coconut Grove Arts Festival

Mid-month. Hundreds of (mostly) talented unknowns line the streets and grassy patches around Coconut Grove's Peacock

Park to display their unusual works, from tree-bark patio furniture to talking mirrors (℡447-0401).

Doral-Ryder Open

Late February to early March. As pro-golfers on the PGA Tour prepare to tackle the famous Doral course nicknamed the "Blue Monster," concerts and games are held during this weeklong event at the posh Doral Golf Resort and Spa near the airport (℡365-0290).

MARCH

Calle Ocho Festival

Early March. A massive festival of Cuban arts, crafts, and cooking along Calle Ocho in Little Havana. A great way to experience the richness of Little Havana's Cuban culture (℡644-8888).

Carnival Miami

Early March. An offshoot of the Calle Ocho festival that carries on for nine days, with Hispanic-themed events across the city, culminating in a parade at the Orange Bowl football stadium (℡644-8888).

Homestead Championship Rodeo

Early March. Professional rodeo cowboys compete in steer wrestling, bull riding, calf roping, and bareback riding competitions in South Miami (℡372-9966).

Asian Arts Festival

Second week in March. Held in South Miami's Fruit and Spice Park, this event celebrates some twenty Asian cultures with handicrafts, music and dance, martial arts, sports tournaments, cooking demonstrations, native costumes, and more (℡954/921-3315).

The Ericsson Open

Late March. Catch tennis's big names in tennis as they compete in the world's fifth largest tennis tournament, held at the Crandon Park Tennis Center in Key Biscayne. Ticket prices are $25 and up (✆446-2200).

APRIL

International Kite Festival

Early April. South Beach's skies fill with multicolored kites of elaborate shapes and enormous sizes as "Kite Masters" come to display their skills. You can build kites for free, take a flying stunt kite lesson, be propelled along the beach in a bicycle-like vehicle powered solely by a kite, or watch Kite Ballet and Precision Kite Flying Teams perform (✆667-7756).

Merrick Festival

Early April. This Coral Gables performing arts festival features opera, theater, ballet, dance, and music on two stages at the Ponce Circle Park, with past performances by the Florida Shakespeare Company, Momentum Dance Company, and the small Coral Gables Opera (✆665-8041).

South Beach Film Festival

Early April. American film directors debut their short independent works at the Colony Theater, 1040 Lincoln Rd, South Beach (✆532-1233).

MAY

The Great Sunrise Balloon Race & Festival

May 9. Held at Homestead Air Force Base, tens of hot-air balloons rise above South Dade to raise money for persons

with disabilities. Hot-air balloon races, food, and family entertainment (©273-3051).

International Hispanic Theater Festival
Late May to mid-June. Held at El Carrusel Theater, this celebration marks Hispanic achievement in the theater arts with
performances by companies from around the world.

JUNE

Art in the Park
Early June. Spread out along the well-manicured lawn of the
South Miami's Charles Deering Estate are a plethora of craft
stalls by local artisans.

Goombay Festival
Early June. A spirited bash in honor of Bahamian culture, in
and around Coconut Grove's Peacock Park (©372-9966).

JULY

America's Birthday Bash
July 4. Music, fireworks, and a laser light show celebrate the
occasion at Bayfront Park in downtown Miami (©358-7550).

Tropical Agriculture Fiesta
Mid-July. Enjoy fresh mangos along with offbeat fruits and
various ethnic foods at the Fruit and Spice Park (©247-5727).

AUGUST

Miami Reggae Festival
First Sunday in August. One of the largest reggae festivals in
the US, this celebration in downtown Miami's Bayfront Park

commemorates Jamaican Independence Day with a full day of local, national, and international musical acts (℃891-2944).

SEPTEMBER

Festival Miami
Mid-September. Three weeks of performing and visual arts events organized by the University of Miami, mostly taking place in Coral Gables (℃284-5500).

OCTOBER

Hispanic Heritage Festival
Month-long celebration of Hispanic culture in Little Havana, with parades, craft fairs, and the like (℃541-5023).

Columbus Day Regatta
Early October. Florida's largest watersport races, which commemorate Columbus's historic voyage. The route runs from Coconut Grove's Dinner Key Marina to Elliott Key and back. Races begin on the weekend closest to Columbus Day (℃858-1733).

West Indian Carnival Extravaganza
Early October. A joyous gathering of soca and calypso bands in Bicentennial Park, downtown Miami (℃435-4845).

NOVEMBER

Miami Book Fair International
Mid-November. A wealth of tomes from across the world spread across the campus of Miami-Dade Community College in downtown Miami (℃237-3032).

Harvest Festival
Mid to late November. A celebration of southern Florida's agricultural traditions including homemade crafts, music, and historical reenactments takes place at the Dade County Fairgrounds in West Dade (✆375-1492).

White Party Week
Late November. Not what you might think from the title, this is one of the gay community's biggest bashes in Miami, open to everyone. The six-day festivities culminate in a lavish ball and fireworks display on the banks of Villa Vizcaya, where the gardens are draped in baroque ornamentation and the partygoers dress up in elaborate white drag costumes. Tickets range from $20 to $499 depending on which events you go to, and proceeds go toward HIV/AIDS research (✆867-1102).

DECEMBER

Indian Arts Festival
Late December. Native American artisans from all over the country gather at the Miccosukee Village to display their work (✆223-8380).

King Mango Strut
Late December. A wacky spoof on the Orange Bowl Parade, where alternative types strut their stuff through Coconut Grove. Recent parade participants include the hysterical "Precision Briefcase Drill Team," twirling monogrammed cases in three-piece suits, the "Marching Freds," for anyone named Fred, and the "Musical Massacre," a sort of free-for-all at the end of the march in Peacock Park, with entrants playing musical instruments and dancing to their own tune (✆445-1865).

Sports and outdoor activities

Miamians are quick to take advantage of the city's sunny weather and lush natural surroundings, making for a place full of fit athletic types. In addition, locals tend to be loyal fans to their **professional** sports teams, following them through all three major seasons: baseball (Florida Marlins), basketball (Miami Heat), and football (Miami Dolphins). As well, there are professional and amateur offerings in **tennis** and **golf** – popular year-round with locals, retirees, and the like – with courts and courses peppered throughout the city. One sport unique to Miami is **jai-alai**, imported from Cuba and today played by both Cubans and Americans alike. Another very Miami activity is watching the **dog races** at the track; though traditionally the province of local old-timers, these races have become somewhat trendy in recent years.

Miami's natural setting and waterfront location provide plenty of participatory options in the sand and surf. **Fishing** is the most visible activity, which locals do just by dropping lines over every conceivable bridge and causeway.

If you want to actually get out on the water, you can opt for deep-sea fishing; opportunities for **snorkeling**, **scuba diving**, and, of course, **swimming** also abound. In addition, the pristine white beaches and South Beach's curvy boardwalk provide a picturesque backdrop for the non-competitive activities of **biking** and **rollerblading**.

BASEBALL

In 1993 the **Florida Marlins** played their first game as a new franchise team for the National League. Just four years later they achieved the ultimate goal by winning the 1997 World Series – the quickest rise from expansion team to champion in the sport's history. In recent years the Marlins haven't fared as well, finishing at the bottom of the league – thanks to the owner trading away all the high-priced players from the team – but Florida fans remain undeterred by this losing streak, and still come to the stadium to watch the fresh young faces. The season runs from April through October with seat prices ranging from $7 to $45. The Marlins play at the Pro Player Stadium, 2269 NW 199th St, sixteen miles northwest of downtown Miami (✆350-5050).

BASKETBALL

Miami's basketball team, the **Miami Heat**, is also a relatively young franchise in the area. Led by Armani-wearing coach Pat Riley, the Heat consistently finish at the top of the league, yet have thus far been unable to win a championship. The team recently said goodbye to the well-aged Miami Arena and now plays in the newly constructed **American Airlines Arena**, in downtown near the Port of Miami (see p.24), which sports a flashy silhouette of a jet on the roof and incredible views of Biscayne Bay. There is also a spherical bandshell for outdoor concerts. Tickets for the new arena are surprisingly more affordable than in the previous venue, ranging from $5 to $150 during the season, which runs from October through April.

In January 2000, the **Miami Sol** (Spanish for "sun") joined the Women's National Basketball League (**WNBA**) and play in a season that begins around the time the men finish. Games take place at the American Airlines Arena, and tickets range from $5 to $25 per game (℃786/777-4765).

FOOTBALL

Florida has three professional football teams, the longest-standing and perennially most successful of which is the **Miami Dolphins**. Though they have won the Super Bowl only once in the past 25-plus years, they remain the only modern National Football Team to have gone through a year undefeated (1972). Long associated with tanned ex-coach Don Shula and quarterback Dan Marino, the team has struggled somewhat in recent years, but always draws a big crowd. The Dolphins' season runs from September through January, and they share the Pro Player Stadium with the Florida Marlins (see "Baseball" opposite). Tickets can be purchased in person at the stadium (Gate G) Mon–Fri 8.30am–6pm and Sat 10am–4pm, or through TicketMaster (℃573-TEAM) and range from $27 to $47.

GREYHOUND RACING

What used to be thought of as a spectator sport for elderly men, **dog racing** in Miami now attracts a much more diverse crowd. The folks come to gamble on dogs, which may not hold the same classy appeal as horse racing but are equally fast and entertaining. The Flagler Greyhound Track,

401 NW 38th Court, Miami ℗649-3000, is the most popular venue in the area; gates open at noon on Tuesday, Thursday and Saturday, and at 6.30pm for nightly races. General admission is free, with clubhouse seating at $3.

JAI ALAI

The term **Jai Alai** comes from the Spanish Basque region and means "merry festival," though what that has to do with what's been dubbed "the world's fastest game" is a bit unclear. The sport is a mix between racquetball and lacrosse and is played in a three-sided court, where a player throws a hard rubber ball against the wall and catches it with a *cesta* (a basket attached to a leather glove that's tied to the hand). The pros play in the gigantic Miami Jai Alai arena near the airport, 3500 NW 37th Ave (daily noon–5pm except Tues; evenings Wed, Thurs, & Fri 7–12pm; general admission $1, reserved seating $3; ℗633-6400). If you'd like to try your hand and test your reflexes, check out the North Miami Jai Alai complex, 1935 NE 150th St, North Miami (℗944-8217), where court time is $6/hour.

BIKING AND ROLLERBLADING

Much of Miami is not great for **biking**, but Coral Gables and Key Biscayne are both lovely – and easy – enough places to cycle, and there's a fourteen-mile cycle path through Coconut Grove and into South Miami, if you're looking at the bike as a mode of transportation. Get hold of the free leaflet *Miami on Two Wheels* from the CVB, 701 Brickell Ave (Mon–Fri 8.30am–5pm; ℗539-3000). Bike **rental** is available in many locations and usually costs somewhere around $20 or so per day, though you can also rent by the hour. Outlets to try include Grove Cycles, 3216

Grand Ave ℂ444-5415; Coral Way Bike Shop, 2237 Coral Way ℂ856-5731; Mangrove Cycles, 260 Crandon Blvd ℂ361-5555; Bike Shop, 923 W 39th St; Bicycle Shop, 824 Washington Ave, ℂ672-5582.

Miami's favorite mode of transportation, **rollerblading,** is most commonly observed in South Beach's environs, especially along Ocean Drive's twisty, oceanfront sidewalk – the famous backdrop for numerous photo shoots and music videos. Try Fritz's Skate Shop, 726 Lincoln Rd (ℂ532-1954), and Skate 2000, 1200 Ocean Drive (ℂ538-8282); and 650 Lincoln Rd (ℂ538-9491). Both shops charge $8/hour and $20–25 for the day.

GOLF

There is no shortage of **golf courses** in Miami, with many of high enough quality to attract professional tournaments such as the PGA and the Doral Open. Two of the best are at the Doral Golf & Spa Resort, 4400 NW 87th Ave, downtown Miami (ℂ592-2030), and Crandon Park, 6700 Crandon Blvd, Key Biscayne (ℂ361-9129), but expect to pay wallet-draining greens' fees. A few more budget-friendly courses can be found at the Bayshore Golf Course, 2301 Alton Rd, Miami Beach (ℂ532-3810), and the Palmetto Golf Course, 9300 SW 152nd St, South Miami ℂ238-2922), where greens' fees range from $25 to $65 depending on the season.

TENNIS

There could hardly be a more perfect setting for **tennis** than Miami – the warm climate and numerous public courts make year-round playing accessible to anyone with a racket. Many neighborhood courts are strictly on a first-come, first-served basis, with no fee to get on or member-

GOLF, TENNIS

ship to have, though some of the bigger recreation centers do charge for usage. Courts in Miami Beach include Flamingo Park, 1000 12th St (℗673-7761), North Shore Park, 501 72nd St (℗673-7730), and in North Miami Beach at Haulover Beach (℗944-3040). You'll find more courts in Coconut Grove's Peacock Park, and in Key Biscayne at Crandon Park, 4000 Crandon Blvd (℗361-5421), the latter of which has both clay and hard courts. For professional matches, Key Biscayne is also home to the Ericsson Open (formerly known as the Lipton Championships) at the Crandon Park Tennis Center in mid-late March (℗446-2200 or 1-800/725-5472). Call the Miami Parks and Recreation at ℗416-1313 for more information.

DIVING AND SNORKELING

Most hotels and resorts have dive centers on their property and offer discount packages that include accommodation and **watersports** passes. The **Miami Watersports Marketing Council**, 1920 Meridian Ave, Miami Beach (℗672-1270 or 1-888/728-2262), can recommend dive shops as well as provide information on wrecks and popular reefs. The most popular operators are **Bubbles Dive Center**, 2671 SW 27th Ave, North Miami (℗856-0565); **South Beach Divers**, 850 Washington Ave, Miami Beach (℗531-6110 or 1-888/331-DIVE); and **Tarpoon Lagoon**, 300 Alton Rd at the Miami Beach Marina, Miami Beach (℗532-1445). Whichever you choose you're likely to get an excellent and up-close look at the colorful array of sea creatures that the waters around the city hold.

> The best snorkeling in the area is done down in the Florida Keys; see Part Three of the guide for details.

FISHING

Whether it's in Biscayne Bay or the Atlantic Ocean, or off some causeway or pier somewhere, you – and the other thousands of novice or professional anglers in the area – shouldn't have a problem finding the perfect spot for **fishing**. In fact, few things incite higher passions in Florida, and people come from all around to do just this, though the Keys are probably more noted for their well-stocked waters than Miami is. **Cobia**, **grouper**, **sailfish**, **barracuda**, **wahoo**, and **skipjacks** are among the hundreds of possible catches, and you can hook many of these whether **sportfishing** from the back of a boat or merely throwing your line out along Key Biscayne's beaches (which is perfectly legal).

You can cast off at the Rickenbacker, MacArthur, Sunny Isles, and 79th St causeways, as well as from the South Point and North Miami Beach piers. Otherwise, try the following **charter boats**, though some may cost quite a bit if you're doing serious sportsfishing out in the deep waters: **Knot Nancy**, 1950 NE 135th Street at the Keystone Point Marina, N Miami Beach (✆620-5896); **Sonny Boy Sportfishing**, Key Biscayne Marina (✆361-2217); **Mark the Shark**, (Biscayne Bay Mariott Marina, downtown (✆759-5297); and the **Reward Fishing Fleet**, 300 Alton Rd at the Miami Beach Marina, South Beach (✆372-9470).

Directory

AIRLINES Air Canada ✆1-888/247-2262; American Airlines ✆1-800/433-7300; British Airways ✆1-800/247-9297; Continental ✆1-800/525-0280; Delta, ✆1-800/221-1212; Northwest Airlines/KLM ✆1-800/225-2525; TWA ✆1-800/221-2000; United ✆1-800/241-6522; US Airways ✆1-800/428-4322; Virgin Atlantic ✆1-800/862-8621.

AREA CODE The telephone code for all Miami numbers is ✆305.

BANKS AND EXCHANGE There are foreign exchange desks at the Miami International airport and at the following banks: Barnett Bank, 701 Brickell Ave (42 branches in Miami; ✆350-7143); First Union National Bank, 200 S Biscayne Blvd (✆599-2265); SunTrust Bank, 777 Brickell Ave (✆592-0800); NationsBank, 1 SE 3rd Ave (✆350-6350) and 1300 Brickell Ave (✆372-0800); Chequepoint, 865 Collins Ave (✆538-5348); Citibank International, 201 S Biscayne Blvd (✆347-1600).

BOAT RENTAL Recreate the opening sequences from *Miami Vice* by skimming over Biscayne Bay in a motor boat. Equipped with 50hp engines, such vessels can be rented at hourly rates at $45 per hour from Beach Boat Rentals, 2380 Collins Ave, Miami Beach (✆534-4307).

CAR RENTAL Alamo, 3355 NW 22nd St (℃633-4132 or 1-800/327-9633); Avis, 2318 Collins Ave, Miami Beach (℃538-4442); Budget, 3901 NW 28th St (℃871-3053 or ℃1-800/527-0700); Enterprise, 3975 NW South River Drive (℃633-0377 or 1-800/325-8007); Hertz, 3795 NW 21st St (℃871-0300 or 1-800/654-3131); Thrifty, 2875 NW 42nd St (℃871-5050 or 1-800/FOR-CARS).

CHILDREN Miami has fairly few amusement parks or kids' museums, but there are a number of places with animals on display, like the Parrot Jungle (p.78) and the Metrozoo (p.79), that are sure to please young ones. There's always the many beaches, too, to occupy the time. If you need babysitting services call ℃856-0550.

COASTGUARD ℃535-4313.

CONSULATES Canada, 200 S Biscayne Blvd, Suite 1600 (℃579-1600); Denmark, PH 1D, 2655 Le Jeune Rd (℃446-0020); France, 1 Biscayne Tower, Suite 1710 (℃372-9798); Germany, Suite 2200, 100 N Biscayne Blvd (℃358-0290); Netherlands, 800 Brickell Ave, Suite 918 (℃789-6646); UK, Suite 2110, 1001 S Bayshore Drive (℃374-1522).

DENTIST For a referral call ℃667-3647.

DOCTOR To find a physician call ℃324-8717.

EMERGENCIES ℃911.

GAY & LESBIAN COMMUNITY HOTLINE ℃759-3661.

GYMS AND DAY SPAS Gables Personal Fitness, 1350 S Dixie Hwy, Coral Gables (℃667-0106); The Gridiron Club, 1676 Alton Rd, South Beach (℃531-4743); Grove Fitness, 2901 Florida Ave, Coconut Grove (℃441-8555);

Shape Up, 1200 West Ave, South Beach (℗538-0660); South Beach Gym, *Clevelander Hotel*, 1020 Ocean Drive, South Beach (℗672-7499); XS Fitness Center, 81 Washington Ave, South Beach (℗532-9989).

HELPLINES Crisis Hotline ℗358-4357; Visitor's Medical Hotline ℗674-2222; Miami Beach Hotline ℗673-7400.

HOSPITALS With emergency rooms in Miami: Jackson Memorial Medical Center, 1611 NW Twelfth Ave (℗585-1111); Mercy Hospital, 3663 S Miami Ave (℗854-4400). In Miami Beach: Mt Sinai Medical Center, 4300 Alton Rd (℗674-2121); South Shore Hospital, 630 Alton Rd (℗672-2100).

INTERNET ACCESS Beach Typewriter Company Inc, 1659 Michigan Ave, South Beach (℗538-6272); *Kafka Kafe*, 1464 Washington Ave, South Beach (℗673-9669); South Beach Online, 924 Lincoln Rd, South Beach (℗538-7868); *Yucaipa*, 428 Española Way, South Beach (℗604-8807).

LAUNDROMATS Check the *Yellow Pages* for the nearest, and note that many hotels will likely have some form of laundry service; handiest for South Beach are: Wash Club of South Beach, 510 Washington Ave (℗534-4298), and Lolita's Laundromat, 405 15th St (℗538-8303); in Coconut Grove try the Coconut Grove Laundry & Cleaners, 3101 Grand Avenue (℗444-1344).

LIBRARIES Miami-Dade County Public Library, 101 W Flagler St, downtown (Mon–Sat 9am–6pm, Thurs until 9pm; Oct–May also Sun 1–5pm; ℗375-2665).

PARKING FINES Parking is a nightmare (see box on p.7), and fines for violations can run from $18 and up.

PHARMACIES Usually open from 8 or 9am until 9pm or midnight. Coconut Grove Pharmacy, 3206 Grand Ave (℡444-0640); 24-hour pharmacy branches of Eckerd at 1825 Miami Gardens Drive (℡932-5740); 1549 SW 107th Ave, downtown (℡220-0147); 2235 Collins Ave, Miami Beach (℡673-9514); 200 Lincoln Rd, South Beach (℡673-9502).

PHOTO PROCESSING Coconut Grove Camera, 3317 Virginia St, Coconut Grove (℡445-0521); Deco Photo, 1238 Washington Ave, South Beach (℡532-6552); The Lab, 1330 Ocean Drive, South Beach (℡674-9808); One Hour Photo, Bayside Marketplace, downtown (℡377-3686); Zalez Photography, 118 Miracle Mile, Coral Gables (℡551-9433).

POLICE For non-emergency: ℡673-7900; emergency: ℡911.

POST OFFICE In downtown Miami, 500 NW Second Ave; in Coral Gables, 251 Valencia Ave; in Coconut Grove, 3191 Grand Ave; in Homestead, 739 Washington Ave; in Key Biscayne, 59 Harbor Drive; in Miami Beach, 1300 Washington Ave and 445 W 40th St. All open Mon–Fri 8.30am–5pm, Sat 8.30am–12.30pm, or longer hours.

RAPE HOTLINE ℡549-7273.

TAX Sales tax is 6.5 percent; room tax a mere 3 percent.

TIME Miami is on Eastern Standard Time, which is five hours behind Greenwich Mean Time and three hours ahead of Pacific Standard Time. Daylight savings takes place between the first Sunday in April and the last Sunday in October.

WEATHER/SURF INFORMATION ℡324-8811 or 229-4522.

WIRE TRANSFERS Western Union has offices all over the city; call ℡1-800/325-6000 to find the nearest.

THE FLORIDA KEYS

Introducing the
Florida Keys

S tretching from the southeastern corner of the state – just about an hour's drive from Miami – all the way to within ninety miles of Cuba, the **Florida Keys** are rightfully as much of a destination for many visitors as the big city itself. Over their length, some hundred miles that skip from island to tiny island – indeed, the name "key" is a variation on the Spanish word *cay*, meaning a small island or bank composed of coral fragments – the Keys parallel the wondrous **Florida Reef**, a great band of living coral not far off the coast. That proximity, not to mention the colorful array of ocean life contained in the waters between, means that opportunities for **snorkeling**, **diving**, and **fishing** are rife throughout the Keys. Even if you're not out in the ocean, the islands themselves hold much allure thanks to the consistently dramatic sunsets on view, tropical ecosystems, and some of the nation's prettiest beaches. Because of these features and their use as a setting in much fiction, film, and folklore, Florida's Keys have earned themselves a romantic and glamorous reputation, though one which has become threatened in recent years by the sheer number of visitors, who have destroyed fragile coral reefs and polluted the area's beaches and forests.

Like most of America, the original inhabitants of the Keys were Native Americans, specifically the Calusa and Tequesta tribes, who were discovered and recorded in the diaries of early shipwrecked Spanish explorers in the 1500s. Mosquitoes and a lack of any way to make a living made it difficult to settle in this area, and for much of the 1800s the Keys, save Key West, remained uninhabited. It wasn't until 1905, when Henry Flagler began to link Florida's mainland with the hundred miles of rocky islands via railroad, that the Keys became a viable option for settlers and visitors alike, and stayed that way until a 1935 hurricane destroyed the rail. Eventually the state built the Overseas Highway to continue access to the Keys, and they in turn continued to thrive, though perhaps even Flagler couldn't have predicted their modern-day popularity.

The Keys are roughly divided into three main sections, with Key West individualistic enough to merit separate discussion. Upon entering the closest of these to the mainland, the **Upper Keys**, which are made up of **Key Largo**, **Tavernier**, and **Islamorada**, you will reach perhaps the best place to visit the reef, the **John Pennekamp State Park**, one of the few interesting parts of Key Largo, even with its inevitable movie associations. Key Largo is rapidly being populated by suburban Miamians, moving here for the sailing and fishing but unable to survive without shopping malls. Despite some of these same problems, Islamorada may be the best local base for fishing, and also has some natural and historical points of note – as does the next major settlement, **Marathon**, which is at the center of the **Middle Keys** and is that group's only real base of operation. This strip, running between Conch Key and the Seven Mile Bridge, has as its main attraction acres of preserved subtropical forest. The **Lower Keys** begin with Bahia Honda Key and run up to Boca Chica Key, the last stop before Key West. They get fewer visitors and less publicity than their neighbors, especially as most are in a rush to hit that final island, but they should not be dismissed; in many ways these are the most unusual and appealing of the whole lot. Covered with dense forests, they are home to the endangered Key deer, as well as a number of rare sea creatures, and boast some of the most untrammeled beaches for miles.

Key West, the final dot of the North American continent before a thousand miles of ocean, is the end of the road in every sense. Shot through with an intoxicating aura of abandonment, it's a small but immensely vibrant place, with a unique laissez-faire atmosphere that's impossible to resist. The only part of the Keys with a real sense of history, Key West was once the richest town in the US – due to the area's successful wrecking industry in which the town took a percentage of all recovered off its shores – and the largest settlement in Florida. There are old homes and museums to explore and plenty of bars in which to while away the hours, as well as a couple of small beaches, something noticeably missing – due to the reef – elsewhere.

The area code for all numbers in the Keys is ©305.

ARRIVAL

Two small **airports** in Marathon and Key West handle all flights into the Keys. However, the only reason you'd fly into Marathon is if you're staying in the Middle Keys and not venturing any further, and Key West is really the more

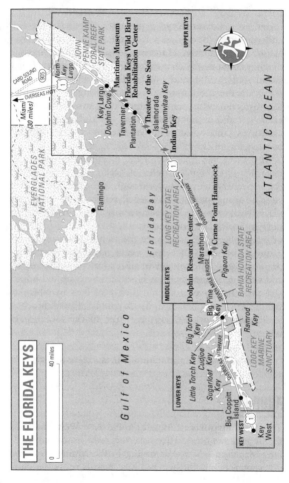

useful of the two. Otherwise, there's only one main road to (and through) the Keys – **Hwy-1**, also known as the **Overseas Highway**, which ends in Key West. It's punctuated by **mile markers (MM)** – posts on which mileage is marked, starting with MM127, just south of Homestead (see "South Miami and Homestead," p.77), and finishing with MM0, in Key West; almost all places of business use mile markers as an address, and throughout this chapter they are tagged with an "MM" (for example, "the *Holiday Inn*, at MM100"). Bear in mind that U-turns are not always possible on the Overseas Highway, so stay alert to avoid missing exits.

By air

Not surprisingly you'll find it cheaper to fly to Miami than to one of the two Keys airports – **Marathon**, MM52 (✆743-2155) and **Key West** (✆296-5439) – but you might find that the price of car rental more than evens things up; in fact, most flights connect in Miami so you might want to consider this when pricing flights. Cape Air (✆1-800/352-0714) flies direct to Marathon from Fort Lauderdale and to Key West from Fort Myers, Naples, and Fort Lauderdale as well. Other airlines that fly into these airports are: American Eagle (1-800/433-7300), Comair (✆1-800/354-9822), Continental (✆1-800/525-0280), Delta (✆1-800/354-9822), Gulfstream International (✆1-800/992-8532; from Miami only), Northwest (✆1-800/225-2525), United Airlines (✆1-800/241-6522), and USAir Express (✆1-800/428-4322).

A **taxi** from the Key West Airport into Old Town will run you around $9 – try Five (✆296-6666) or Friendly Cab (✆292-0000). Shuttles run between Miami International Airport and the Keys but at a hefty price – you'd be better off taking Greyhound (see overleaf).

ARRIVAL: BY AIR

197

A novel means of getting from Miami into Key West is Chalk's International Airlines **seaplane** service (©1-800/424-2557; about $190 round trip), which runs daily to Key West Harbor and includes a free water taxi transfer to Mallory Square.

By car

Arriving from Miami there are two options. Either take the **I-95** south to Hwy-1, or, for a shorter route, take the Florida Turnpike Extension toll route south and pick up Hwy-1 at Florida City.

The clever and more scenic way to arrive in the Keys is with **Card Sound Road** (**Hwy-905A**; $1 toll), which branches off Hwy-1 a few miles south of Homestead. Doing so avoids the bulk of the tourist traffic, and, after passing through the desolate southeastern section of the Everglades, gives soaring views of the mangrove-dotted waters of Florida Bay (where a long wait and a lot of luck might be rewarded with a glimpse of a rare American crocodile).

Approaching the end of the line in Key West, Hwy-1 becomes known as Roosevelt Boulevard, Truman Avenue, or Whitehead Street at various stages on the island. And though cars are the main mode of transportation when getting to Key West, they're best left parked once you arrive as parking is scarce (though some hotels and guesthouses have small lots) and walking is free.

By bus

Greyhound (©1-800/231-2222) services the Keys four times daily from Miami, and the main station in Key West is located at 3531 S Roosevelt Blvd. Scheduled stops are in North Key Largo (Central Plaza, 103200 Overseas

Highway; 1hr 55min; ✆451-6280); Islamorada (*Burger King*, MM82; ✆852-4266); Marathon (6363 Overseas Highway; ✆743-3488); Big Pine Key (MM30.2; ✆872-4022); and Key West (615 1/2 Duval St; ✆296-9072). You can flag down a bus anywhere along the Overseas Highway and purchase your ticket onboard.

By boat

Since it's surrounded by water, a natural approach to Key West is via **boat**. Unless you've got your own, try the Key West Shuttle ($55 one way, $99 round trip; ✆1-888/key-boat), which departs from two of Florida's West Coast cities, Naples and Fort Myers, and drops you off in Key West's Mallory Square – either trip will take from 3hr 30min to 4hr, one way.

Swimming with dolphins

Dolphins are a common sight around the Florida Keys and are the star attraction of the state's many marine parks – though watching them perform somersaults in response to human commands gives only an inkling of their potential. Although you pay through the nose for doing so, one of the best experiences you can have while in the Keys is to swim with them, which you can do at the locations listed below (fuller details appear in the text).

Key Largo Dolphins Plus, MM100 (✆451-1993); Dolphin Cove, MM102 (✆451-4060).

Islamorada Theater of the Sea, MM84.5 (✆664-2431).

Marathon Dolphin Research Center, MM59 (✆289-1121); Dolphin Connection, MM61 (✆743-7000 ext. 3030).

GETTING AROUND

If you're planning on exploring the Keys at any length, a **car** is essential for ducking offroad and setting your own pace for sightseeing, as well as for doing any serious island hopping. Traffic tends to get heavy on Friday and Sunday evenings when mainland residents make weekend trips to the shore, and you should beware that cops tend to lurk throughout the Keys.

There are no real effective public transportation systems between the Keys, so if you're not reliant on a car, you might want to consider renting a **moped** as your primary means of getting around; these typically cost about $25–30 per day, and you'll find rental places in the major settlements, like Key Largo, Marathon, and Key West.

ACCOMMODATION

Accommodation options in the Keys are certainly abundant but tend to be more expensive than on the mainland. During high season, November to April, budget for at least $50–85 a night, $40–60 the rest of the year, though if you're staying in Key West, plan on spending a bit more. **Camping** is considerably less expensive and is well catered for throughout the Keys. Unless you're traveling with children or in a group, choosing one of the **guesthouses/bed & breakfasts** is far more fun than staying in an impersonal hotel – most **hotels** are either stationed directly off the busy and charmless US-1, or are a bit over-hyped and priced to match.

INFORMATION

Various visitor centers dot Hwy-1, beginning in **Key Largo** at the Chamber of Commerce (COC), MM106 (daily 9am–6pm; ℂ451-1414). **Islamorada**'s COC is inside a reconditioned railroad car at MM82.5 (Mon–Fri 9am–5pm; ℂ664-4503 or 1-800/322-5397), and the helpful **Marathon** COC is at MM53.5 (Mon–Fri 9am–5pm; ℂ743-5417; 1-800/262-7284). There is a very small information center for the **Lower Keys** in Big Pine Key at MM31 open Mon–Fri 9am–5pm and Sat 9am–3pm. **Key West** has several outlets for information: as you approach the island by car you'll hit the information-packed **Welcome Center** (Mon–Sat 9am–7.30pm, Sun 9am–6pm; ℂ296-4444) on North Roosevelt Boulevard. If you don't feel like stopping here, press on and use the **Greater Key West Chamber of Commerce**, 402 Wall Street at Mallory Square (daily 8.30am–5pm; ℂ294-2587), for free tourist pamphlets and discount vouchers.

Details of Key West tours can be found on p.245.

Key West also has a good number of **free publications** found at most pharmacies and newsstands throughout town, though these will mostly just clue you in on local happenings rather than listings throughout the Keys. These include *Solares Hill* (monthly), *The Conch Republic* (monthly), *Island Life* (weekly), and the gay-oriented gossip sheet *What's Happening* (weekly).

INFORMATION

The Upper Keys

The northernmost portion of the Florida Keys, and the one you'll first encounter if you're coming by car, is known, appropriately enough, as the **Upper Keys**, roughly made up of three major communities – Key Largo, Tavernier, and Islamorada – between which there's a scattering of remote islands, many of which are only accessible by boat. **Key Largo** is the biggest although not the prettiest of the Keys, and has the **John Pennekamp Coral Reef State Park** as its main attraction. Further on, the little town of **Tavernier** is really a place to pass through on the way to bigger and livelier **Islamorada** – mostly made up of a string of state parks.

> **Right before you approach Key Largo, Hwy-905 merges with Hwy-1. Known from here on as the Overseas Highway, Hwy-1 is the main – and only – road all the way to Key West.**

KEY LARGO

Thanks to the 1948 film *Key Largo*, in which Humphrey Bogart and Lauren Bacall grapple with Florida's best-known features – crime and hurricanes – almost everybody has heard of **Key Largo**. Yet the film's title was chosen for no other reason than it suggested somewhere warm and exotic, and the film was almost entirely shot in Hollywood – hoodwinking countless millions into thinking that paradise was a town in the Florida Keys.

Recognizing a potential tourist bonanza, businesspeople here soon changed the name of their community from Rock Harbor to Key Largo (a title that until then had applied to the whole island, derived from *Cayo Largo* – Long Island – the name given to it by early Spanish explorers), and tenuous links with Hollywood are maintained even today. The steam-powered boat that starred alongside Bogart in *The African Queen* is moored, when not on promotional tours, in the marina of the *Holiday Inn* at MM99.7, and the hotel's lobby displays a selection of stills of Bogart and co-star Katharine Hepburn acting their hearts out – in England and Africa.

Clinging to this image, which is based more in movies than reality, the town of Key Largo is a fairly unappealing jumble of filling stations, shopping plazas, and fast-food outlets. There are one or two low-key attractions besides the *African Queen*, such as a wild bird rehab center and a maritime museum, which will take up a half-day's time at best. The compelling reason for a longer stay is to explore the extensive coral reefs at the John Pennekamp Coral Reef State Park, miles of brilliant underwater life around which you can snorkel, or see from the bottom of a glass boat.

North Key Largo

The bulk of **North Key Largo**, where Hwy-905 touches ground, is pretty much development-free, marked only by the odd shack amid a rich endowment of trees. In fact, despite elaborate plans to turn the area into a city called "Port Bougainvillea," with high-rise blocks and a monorail (a terrifying prospect ended by sudden bankruptcy), much of the land here is now owned and protected by the state. There are plenty of scare stories about the region, usually involving drug smugglers and practitioners of the Voodoo-like *Santeria*, though they're designed as much to ward off visitors as anything else, and in reality there's no more drug smuggling here than anywhere else in the Keys – and magic merchants come not to sacrifice tourists but to gather herbs for use in their rituals. Indeed the most sinister thing about this part of Key Largo is probably the exclusive **Ocean Reef Club**, whose golf course you'll spot after a few miles if you turn left where Hwy-905 splits; it's regarded by the FBI as the country's most secure retreat for very important people – watch out for nervous, armed men in dark suits.

Islands off Key Largo

The tiny, uninhabited **islands** just off Key Largo make glorious forays, and there's no better way of exploring them than hiring a boat or catamaran. Signs abound for boat rentals, but the most reliable and user-friendly option is Robbie's Boat Rentals and Charters, located bayside behind the *Hungry Tarpon* restaurant, MM77.5 (℗664-9814). A rugged, Hemingwayesque personality, Captain Tim (everone goes by their first name in the Keys) will take good care of you whether you rent a boat to explore Indian Key or to snorkel in Alligator Reef with jellyfish warrior Captain Keith. They can also customize overnight boating trips that include snorkeling, dive certification, and deep-sea fishing. If you decide to go it alone, do heed their advice about the varying shades of shallow waters to avoid grounding your boat. If a glass-bottomed boat tour is more up your alley, head to the *Holiday Inn* docks at MM100 (℗451-4655), from where you can take two-hour cruises at 10am, 1pm, and 4pm – prices start at $25.

John Pennekamp Coral Reef State Park

Daily 8am–sunset; cars and drivers $3.75 plus 50¢ per passenger, pedestrians and cyclists $1.50.

The one essential stop on Key Largo is the **John Pennekamp Coral Reef State Park**, at MM102.5. At its heart is a protected 78-square-mile section of living coral reef, part of the reef chain that runs from here to the Dry Tortugas, five miles off Key West.

Just a few decades ago, great sections of the reef were dynamited or hauled up by crane to be broken up and sold as souvenirs. These days, collecting Florida coral is illegal, and any samples displayed in tourist shops were most likely imported from the Philippines. Despite the damage wrought by tourism, however, experts still rate this as one of the most beautiful reef systems in the world. Whether you opt to visit the reef here or elsewhere in the Keys (such as Looe Key, p.237), make sure you visit it somewhere; it's every bit as good as it's cracked up to be.

How to see the park

Since most of the park lies underwater, you'll need to arrange your transportation carefully; for this, stop by the **visitor center** (daily 8am–5pm; ©451-1621), located in the park's center at the foot of a 75-foot observation tower, which will arrange your trip. One of the best ways to take it all in is on a **snorkeling tour** (9am, noon, & 3pm; adults $24.95, under 18s $19.95), or, if you're qualified, a **guided scuba dive** (9.30am & 1.30pm; $31.50 excluding equipment; diver's certificate required). If you prefer to stay dry, a remarkable amount of the reef can be enjoyed on the two-and-a-half-hour **glass-bottomed boat tour** (9.15am, 12.15pm, & 3pm; adults $18, under 12s $10). You can also **rent a boat** – everything from a single-person kayak to a power boat – from the dive and boat

JOHN PENNEKAMP CORAL REEF STATE PARK

rental shop next to the visitor center (©451-6322); single kayaks cost $10, $15 for doubles; a 19-foot power boat is $27.50 per hour ($90 for half a day), a 28-foot boat $50 per hour ($185 per half day).

Note that only during the summer are you likely to get a place on these tours or obtain a boat without **booking ahead**. To be sure, call the dive center at ©451-6322 or try one of the local diving shops: American Diving Headquarters, MM106 (©1-800/322-3483), and the highly entertaining Captain Slate's Atlantis Dive Center, at MM106.5 (©451-1325), operate their own trips out to the reef – and cover a larger area than park tours – for around the same rates (see p.208 for a more comprehensive list of dive centers).

What to see in the park

Only when you're **at the reef** does its role in providing a sheltered environment for a multitude of crazy-colored fish and exotic sea life become apparent. Even from the glass-bottomed boat you're virtually guaranteed to spot lobsters, angelfish, eels, and wispy jellyfish shimmering through the current, shoals of minnows stalked by angry-faced barracudas – and other less easily identified aquatic curiosities.

Despite looking like a big lump of rock, the **reef**, too, is a delicate living thing, composed of millions of minute coral polyps that extract calcium from the seawater and grow from one to sixteen feet every 1000 years. Coral takes many shapes and forms, resembling anything from staghorns to a bucket, and comes in a paint-box variety of colors due to the plants (*zooxanthellae*) living within the coral tissues. Sadly, it's far easier to spot signs of death rather than life on the reef: white patches show where a carelessly dropped anchor or a diver's hand have scraped away the protective mucus layer and left the coral susceptible to lethal disease.

This destruction was so bad at the horseshoe-shaped

Molasses Reef, about seven miles out (so called because a Jamaica schooner carrying sugarcane ran aground here a century or so ago), that the authorities sank two obsolete Coast Guard cutters nearby to create an alternative attraction for divers. The environmental disruption has slowed due to better public awareness, and today you'll be able to enjoy some great snorkeling around the reef and the cutters. If you like wrecks, head for **The Elbow**, a section of the reef a few miles northeast of Molasses, where lie a number of intriguing, barnacle-encrusted nineteenth-century specimens; like most of the Keys' diveable wrecks, these too were deliberately brought here to bolster tourism in the Seventies, and you definitely won't find any treasure.

By far the strangest thing at the reef is the **Christ of the Deep**, a nine-foot bronze statue of Christ intended as a memorial to perished sailors. The algae-coated creation, twenty feet down at **Key Largo Dry Rocks**, is a replica of Guido Galletti's *Christ of the Abyss*, said to be similarly submerged off the coast of Genoa, Italy, and is surely the final word in Florida's long-established fixation with Mediterranean art and architecture. Glass-bottomed boat trips, by the way, don't visit The Elbow or the Christ of the Deep.

The rest of the park

Provided you visit the reef early, there'll be plenty of time left to enjoy the terrestrial portion of the park. The ecological displays at the visitor center (see above) provide an inspiring introduction to the flora and fauna of the Keys and will give you a practical insight into the region's transitional zones – the vegetation changes dramatically within an elevation of a few feet.

You can't miss the trail signs outside the visitor center pointing you to any one of the park's tropical hardwood **hammock trails**, which meander through red mangroves,

JOHN PENNEKAMP CORAL REEF STATE PARK

Dive operators

Tropical fish, colorful reefs, exotic plant life, and sunken treasure all await beneath the water's surface throughout the Keys. In the Upper Keys there are some particularly good dive shops to aid you in your underwater excursions – which promise to be unforgettable.

American Diving Headquarters, MM106 (©1-800/322-3483).

Aqua-Nuts, MM104.2, at *Kelly's on the Bay* (©451-1622 or 1-800/226-0415).

Captain Slate's Atlantis Dive Center, MM106.5 (©451-3020 or 1-800/331-3483).

HMS Minnow, MM100 at the *Holiday Inn* (©451-7834 or 1-800/366-9301) who incidentally *do* have "three-hour tours."

Ocean Divers, MM100, 522 Caribbean Drive (©451-1113).

Silent World Dive Center, Inc, MM103.2 (©451-3252 or 1-800/966-DIVE).

pepper trees, and graceful frangipani. Racoon, heron, and fiddler crab tracks are everywhere, and hairy-legged, golden orb spiders dangle from many a branch. The park also boasts some fine man-made **beaches** on the bayside of the park, but note that the coral is very unforgiving to bare feet. Another option for exploring the park is to rent a **canoe** ($10 per hour) and glide around the mangrove-fringed inner waterways.

Dolphin Cove

Daily 8am–5pm; $8 entrance fee, $100 to swim with the dolphins.

Dolphin Cove, a five-acre marine environment research center just south of MM102, is one of the best of several dolphin encounter programs in the Keys. It's expensive, but worth every penny to swim with one hand planted firmly on a dolphin's slippery dorsal fin – and if your budget can't stretch to it you can always watch others doing it as a non-swimming observer. Sessions are at 9am, 1pm, & 3pm. Dolphin Cove is also the departure point for Captain Sterling's Crocodile Tours (©853-5161), one of the more knowledgeable **tour operators** in the area.

For information on other locations to swim with the dolphins, see Chapter 19, "Introducing the Florida Keys," p.199.

Maritime Museum of the Florida Keys

Mon–Fri 8am–4pm, Sun 10am–3pm, closed Sat; $3.

Housed in a fake castle, the **Maritime Museum of the Florida Keys**, MM102, looks a kitschy kind of place from the outside; inside the not-for-profit organization that runs the place tries, through a series of small exhibits, to stress the role that the profitable wrecking industry played in the Keys' history. Back in the eighteenth and nineteenth centuries, ships would come close to shore and instantly become vulnerable to the jagged reefs and swift currents hereabouts – and salvaging became a mainstay operation. On display is a collection of artifacts salvaged from those wrecks – leg and arm irons from the slave ship *Henrietta Marie* which sank in 1700, dishes and glasswear, coins, and various gleaming jewels among them.

Florida Keys Wild Bird Rehabilitation Center

Daily 8.30am–5.30pm; free but dependent on donations.

Just before crossing into Tavernier, at MM93.6, the **Florida**

KEY LARGO

An African Queen in Key Largo

Key Largo was known as Rock Harbor until a film crew came down in 1948 to make the legendary movie *Key Largo*, and local officials searching for tourist dollars quickly changed the name. In reality, the only scenes shot in the area were at the *Caribbean Club Bar* at MM103.5 (see p.213); the rest of the movie was filmed in Hollywood. A more exciting movie relic is the original workboat used in the movie **African Queen**, starring Humphrey Bogart and Katherine Hepburn, which is moored at the Key Largo Marina at the *Holiday Inn*, MM99.7 (©451-2121). You can gawk at the badly aged boat in the marina for free or you can take a spin in it by appointment only (tours run on a "by demand basis" through the *Holiday Inn* gift shop; ©451-2121).

Keys Wild Bird Rehabilitation Center is an inspirational place where volunteers rescue and rehabilitate birds who have been orphaned or have met with other common catastrophes like colliding with cars or power lines. A wooden walkway is lined with huge enclosures, and signs detail the birds' histories. You'll see spoonbills and pelicans and osprey, as well as many rare and endangered birds, such as the Schaus swallowtail butterfly and the Key Largo wood rate.

Accommodation

Economy Efficiency (also known as Ed & Ellen's)
103365 Overseas Highway ©451-4712.
A standard motel with clean, basic rooms – at a price unbeatable for the area. **②**.

Jules' Undersea Lodge

51 Shoreland Drive ℂ1-800/858-7119 or 451-2353.

Very costly, but a definite adventure, this tiny "hotel" is
anchored thirty feet below the ocean's surface – and is only
accessible by diving. It's sort of like staying in a submarine, save
that the accommodations, linked to land by an intercom system, have comfortable beds, private bath, and tasteful furniture.
The two-person luxury option (for $1000) comes complete
with caviar and flowers. Just remember your diver's certificate –
otherwise you'll have to take the hotel's three-hour crash
course ($75) before you'll be allowed to unpack. ⑧.

Kona Kai Resort

97802 Overseas Highway, MM98 ℂ852-7200.

A little pricier than its neighbors, but the chalets that make up
this resort are huge and stylish, a dozen strains of banana grow
in the lovely garden, and the hotel has its own art gallery. ⑦.

Largo Lodge

101740 Overseas Highway, MM101.5 ℂ451-0424 or
1-800/IN-THE-SUN.

Comfortable one-bedroom cottages with private screened
porches, kitchenettes, and direct beach access, in a relaxing
bayfront setting. ⑤.

Seafarer Fish and Dive Resort

MM97.8 ℂ852-5349 or 1-800/599-7712; fax 852-2265.

Located about five miles from the John Pennekamp State Park,
this hotel offers clean, inexpensive rooms, each with private
bath. The deluxe cottages are a good deal too, each with a
roomy sundeck and kitchen. ②–⑤.

**For an explanation of the accommodation price
codes, see p.88. For eating price categories see p.104.**

KEY LARGO

Eating

Ballyhoo's
MM98 opposite the *Seafarer Hotel* ℗852-0822. Inexpensive.
Opened twenty years ago by a couple of fishermen, this place
serves legendary breakfasts, with mounds of pancakes,
omelettes, croissants dipped in orange and egg, and a wide
selection of grilled sandwiches.

Crack'd Conch
MM105 ℗451-0732. Inexpensive.
A local favorite, with popular items on the menu including
Keys' specialties like fried alligator and conch salad, all of
which are tasty and affordable. More than one hundred beers
on tap as well.

Frank Keys Café
100211 Overseas Highway ℗453-0310. Moderate–Expensive.
Set in an attractive cottage hidden away from the highway, this
sweet café offers slightly more sophisticated – and more expensive – seafood and classic American fare.

Mrs Mac's Kitchen
MM99.4 ℗451-3722. Inexpensive.
This local favorite is well-known for its bowls of ferociously
hot chili and other home-cooked goodies – definitely a good
pit stop when you're on the go.

Snappers Raw Bar
MM94 at Ocean View Boulevard ℗852-5956. Inexpensive.
A good choice for alligator and atmosphere; enjoy the water-
side, candlelit setting with a 'gator starter, or swing by for the
Sunday brunch (10am–2pm).

Key Largo also has one of the Keys' biggest
supermarkets, Winn-Dixie (MM105), which is ideal
for loading up on supplies for the journey ahead.

Drinking

Caribbean Club Bar
MM103.5 ℂ451-9970.

Unlike its classy depiction in *African Queen*, this is more the
place to drink if you have no fear of tropical shorts and want to
shoot some pool. The crowd is particularly lively, especially
when the occasional band takes to the stage – plus you can take
your frozen drink outside and watch a glorious Florida Bay
sunset.

Coconuts
Marina del Mar Resort, MM100 ℂ451-4107.

A mellow crowd knocks 'em back at this breezy watering hole
frequented by locals and visitors alike. It's a great spot for a cold
beer and no attitude.

TAVERNIER

Ten miles south of Key Largo on the Overseas Highway,
Tavernier is a small, homey town that was once the first
stop on the Flagler railway (the Keys' first link to the mainland; see "Marathon," p.222). There's not a whole lot here,
but Tavernier's historic buildings and decent Cuban café
(see p.215) make it a worthy short stop.

The old architecture found here is a rarity in the Keys,
outside of Key West, and has thus been designated a **historic district**, between MM91 and MM92 – turn bayside

at the *Tavernier Hotel* and then take the first right up Atlantic Circle Drive to get there. In addition to the plank walls and tin roofs of the turn-of-the-century Methodist Church (now functioning as a small visitor center) and post office, you'll see some of the "weather proof" Red Cross buildings erected after the 1935 Labor Day hurricane – which laid waste to a good chunk of the Keys. Before locals could find out if they were waterproof and therefore capable of withstanding another similar hurricane, the structures crumbled due to saltwater being used in the concrete mix – which eventually eroded the buildings' walls and rusted the steel frames.

Accommodation

Bay Breeze Motel

MM92.5 ©852-5248 or 1-800/937-5650.
A small waterfront motel with basic accommodation. Extras include free rowboats, a heated pool, and the largest private beach in Tavernier. ②–③.

Tavernier Hotel

MM91.8 ©852-4131.
A quaint, classic hotel painted bubble-gum pink that was originally built as an open-air theater. ④–⑤.

Eating

The Copper Kettle

91865 Overseas Hwy, MM91.8 ©852-4131. Moderate.
Next door to the *Tavernier Hotel*, this is a cozy place for candlelit dinners of honey Cajun shrimp and other regional delights.

Sunshine Café

MM91.8 (no phone and no English spoken). Cheap.

Don't let the dingy exterior put you off from discovering this hidden gem. Get a jolt of top-notch Cuban coffee for $1 and choose from loaded trays of Cuban treats like *tamales* (corn tortillas stuffed with pork and served with fried plantain) and black beans and rice.

ISLAMORADA

Once over Tavernier Creek, you're at the start of a twenty-mile strip of small islands – Plantation, Windley, and Upper and Lower Matecumbe – which is collectively known as **Islamorada** (pronounced "eye-la-more-ah-da"). More than any other section of the Keys, fishing is the big thing here. Tales of monstrous tarpon and blue marlin captured off the coast are legendary, and there's no end to the smaller prey routinely hooked even by total novices.

For non-fishing folk, there's little in Islamorada to warrant an extended stay. The **Chamber of Commerce**, at MM82 (Mon–Fri 9am–5pm, ℂ664-9767; fax 664-4289), is packed with general information and details on the latest cut-rate accommodation deals. Half a mile further south, an Art Deco **monument** marks the grave of the 1935 Labor Day hurricane's 425 victims, killed when a tidal wave hit their evacuation train.

Tours and getting around

Islamorada has three state parks – **Indian Key**, **Lignumvitae Key**, and **Long Key** – at its southern end which offer a broader perspective of the area than just fishing and diving. The **guided tours** to Indian Key and Lignumvitae Key are particularly enchanting and reveal a near-forgotten chapter of the Florida Keys' history and a

ISLAMORADA

virgin forest respectively (see p.218). A two-hour **Indian Key tour** (Thurs–Mon 8.30am to 12.30pm) departs from Robbie's Marina, MM77.5 (©664-4196; $15; children $10), as does the **Lignumvitae tour** (daily 9.30am–12.30pm, plus an evening cruise one hour before sunset; $15). Alternatively, a tour of both Keys runs from **Papa Joe's Marina**, MM80 (daily for two or more people at 8.30am; $24; children $14; ©664 5005).

Fishing, snorkeling, and diving

If you'd like to do some **fishing** yourself, there's lots of opportunity. You can either rent a fishing boat or, for much less, join a fishing party boat from any of the local marinas. The widest array of options is at the *Holiday Isle* hotel, 84001 Overseas Highway (©1-800/327-7070), and Bud 'n' Mary's, MM80, which also sports a modest **Museum of Fishing** (Mon–Sat 10am–5pm; free), with its small collection of "the fish was this big" photographs, antique reels and tackle, plus some nasty-looking shark teeth.

There's notable **snorkeling** and **diving** in the area, too. Crocker and Alligator reefs, a few miles offshore, both have near vertical sides, whose cracks and crevices provide homes for a lively variety of crabs, shrimps, and other small creatures that in turn attract bigger fish looking for a meal. Nearby, the wrecks of the Eagle and the Cannabis Cruiser provide a home for families of gargantuan amberjack and grouper. Get full snorkeling and diving details from the marinas or any dive shop on the Overseas Highway.

Other operators to try out include: Caribbean Watersports, MM82 (©664-9598); Rainbow Reef Dive Center, MM85 (©664-4600); or World Down Under, MM81.9 (©664-9312).

The Theater of the Sea

Daily 9.30am–4pm; adults $16.75, under 13s $10.25.

Back on dry land, you might want to pass a couple of hours at the **Theater of the Sea**, MM84.5, but only if the price doesn't put you off and you haven't already seen one of the better marine parks in southern Florida. Sea lions, dolphins, and a half-dozen tanks full of assorted fish and crustaceans are introduced by a knowledgeable staff, and, if you reserve ahead, you can swim with the dolphins or sea lions ($95 and $65 respectively; see p.199).

Indian Key

You'd never guess from the highway that **Indian Key**, one of many small, mangrove-skirted islands off Lower Matecumbe Key, was once a busy trading center, given short-lived prosperity – and notoriety – by a nineteenth-century New Yorker called Jacob Houseman. After stealing one of his father's ships, Houseman sailed to Key West looking for a piece of the lucrative wrecking (or salvaging) business. Mistrusted by the close-knit Key West community, he bought Indian Key in 1831 as a base for his own wrecking operation. In the first year, Houseman made $30,000 and furnished the eleven-acre island with streets, a store, warehouses, a hotel, an observation tower, and a permanent population of around fifty. However, the income was not entirely honest: Houseman was known to lead donkeys with lanterns along the shore to lure ships toward dangerous reefs, and he eventually lost his wrecking license for "salvaging" from an anchored vessel.

In 1838, Indian Key was sold to physician-botanist Henry Perrine, who had been cultivating tropical plants here with an eye to their commercial potential. A Seminole attack in 1840 burned every building to the ground and

ended the island's habitation, but Perrine's plants survived
and today form a swathe of flowing foliage that includes
sisal, coffee, tea, and mango plants. Besides allowing ample
opportunity to gaze at the flora, the **two-hour tour** (see
p.216) takes you around the now deserted streets, up the
observation tower and past Houseman's grave – his body
was brought here after he died working on a wreck off Key
West.

Lignumvitae Key

Lignumvitae Key is a relatively tiny, 280-acre hammock
known for its tongue-twisting assortment of hardwood trees
such as strangler figs, pigeon plums, poisonwoods, mastics,
mahoganys, and gumbo limbos. In fact, the word
"lignumvitae" comes from the Latin phrase "wood of life,"
which sums up the character of the island quite nicely. It
escaped major development due to its slightly askew location that didn't line up with the Flagler's railroad trying to
connect the Keys with the mainland. And as a consequence
it tries to retain as much isolation as possible, allowing only
fifty people at a time on its shores. Unless you're taking a
tour from Robbie's Marina (see p.216), private boaters must
contact a park ranger for access to Lignumvitae Key.

One unusual feature of the island is the sizable spiders,
such as the golden orb, whose silvery web regularly
spans entire pathways.

The trail through the forest was laid out by a wealthy
early Miamian, W. J. Matheson, whose 1919 limestone
house is the island's only sign of habitation and shows the
deprivations of early island living – even for the well-off.
The house actually blew away in the 1935 hurricane, but
was found and brought back.

Long Key State Recreation Area

Daily 8am–sunset; cars $3.75 plus $1 per passenger, pedestrians
and cyclists $1.50.

An aerial shot of **Long Key** makes it look like a snake about
to strike, a feature that earned it the nickname of "Cayo
Vivora" – rattlesnake key. But there are no rattlesnakes here;
rather you'll find Long Key populated by many West Indian
and Caribbean varieties of trees and shrubs similar to those on
Lignumvitae Key, and including Jamaica dogwoods and crab-
woods. There are two nature trails – a fifteen-minute one that
weaves along the bayside, and a forty-minute hike along the
beach and on a boardwalk over a mangrove-lined lagoon. Or,
better still, you can rent a canoe ($4 per hour) and follow the
simple **canoe trail** through the tidal lagoons in the company
of some mildly curious wading birds. **Camping** in the park is
also available – call the visitor center (daily 9am–5pm; ℭ664-
4815) for details on canoe rental and camping.

Accommodation

Cheeca Lodge
MM82 ℭ664-4651 or 1-800/327-2888.
This resort is anything but a "lodge." The complex includes
140 rooms, a golf course, six tennis courts, boating, fishing,
and parasailing options – reservations and details at the front
desk – as well as babysitting services. Rooms are spacious and
clean, and the resort itself is very quiet and serene. ⑦–⑧.

Fiesta Key KOA Resort
MM70 ℭ664-4922 or 1-800/562-7730; fax 664-8741.
This is primarily a full-service campground, but it also has
twenty small (and very basic) motel rooms. Most importantly
– it's right on the beach. ②–③.

ISLAMORADA

Holiday Isle Beach Resort

84001 Overseas Highway, MM84 ℗1-800/327-7070.

Reminiscent of a Spring Break flashback, this popular resort is a psychedelic trip: vivid citrus-colored plastic ornaments and tiki huts fill the vacation village, which incorporates several hotels. The atmosphere is youthful and friendly and the main hotel itself is very comfortable, with nightly entertainment at the tiki bar. Rooms are small but clean, but you may not be here to sleep anyway. ③–④.

Key Lantern Motel and Blue Fin Inn

MM82 ℗664-4572.

You won't find a cheaper deal in Islamorada than here. Spacious rooms with kitchenettes, TVs, and air-conditioning, along with laundry facilities and grills on-site. A perfect location, right on the water. ②–③.

Smugglers Cove Resort and Marina

MM.85 ℗664-5564; fax 664-2953.

Waterfront hotel rooms and efficiencies – studios with a small kitchen among a full-service resort with plenty of watersports to choose from just outside your door. ③–④.

You're unlikely to find accommodation in Islamorada for under $70 a night, although price wars among the bigger hotels can reveal occasional finds, and campgrounds usually offer motel-style rooms at lower prices than standard hotels.

Eating

Grove Park Café

MM81.7 ℗664-0116. Moderate.

Tucked away from the highway, this small, self-consciously cute café serves sophisticated American dishes (try their conch chowder or the crab cakes), sandwiches, and good homemade bread. They also make picnic lunches to go. Highly recommended.

Islamorada Fish Company
MM81 ©664-9271. Inexpensive–Moderate.
You can actually watch your dinner arrive from the docks while sitting seaside at this relaxed, ideally located – it's right on the water – restaurant. Daily specials are the ones to order here, but watch out, it fills up fast so try and get here before 6pm.

Little Italy
MM68.5 ©664-4472. Moderate.
When you've eaten enough seafood to last you a lifetime, this Italian stop is a good option. Great light pasta dishes, plus chicken, veal, and steak are on offer and there's a good wine list too.

Manny & Isa's
MM81.5 ©664-5019. Cheap.
An informal joint, which serves up hearty portions of high-quality, low-cost Cuban food.

Papa Joe's
MM79.7 ©664-8756. Inexpensive.
Like many restaurants in the Keys, this creaky place has been around forever, surviving hurricanes and serving as a Coast Guard barrack during World War II. And the food isn't bad either, including an award-winning seafood bisque and key lime pie made to the previous owner's secret recipe. Absolutely worth stopping for.

ISLAMORADA: EATING

The Middle Keys

T he Atlantic Ocean meets the Gulf of Mexico below Long Key Bridge, which links the Upper Keys to the more sedate and smaller **Middle Keys**, stretching from Conch Key (MM65) to the **Seven Mile Bridge** (MM47). The largest of these keys is **Vaca** – once a shanty-town of railway workers – which is home to the area's only settlement, **Marathon**, on its western boundary.

Though sights are few, the natural hammock in Marathon is considered to be the most environmentally significant property in the Keys due to the diverse ecosystems it sustains and the dolphin rehabilitation program here, which is at the forefront of advanced aquatic research. A few of Henry Flagler's railroad relics remain as well, inspiring a small museum on Pigeon Key and creating some great fishing piers put to use by local enthusiasts.

If you're planning on staying in the Middle Keys, **accommodation** is not a problem, particularly in Marathon where there are plenty of places to **eat and drink** at a reasonable cost.

MARATHON

With 12,000 residents, **MARATHON** is the second largest community in the Keys, surpassed only by Key West. It is a town dedicated to fishing, both as an industry and as a sport. Its populace is mostly made up of long-time vacationers and retirees, happy to spend their days fishing off the abandoned bridges of Flagler's old railroads and boating around the Keys' waterways.

Marathon also has a couple of small **beaches** worth checking out. **Sombrero Beach**, along Sombrero Beach Road (off the Overseas Highway near MM50), is a slender strip of sand with good swimming waters and shaded picnic tables. Four miles north, **Key Colony Beach** is prettier and quieter, a man-made beach dredged into existence during the Fifties to entice potential home-buyers to the area. And although there is little to do in Marathon itself, the area's tourist draws support the Middle Keys' only **restaurants** and **accommodation**.

Marathon festivals

If you're here in late March or mid-April there are two festivals in Marathon worth checking out. During the last weekend in March the **Marathon Seafood Festival** (exact locations vary) is one of the hottest food festivals in the Keys – while at the same time it helps support local tourism and fishing industries. Stuff yourself silly with all things fish including Keys specialties like Florida lobster, conch prepared every possible way, and delicious wahoo, grouper, and cobia (℗743-5417; $2).

In Mid-April, the **Seven Mile Bridge Run** takes over the island and if you're planning on driving around Marathon at this time check the exact date – otherwise you might be caught in the tail end of close to 1500 runners. Competitors begin at the crack of dawn and race along seven miles of one of the world's longest bridges – nothing but ice blue water surrounding them in this annual scenic run that stretches from Marathon to Little Duck Key (℗1-800/262-7284; $25 entrance fee).

MARATHON

Crane Point Hammock

MM50.5. Open Mon–Sat 10am–5pm, Sun noon–5pm; $7.50, includes admission to both museums and all trails.

Hidden away, but in the heart of Marathon, the **Crane Point Hammock** is 64 steamy acres of subtropical forest untouched by the human hand. The park is made up of two museums, some nature trails, and a visitor center dedicated to native birds and wildlife. A free booklet gives details of the trees you'll find along the handful of **nature trails**, and along the aptly named Bahama House Trail you'll see the Adderley House, built in 1903 by Bahamian immigrants – one of the last examples of Bahamian architecture in the US (for others see "Key West," p.241).

Of the hammock's two museums, the excellent **Museum of Natural History of the Florida Keys** gives a solid rundown of the area's history – starting with the Caloosa Indians (who had a settlement on this site until they were wiped out by disease brought by European settlers in the 1700s), and continuing with the story of early Bahamian and American settlers. Not to be missed is the motley collection of artifacts near the museum shop, including a raft made of inner tubes that carried four Cuban refugees across ninety miles of ocean in the early 1990s – a poignant exhibit given the recent Elian Gonzalez affair.

....

A large section of the Natural History Museum features interactive displays designed to introduce kids to the Keys' complex, subtropical ecosystems, including the hardwood hammocks and reefs.

....

Much the same ground is covered at the adjoining **Florida Keys Children's Museum**, which houses a tropical aquarium, a hawk habitat, an iguana exhibit, a terrarium, and a 15,000-gallon artificial saltwater lagoon where you can feed the fish. Beware that the hammock's resident mosquitoes are a painful nuisance – particularly here – so consider investing in the bug sprays sold at the pharmacy directly across the highway.

> For a closer look at the Keys' natural life, take the waterborne ecology tour (Thurs–Sat, 10am & 2pm; $15; ℗743-7000 – ask for the marina of the ultra-pricey *Hawks Cay Resort* on Duck Key, reached by way of a causeway at MM61. Led by a radically minded local naturalist, the two-hour trip to an uninhabited island furnishes you with a wealth of information on the makeup of the Keys and the creatures who live in them.

DOLPHIN RESEARCH CENTER

Daily 9am–4.30pm; $12.50 adults, $7.50 children 4–12; $110 to swim with the dolphins. ℗289-1121.

Look for the giant dolphin sign just east of Marathon, and you'll find the **Dolphin Research Center**, MM59 at Grassy Key, an institute at the forefront of dolphin research which uses dolphins in therapy programs for cancer-sufferers and mentally handicapped children. The exceptional patience and gentleness displayed by the dolphins (all of whom are free to swim out to sea whenever they want) in this work suggest that their sonar system may allow them to make an X-ray-like scan of a body to detect abnormalities and perhaps even to "see" emotions. Averaging seven feet long, dolphins look disconcertingly large at close quarters – and will lose interest in you long before you tire of their company – but if you do get the opportunity to join them, it's an unforgettable experience. They have several different

On the water

The choice locale for the pursuits of **snorkeling** and **scuba diving** is **Sombrero Reef**, marked by a 142-foot-high nineteenth-century lighthouse, whose nooks and crannies provide a safe haven for thousands of darting, brightly colored tropical fish. The best time to go out is early evening when the reef is at its most active, as the majority of its creatures are nocturnal. The pick of local **dive shops** is *Hall's Dive Center* (©1-800/331-4255), on the grounds of *Faro Blanco Marina Resort*, MM48.5, which offers five-day Basic Open Water Scuba Certificate courses ($385) to novice divers; night diving, wreck diving, and Instructor's Certificate courses are available for the experienced. Once certified, you can rent equipment ($55) and join a dive trip (9am, 1pm, 5.30pm; $40).

Around Marathon, **spearfishing** is permitted a mile offshore (there's a three-mile limit elsewhere), and the town hosts four major **fishing tournaments** each year, which you can learn about at the **Visitor Center**, 3330 Overseas Highway (Mon–Fri 9am–5pm; ©1-800/842-9580). Boats take out up to six people and charge between $400 and $850 for a full day's fishing (daily 7am–4pm), including bait and equipment. If you can't get a group together, join one of the countless group boats for about $40 per person for a full day's fishing – remember, though, that it's easier to catch fish with fewer people aboard.

Although most of the boats at the local marinas are large power vessels designed for anglers, Marathon is also a major **sailboat** base, offering vessels for charter – with or without a captain – as well as sailing courses. A reliable source of both is *A–B–Sea Charter* (©289-0373), at the *Faro Blanco Marina Resort*, MM48.5.

dolphin "encounter" programs, the most popular being the chance to swim with them, but there are also learning sessions on dolphin training, a non-water contact encounter, and accredited college courses. Reservations are a must, except for the training session, which you can sign up for when you enter the center. If you'd rather see the dolphins from afar and get the behind-the-scenes spiel, you can join one of the daily **tours** (10am, 11am, 12.30pm, 2pm, and 2.30pm).

Not to be outdone by the sleek mammals, a plethora of felines call the center home too, strolling next to the sea lion tank or stretched out along the edge of the manatee lagoon – most of them stray "Hemingway cats" (see p.256) which sport an extra toe on their paws.

PIGEON KEY

During the construction of Flagler's railroad, from 1908 through 1935, the laborers lived on tiny **Pigeon Key**. Until recently, the Key was used by the University of Miami for marine science classes, but recently the five-acre island was added to the National Register of Historic Places. On the island are seven original houses, including the **Assistant Bridge Tender's House**, renovated to look as it did in 1912, and a small **museum** which displays a selection of photographs documenting the bridge's construction and its workers. Tours of the museum cost $7.50, a fee which is included in the price of the shuttle (daily 10am–5pm) that runs here from Knights Key, at the western end of Marathon. Alternatively, you can walk or bike over the old bridge (see below), and pay the museum fee at the door.

In early February look out for the Pigeon Key Arts Festival held under the old Seven Mile Bridge on Pigeon Key. A kaleidoscope of watercolors, metallic jewelry, pottery, and paintings by local and

**international artists are judged and celebrated over a
festive weekend. Listen to live bands and sample food
from area restaurants while you browse along the
beach (℗289-0025; $7.50 adults).**

THE SEVEN MILE BRIDGE

Bridging the Middle Keys gave Henry Flagler's engineers
some of their biggest headaches. North of Marathon, the
two-mile-long **Long Key Viaduct**, a still-elegant structure
of nearly two hundred individually cast arches, was Flagler's
personal favorite and was widely pictured in advertising
campaigns. Yet a greater technical accomplishment was the
Seven Mile Bridge (built from 1908 to 1912) to the south,
linking Marathon to the Lower Keys. At one point, every
US-flagged freighter on the Atlantic was hired to bring in
materials – including special cement from Germany – while
floating cranes, dredges, and scores of other crafts set about a
job that eventually cost the lives of 700 laborers. When the
trains eventually started rolling (doddering over the bridges
at 15mph), passengers were treated to an incredible panora-
ma: a broad sweep of sea and sky, sometimes streaked by lus-
cious red sunsets or darkened by storm clouds.

    The Flagler bridges were strong enough to withstand
everything that the Keys' volatile weather could throw at
them, except for the calamitous 1935 Labor Day hurricane,
which tore up the railway. In 1982, a $45-million renova-
tion effort went into building a new Seven Mile Bridge
between Key Vaca and Bahia Honda Key, which certainly
improved traffic flow but also put an end to the fabulous
view, with walls that are just high enough to block the
sights. Today, the old bridges make extraordinarily long
fishing piers and jogging strips, and a section of the former
Seven Mile Bridge also provides land access to Pigeon Key.

ACCOMMODATION

Anchor Lite

11699 Overseas Highway, MM53 ℂ743-7397.

Right on the ocean, all rooms have air-conditioning, private baths, and good-sized kitchens, plus use of the private dock. An inexpensive option with lots of character. ②–④.

....

For an explanation of the accommodation price codes, see p.88. For eating price categories see p.104.

....

Cocoplum Beach and Tennis Club

109 Cocoplum Drive, MM54.5 ℂ743-0240 or 1-800/228-1587. This is a gem in the Middle Keys, an oceanfront property tucked off the main road. The complex consists of twenty individual two-story octagonal-shaped homes, each with two bedrooms, two baths, a large wraparound screen porch, full kitchen, and dining room. There's also a pool, an outdoor hot tub, and tennis courts. Works best if you're traveling with four or more people. ⑧.

Conch Key Cottages

62250 Overseas Highway, MM62.3, Walkers Island ℂ289-1377 or 1-800/330-1577.

Nestled on their own private island, these cottages come in a variety of sizes – some with private porches and barbecues – but all with access to a private beach. If you're traveling in a small group, they're a reasonable option; if you can afford it, push for the ones with waterfront views. The adjoining marina takes care of all your watersport amenities. ③–⑦.

Faro Blanco Marine Resort

1996 Overseas Highway, MM48.5 ℂ743-9018 or 1-800-759-3276.

ACCOMMODATION

A pristinely placed resort, whose small cottages and houseboats offer beautiful views of the mangroves. Everything is done well here – clean spaces, tasteful decor, and reliable staff. ③–⑧.

Flamingo Inn

MM59, at Grassy Key ✆289-1478 or 1-800/439-1478.
Very comfortable beds, big clean rooms, and a pool – the best deal in the area. ②–③.

Tropical Cottages

243 61st St, MM50 ✆743-6048.
There are ten inexpensive cottages that make up this sandy complex, complete with kitchenettes, TVs, and air-conditioning. They even offer free dockage here in case you arrive by boat. It's a pleasant and private place to stay for a great price and makes a nice stop-off point between Miami and Key West. ①–②.

EATING

Crocodiles on the Water

MM48, down 15th St ✆743-9018. Moderate–Expensive.
Part of the classy *Faro Blanco Marine Resort*, this restaurant offers a more upscale dining experience than its neighbors. Cuban fish and oyster dishes are standouts on the menu. However, good daily specials and salads as well as a mouth-watering dessert tray should accommodate anyone's tastes.

Porky's

1400 Overseas Highway, MM47.5 ✆305/289-2065. Cheap.
While the name is a bit off-putting, the barbecue specials and burgers, along with excellent conch fritters and other local seafood, will keep you coming back. For a twist, they also offer free sunset cruises.

The Quay

12650 Overseas Highway, MM54 ©305/289-1810. Inexpensive.
Skip the pricey main restaurant and follow the music at the
thatched tiki bar in the back. Here you'll find good fish sandwiches and fresh seafood as well as some chicken dishes and
assorted veggies.

The Seven Mile Grill

1240 Overseas Highway ©743-4481, just east of the Seven Mile
Bridge. Inexpensive.
The locals flock here for fine conch chowders and shrimp
steamed in beer. It's very Florida in feel, with its mellow location, seafood specials, and steady flow of beer and people.

DRINKING

Bacchus Tiki Bar

MM47.6 down 11th St (no phone).
A cool place to drink, just north of the Seven Mile Bridge,
with a laid-back clientele and tasty piña colada specials.

Gary's Pub and Billiards

MM50 ©743-0622.
A big bar where the locals congregate for its pool tables and
jukebox.

Herbie's Bar

MM50.5 ©743-6373.
Endless mugs of cold beer flow from the taps in this hut-like bar.
They also serve conch fritters and other munchies. Closed Sun.

Hurricane Raw Bar

MM49.5 ©743-5755.
More karaoke than you could ever imagine, in a fun waterfront
setting. Cheap drink specials keep a youthful crowd packed in.

DRINKING

Shuckers Restaurant

725 11th St ✆743-8686.

A pleasant waterfront tiki bar, which is also a prime vantage-point for sipping a drink as the sun goes down.

The Lower Keys

The end of the Seven Mile Bridge marks the beginning of the quiet, heavily wooded, and predominantly residential **Lower Keys**, punctuated with cheery names like **Big Pine**, **Little Torch**, **Summerland**, and **Sugarloaf**. Aligned north–south and built on a limestone rather than a coral base, these islands boast a lush variety of flora and fauna – hardwood trees, silver palms, saw palmettos, tropical fruits like tamarinds, papayas, and starfruit, and some magnificent birdlife – much of it tucked miles away from the **Overseas Highway**, which runs throughout the chain.

Accommodation and eating options are scattered throughout the Lower Keys – with no one island serving as much of a central base – and are listed at the end of the chapter.

Most visitors speed through the area on the way to Key West, just forty miles further from the end of the Seven Mile Bridge, but the area's lack of rampant tourism and easily found seclusion make it a good place to linger for a day or two. Its main settlement, Big Pine Key, is not much of a place to hang out, but it does hold what shrinking habitat there is for the dainty and endangered **Key deer**; as you approach, signs with very slow speed limits will pop up with more frequency, all of which you'd be advised to heed.

BAHIA HONDA STATE RECREATION AREA

Daily 8am–sunset; cars with one person $2.50, two people $5, and 50¢ for each additional person; pedestrians and cyclists $1.50.

The first place of consequence you'll hit after crossing the Seven Mile Bridge is the 300-acre **Bahia Honda State Recreation Area**, on Bahia Honda Key, one of the Keys' prettiest spots and home to much attractive wildlife. Clean white **beaches**, framed by exotic plants and picturesque views, lie on either side of the park, allowing for sun-bathing and swimming both bayside and oceanside.

Once inside the park, you should ramble on the **nature trail**, which loops from the shoreline through a hammock of silver palms, geiger, and yellow satinwood trees, passing rare plants such as dwarf morning glory and spiny catesbaea. Keep a look out for white-crowned pigeons, great white herons, roseate spoonbills, and giant ospreys (whose bulky nests are plentiful throughout the Lower Keys, often atop telegraph poles). Nature programs start at 11am and you can ask about organized **walks** through the park, though it's pleasant enough without a guide.

The waters at the park's southern end are good for swimming (beware, though, that currents here can be very swift), as well as for snorkeling, diving, and especially windsurfing – rent equipment from the Bahia Honda marina's dive shop where you'll also notice the two-story **Flagler Bridge**. The unusually deep waters here (Bahia Honda is Spanish for "deep bay") made this area the toughest of the old rail-way bridges to construct, and widening it for the road proved impossible: the solution was to put the highway on a higher tier. It's actually far safer than it looks and there's a fine view from the top of the bridge over the Bahia Honda channel toward the rest of the forest-coated Lower Keys.

BIG PINE KEY

Second in size among all the Keys to Key Largo, **Big Pine Key**, which you'll cross on to at MM33, is mostly residential, but it manages to attract a number of visitors to its large wildlife refuge, who come in the hopes of spotting a member of the endangered **Key deer** species. The deer, no bigger than large dogs, were first documented in the journal of a shipwrecked Spanish explorer in the 1500s, and it is thought that they migrated thousands of years ago when the Keys were still joined to the mainland. For many years, they provided food for sailors and Key West residents, but hunting and the destruction of their natural habitat led to near extinction by the late 1940s. The **National Key Deer Refuge**, spread over Big Pine Key and neighboring **No Name Key**, was set up here in 1954 to safeguard the animals – one refuge manager went so far as to burn the cars and sink the boats of poachers – and their population has now stabilized between 250 and 300.

Admission is free to the refuge, though you should still stop at the **refuge headquarters** (Mon–Fri 8am–5pm; ©872-2239), at the western end of Watson Boulevard, off Key Deer Boulevard, for information, maps, and orientation. There, park rangers can point you to one of three established public areas of the refuge. Perhaps the best place for spotting one of the deer is on No Name Key, to which Key Deer Boulevard leads; try to arrive either early morning or late afternoon, when temperatures are cooler. While the deer are definitely worth catching a glimpse of, make sure not to feed them (there are fines of up to $25,000) and be cautious when driving – signs alongside the road state the number of road-kills to date during the year.

Also part of the refuge, and a place you can get out of the car for a stretch, is **Watson's Nature Trail**, a relatively short trail in the refuge's hardwood hammock, open from December through March. You can walk the trail alone or call ahead of time to arrange a guide. Three and a half miles down from the refuge headquarters on Key Deer Boulevard is **Blue Hole**, the third open area, a freshwater lake with a healthy population of soft-shelled turtles and at least one alligator, who now and then emerges from the cool depths to sun itself – parts of the lakeside path may be closed if he's staked out a patch for the day.

TORCH KEYS AND AROUND

An even more peaceful atmosphere prevails on the Lower Keys south of Big Pine Key, despite the efforts of property developers to commercialize this patch of nature. The **Torch Keys** (made up of Little Torch Key and Big Torch Key), so-named for their forests of torchwood – used for kindling by early settlers – can be swiftly bypassed on the way to **Ramrod Key**, about five miles west from Big Pine Key, where **Looe Key Marine Sanctuary** is a terrific place for viewing the coral reef.

Perhaps the most expensive thing you'll see anywhere in the Keys is the blimp-like "aerostat" hovering over **Cudjoe Key**. It was built and put in place by the US Government in the early 1970s in order to beam TV images of American-style freedom – baseball, sitcoms, soap operas – to Cuba. Called *TV Martí*, the station was named after the late-nineteenth-century Cuban independence fighter, José Martí. In July 1993 the Clinton administration decided to end the broadcasts, and the aerostat's future is uncertain.

Looe Key Marine Sanctuary

Mon–Fri 8am–5pm.

Keen underwater explorers should home in on **Looe Key Marine Sanctuary**, clearly marked on the Overseas Highway on Ramrod Key. Not an actual separate key, this five-square-mile protected reef area was named after the *HMS Looe*, a British frigate that sank here in 1744. The ballast stones of the *HMS* are still visible in the reef, which is every part the equal of the more-publicized John Pennekamp Coral Reef State Park, up in Key Largo (see p.205). The transparent waters and reef formations create an unforgettable spectacle; rays, octopus, and a multitude of gaily colored fish flit between tall coral pillars, big brain coral, complex tangles of elk and staghorn coral, and soft corals like purple seafans and sea whips. Twists and turns of underwater slopes, ledges, caves, and a coral "nursery" – where they rehabilitate damaged coral – make the dive even more exciting.

The **sanctuary office** is actually located down in Key West (℃292-0311) and provides free maps and information. In any case, you'll have to check in somewhere besides the sanctuary first, as you can only visit the reef on a trip organized by one of the many diving shops throughout the Keys; the nearest is the neighboring **Looe Key Dive Center**, MM27.5, Ramrod Key (℃1-800/942-5397). You might also want to plan your visit to coincide with the **Underwater Music Festival** (℃872-9100) at Looe Key, the second Saturday of July, where the organizers drop waterproof speakers underwater and pipe in music. The effect is surreal – snorkelers and divers are treated to six hours of slightly distorted reggae, New Age, and jazz wafting through the waters.

LOOE KEY MARINE SANCTUARY

SUGARLOAF KEY AND BEYOND

On the sizable but mostly uninteresting **Sugarloaf Key**, fifteen miles from Ramrod Key, the 35-foot **Perky's Bat Tower**, MM17, stands as testimony to one man's misguided belief in the benefits of bats. A get-rich-quick book of the 1920s, *Bats, Mosquitoes and Dollars*, led Richter C. Perky, a property speculator who had recently purchased the island from an English farmer named W. C. Chase, into thinking bats would be the solution to the Keys' mosquito problem. With much hullabaloo, he erected this brown cypress lath tower, and dutifully sent away for a costly supply of bats to solve his woes. It didn't work: no bat ever showed up, the mosquitoes stayed healthy, and Perky went bust soon after. The background story is far more interesting than the actual tower, but if the tale tickles your fancy, you can view the tower from the bumpy road just beyond the sprawling *Sugarloaf Lodge*, at MM17 (see opposite).

There's not much more to see between here and the fifteen miles remaining until Key West, just uninspiring **Boca Chica Key**; best to continue on your way.

ACCOMMODATION

Caribbean Village

MM10.7, 1211 Overseas Highway, Big Coppitt Key (off Boca Chica Key) ©296-9542.

The crisp blue-and-white Bahamian-style home is the last motel before Key West, and is a perfect (and cheap) alternative to the craziness of that wild island. All rooms face the water, some with balconies and full kitchens, and a few are even "floating rooms," though fortunately you can't feel the floor moving. Rooms start at an amazing $35–65 per night. ①–②.

For an explanation of the accommodation price
codes, see p.88. For eating price categories, see p.104.

Parmer's Resort

MM28.5, 565 Barry Ave, Little Torch Key ℗872-2157.
Motel rooms, one-bedrooms, and efficiencies with full kitchens
and decks make up this spectacular waterfront resort. A garden
pool and numerous boat slips are added bonuses, and the resort
is close to the beautiful beaches of Bahia Honda and the Looe
Key National Marine Sanctuary. ③–④.

Sugarloaf KOA

MM20, Summerland Key ℗745-3549 or 1-800/562-7731.
Just twenty miles from Key West, this fully functioning campground provides a freshwater pool, hot tub, watersport rentals,
and a waterfront restaurant and bar. You can snorkel, dive, or
fish directly from the private beach. RV ($110–169) and tent
($39.95) accommodation only.

Sugarloaf Lodge

MM17, Sugarloaf Key ℗745-3211.
All rooms and efficiencies overlook either Sugarloaf Bay or the
canal by the marina. This comfortable lodge has been run by
the same family for 25 years, and it comes with special extras
like a miniature golf course, tennis courts, a freshwater pool,
even a library. There is a small home-style restaurant and a
waterfront tiki bar with awesome strawberry daquiris. Its proximity to the adjoining Great White Heron National Wildlife
Refuge assures borders they'll see some amazing wildfowl flying outside their window. Extremely reasonable rates the whole
year. ②–④.

ACCOMMODATION

EATING

Big Pine Coffee Shop
MM30, Big Pine Key ©872-2790. Inexpensive.
Open for breakfast, lunch, and dinner, this coffee shop has
formica tables at which you can sit and gorge yourself on crab
salads and steamed shrimp by the half pound.

Coco's Kitchen
MM29, 283 Key Deer Blvd, Big Pine Key ©875-4495. Cheap.
This is an inexpensive Cuban restaurant, serving traditional
dishes like pulled pork sandwiches and rice and beans.
Everything is packed with flavor and everything is good.

MangroveMama's
MM20, Sugarloaf Key ©745-3030. Moderate.
Dinner only at this semi-pricey restaurant – at least for the area
– but worth checking out for its rustic atmosphere, great
seafood, and home-baked bread. Closed Sept.

No Name Pub
MM28, 1/4 mile south of No Name Bridge, Big Pine Key ©872-9115.
Inexpensive.
Good jukebox, cold beers, and lots of burgers, fries, and other
grilled delights are in supply here. Many have dinner and then
retire to the bar until closing – around midnight.

Key West

A mere ninety miles from Cuba – closer than it is to mainland Florida – **Key West** can often seem far removed from the rest of the US. Famed for their tolerant attitudes and laid-back lifestyles, its 30,000 islanders seem adrift in a great expanse of sea and sky. Despite the million tourists who arrive each year, the place resonates with an anarchic and individual spirit initiated by locals, known as "conchs" (after the giant sea snails eaten by early settlers), who shoot the breeze on street corners and smile at strangers.

Yet as wild as it may first appear, Key West today is far from being the misfits' haven that it was just a decade or so ago. Much of the sleaziness has been gradually brushed away through a steady process of restoration and revitalization, paving the way for a sizable vacation industry that at times seems to revolve around party boats and heavy drinking. Still Key West has retained its nonconformist edge and liberal attitude, creating a particularly welcoming environment that has attracted a large gay population. Indeed, it is now estimated that one in five of Key West residents is gay – and this segment of the population has taken a leading role in local business and politics.

The sense of isolation from the mainland – much stronger here than on the other Keys – and the camaraderie of the locals are best appreciated by adjusting to the mellow pace and joining in. Amble the side streets, make meals last for hours, and pause regularly for refreshment in the numerous bars. Key West's knack for tourism can be gaudy, but it's quite simple to bypass the commercial traps and discover an island as unique for its present-day society as for its remarkable past.

The square mile of the **Old Town** – in essence the westernmost chunk of the island – contains most of the main attractions you'll want to see and is the best place for taking in Key West's wild characters, raucous nightlife, and scrumptious seafood. Tourists are plentiful around the main streets, but the relaxed, casually hedonistic mood affects everyone, no matter how long you've been here. All of Old Town's sights can be seen on foot in a couple of days, though you may well want longer to fully soak in the vibe.

The tourist epicenter of Old Town is **Duval Street**, whose northern end is marked by **Mallory Square**, a historic landmark that is now home to a brash chain of bars that entirely ignores the whimsical, freethinking spirit of the island. But just a few steps east of here is Key West's historic section, a network of streets teeming with rich foliage and brilliant blooms draped over curious architectural gingerbread molding and "eyebrow" roofs, whose slanted overhangs cover upstairs windows like eyelids. This area boasts many of the best guesthouses, zany eateries, and wacky galleries.

Just southwest, Key West's military history becomes obvious, beginning with the **Truman Annex**, a naval base established in 1822 to help control piracy. It has little to hold your attention but it does provide access to the **Fort Zachary Taylor State Park and Beach**, an uncrowded place to relax. There are also vestiges of military activity in two Civil War-era lookout points further afield, one of which, the **East Martello** tower near the airport, is worth the trek out.

A five-minute walk east from Fort Zachary will take you to the **Bahama Village**, a couple of blocks of dusty lanes where you can see some of the last Bahamian architecture left in the Keys. This unique enclave from yesteryear boasts some of the best restaurants on the island, although developers are already speculating on the area's future.

....

A detailed color map of Key West's Old Town can be found at the back of the guide.

....

Some history

Piracy was the main activity around Key West – first settled in 1822 – before Florida joined the US and the navy established a base here. This cleared the way for a substantial **wrecking industry**. Millions of dollars were earned by lifting people and cargo off shipwrecks along the Florida reef, and by the mid-nineteenth century, Key West was the wealthiest city in the US.

....

Juan Pablo Salas, a Spanish soldier, received Key West as a grant in 1815 and sold it to John Simonton, a developer on the island, for a mere $2000 in 1822.

....

The building of reef lighthouses sounded the death knell for the wrecking business, but Key West continued to prosper. Many **Cubans** arrived with cigar-making skills, and migrant **Greeks** established a lucrative sponge enterprise (the highly absorbent sea sponges, formed from the skeletons of tiny marine creatures, were the forerunners of today's synthetic sponges). Industrial unrest and a sponge blight drove these businesses north to Tampa and Tarpon Springs, and left Key West ill-prepared to face the **Depression**. By the early Thirties, its remaining inhabi-

KEY WEST

tants – die-hard locals who defied the suggestion that they move to the mainland – were living on fish and coconuts. In July 1934 the city finally declared bankruptcy, and under Roosevelt's New Deal, Key West was tidied up and readied for tourism. Unfortunately, the 1935 Labor Day hurricane blew away the Flagler railway – Key West's only land link to the outside world.

An injection of naval dollars during World War II, along with the island's geographical location, ideal for surveying communist Cuba, eventually saved Key West and provided the backbone for its future economy.

Tourists started arriving in force during the Eighties, just as a taste for independence was rising among the locals. In April 1982, US border patrols in relentless pursuit of drugs and illegal aliens began stopping all traffic leaving the Keys. Locals promptly proclaimed the town to be the capital of the "**Conch Republic**." Partly an excuse for a booze-up, this declaration (followed immediately by surrender and a request for aid) made a humorous but serious political point: the community – already separated geographically from the mainland – would always strive to maintain a social separation as well.

Getting around

For **getting around** the narrow, pedestrian-busy streets of Key West, you're far better off walking than driving (although there is a cheap **parking garage** on the corner of Caroline and Grinnell streets that charges $6/day), and **renting a bike** ($7–10 per day) is one of the most pleasant ways to see the nooks and crannies of the island. Hard-to-find street signs are painted vertically on the base of each junction lamppost, though many are peeling off. If you're planning to venture further afield, **renting a moped** ($25–30 per day) is a popular mode of transportation among

Key West tours

For a quick spin around Key West's main sights, the **Conch Tour Train** (Mallory Square; every 20–30min 9am–4pm; $12) and the **Old Town Trolley** (board at any of the marked stops around the Old Town; every 30min 9am–4.30pm; $14) both dole out lots of loud-speakered facts and trivia, but unfortunately don't really foster an appreciation of the island's atmosphere.

For that, you may be better off with the hands-on learning experience provided on a **bike tour** with environmentalist Lloyd Mager, which is anything but a relaxing ride through Key West's hidden streets. Mager, a transplanted New Jersey native, who has sworn off cars and other motorized transportation, will have you talk to the Parrot Lady, explore a Zen meditational garden, taste hand-plucked tamarinds and coconuts and treat you to an animated and enthusiastic recounting of the island's past and present ($15; tours meet at the Moped Hospital ⓒ294-1882).

Similary environmentally conscious, Dan McConnell, based at Mosquito Coast Island Outfitters, 1107 Duval St (ⓒ294-7178), runs six-hour **kayak tours** of back-country mangroves ($48.15 per person) filled with facts on the ecology and history of the Keys. To explore the reef by boat, join the informative half- or full-day tours aboard the 65-foot schooner *Reef Chief* (phone ⓒ292-1345 for details).

visitors, much to the chagrin of the locals who get their kicks from watching numerous "scooter wipeouts" from unskilled riders. Remarkably, although it's entirely walkable, there is a **bus service** (75¢ exact change; ⓒ292-8164) in Key West: two routes, one clockwise and the other counterclockwise, loop around the tiny island roughly every fifteen minutes between 7am and 9am and between 2.30pm and 5.30pm. If you're pressed for time, or feel like having a guide along with you, you may wish to take one of the **tours** outlined in the box on p.245.

DUVAL STREET

Anyone who saw Key West two decades ago would today barely recognize the main promenade, **Duval Street**, which cuts a mile-long swathe right through the Old Town. Teetering precariously on the safe side of seedy for many years, the street is now a well-manicured strip of beachwear and T-shirt shops mostly catering to vacationers. Balanced by the presence of colorful local characters and round-the-clock action, Duval Street is still an interesting place to hang out.

Most of the action is along the northern part of the street, but as you head south, everything begins to advertise itself as "the southernmost" of its kind. In actuality, the **southernmost point** in Key West, and consequently in the continental US, is to be found at the intersection of Whitehead and South streets, where a giant, striped **buoy** marks the precise spot.

Wrecker's Museum and around

Map 8, D4. 322 Duval St. Daily 10am–4pm; $4.

Other than shops and bars, few places on Duval Street provide a break from tramping the pavement; an exception is the **Wrecker's Museum**, located within the oldest house in Key West – a fact also hyped as a selling point. The museum provides plenty of background on the industry of salvaging cargo from foundering vessels. In the days before radio and radar, wrecking crews simply went out in bad weather and sailed as close as they dared to the menacing reefs, hoping to spot a grounded craft. Judging by the choice furniture that fills the museum, including the likes of antique European mirrors and some early American dining-room pieces, Captain Watlington, the wrecker who lived here during the 1830s, did pretty well. On the top floor cartoons recount several Key West folktales, including the dunking of a preacher who dwelled too long on the evils of drinking, and there's a spectacular miniature dollhouse that was built for the Captain's nine daughters.

A few blocks from the museum, **St Paul's Episcopal Church**, at no. 401, is worth entering briefly for a look at its rich, stained-glass windows; otherwise, you'll likely find the interior fairly standard. If overwhelmed by piety, you might scoot around the corner to the **Old Stone Methodist Church**, 600 Eaton Street. Built in 1877, it's the oldest church in Key West, standing comfortably under the shade of a giant Spanish laurel tree in its front yard.

The San Carlos Institute

Map 8, D5. 516 Duval St. Tues–Sun 11am–5pm; free but donations accepted.

Now affiliated with the Smithsonian Institute, the **San Carlos Institute** has played a leading role in Cuban exile life since it was founded by Cuban immigrants in 1871 to serve the community as Florida's first bilingual and integrated school. Financed by a $100,000 grant from the Cuban government, the present building dates from 1924. The soil on its grounds is from Cuba's six provinces, and a corner-stone was taken from the tomb of legendary Cuban independence campaigner José Martí, who rallied the exiles on the Institute's balcony and nicknamed the home "La Casa Cuba." Following the break in diplomatic ties between the US and Cuba in 1961, the building fell on hard times – and was briefly used as a cinema, much to the annoyance of local Cubans – until it was revived by a million-dollar

DUVAL STREET

247

restoration project in 1992. Today, besides staging opera in its acoustically excellent auditorium and maintaining a well-stocked research library (including, most notably, the records of the Cuban Consulate from 1886 to 1961), it has a first-rate permanent exhibition, with busts and statues of famous Cuban patriots like Martí, paintings of the homeland, and historical timelines on the history of Cubans in the US and, in particular, Key West.

MALLORY SQUARE AND AROUND

In the early 1800s, thousands of dollars worth of marine salvage was landed at the piers, stored in the warehouses, and sold at the auction houses on **Mallory Square**, just west of the northern end of Duval Street. The square's present-day commerce, however, is based on tourism, and little remains from the old days. By day, the square is a plain souvenir market selling overpriced ice cream, trinkets, and T-shirts, but at night it is transformed for the **sunset celebration**, when jugglers, fire-eaters, and assorted loose-screw types create a merry backdrop to the sinking of the sun. The celebration, which began in the Sixties as a hippie excuse for a smoke-in, has grown to include handmade arts and craft stands, food vendors, and other signs of commercialization, though it's still well worth checking out.

Historic Sculpture Garden

Map 8, C3. Mallory Square next to the Chamber of Commerce. Open daily; free.

Just a block up Wall Street from the center of Mallory Square is the **Historic Sculpture Garden**, a bizarre, faux graveyard lined with bronze sculpted heads of the men and women who have influenced Key West, like Asa Tift, Robert Audubon, and Henry Flagler. The garden looks more like a wax-work chamber of horrors than an austere tribute, but informative plaques running throughout the garden disclose the interesting origins of Key West's road names, and the whole experience makes for a fun history lesson. The grounds are paved with engraved bricks, and, for $60, you can help preserve the area and know that thousands of tourists are trampling on – and maybe even reading – your name.

Shipwreck Historeum

Map 8, C4. Whitehead St at Mallory Square. Daily shows begin at 9.15am and run every 30 mins until 4.45pm; adults $8; under 12s $4.

On the opposite side of Mallory Square from the garden, at the junction of Whitehead and Wall streets, is the excellent **Shipwreck Historeum**, where costumed guides recount the history of wrecking in Key West. Visitors are swept inside by a famous modern wrecker, Asa Tift, and then "recruited" as crew members preparing for their first salvage mission. After a quick film and an impassioned send-off by Tift, you're free to stroll through the two-story museum designed to look like the inside of a cargo ship. Its collection boasts some fine treasures from the *Isaac Allerton*, which sank in 1856 and remained undiscovered until Tift found it in 1985. Better still is the panoramic view from the top of the reconstructed viewing tower.

Key West Aquarium

Map 8, B4. 1 Whitehead St at Mallory Square. Daily 10am–7pm; adults $8, under 15s, $4.

More entertaining than the square during the day is the small gathering of sea life inside the adjacent **Key West Aquarium**, where ugly creatures such as porcupine fish and longspine squirrel fish lurk behind the glass, and sharks (the smaller kinds such as lemon, blacktip, and bonnethead) are known to jump out of their open tanks during the half-hour **guided tours** (11am, 1pm, 3pm, and 4.30pm). And if you intend to eat conch, a rubbery crustacean sold as fritter or chowder all over Key West, do so before examining the live ones here – they're not the world's most aesthetically pleasing creatures.

Mel Fisher's Treasure Museum

Map 8, C4. 200 Greene St. Daily 9.30am–5pm; adults $6.50, children 13–18 $4.

Down the road from the aquarium, **Mel Fisher's Treasure Museum** collects skillfully crafted decorative pieces, a highly impressive emerald cross, a liftable gold bar, plus countless vases and daggers alongside an impressive looking cannon, all salvaged from two seventeenth-century wrecks. As engrossing as the ensemble is, it's really a celebration of an all-American rags-to-riches story. Now the high priest of Florida's many **treasure seekers**, Fisher was running a surf shop in California before he arrived in the Sunshine State armed with ancient Spanish sea charts. In 1985, after years of searching, he discovered the *Nuestra Señora de Atocha* and *Santa Margarita*, both sunk during a hurricane in 1622, forty miles southeast of Key West – they yielded a haul said to be worth millions of dollars. Among matters you won't find mentioned at the exhibit is the raging dispute between Fisher and the state and federal governments over who owns what, and the ecological upsets that uncontrolled treasure-seeking has wrought upon the Keys.

THE TRUMAN ANNEX

Map 8, C4–C6.

The old naval complex that contains the Fisher trove was once part of the **Truman Annex**, a decommissioned section of a naval base established in 1822 to keep a lid on piracy around what had just become US territory. Some of the buildings subsequently erected on the base, which spans a hundred acres between Whitehead Street and the sea, were – and still are – among Key West's most distinctive, with many homes constructed with the wood from ship-wrecked vessels and featuring breezy Bahamian slatted shutters, glazed hardwood floors, and small window openings close to the roof to let hot air escape from the attics.

> **President Harry S. Truman spent so much time in Key West that the naval station was renamed the Truman Annex and the Navy base commandant's home renamed the Little White House.**

In 1986, the Annex passed into the hands of a young property developer who purchased it for $17.25 million. The developer made a lot of fast friends by throwing open the weighty **Presidential Gates** on Caroline Street (which had previously parted only for heads of state) and encouraged the public to walk or cycle around the complex. Today, the Annex's 45 acres are mainly vacation and rental properties sitting among historic naval buildings, but the Annex has access to Fort Zachary Taylor and its long stretch of beach. If you feel so inclined, get the free **walking guide** of the Annex from the well-marked sales office and embark on a building-by-building tour – the buildings' interiors, unfortunately, are closed to the public.

Harry S. Truman Little White House Museum

Map 8, C4. 111 Front St. Daily 9am–5pm; adults $7.50, under 12s $3.75.

The most famous building in the Annex is the modest, ten-room West-Indian-style home nicknamed the **Little White**

House, at the junction of Caroline and Front streets. Truman began visiting here in 1946 and allegedly spent his time playing poker, cruising Key West for doughnuts, and swimming. The house has been converted into a museum which chronicles the Truman years with relics like his original piano and poker table, along with a collection of presidential photographs of Kennedy, Eisenhower, and Carter, all of whom stayed at the home, on display. Eisenhower, visited during his recuperation from a heart attack, Kennedy rested here before the Bay of Pigs fiasco, and Carter made a brief pleasure visit in 1996.

Fort Zachary Taylor

Map 8, A8. Daily 8am–sunset; cars $2.50 plus $1 per person, pedestrians and cyclists $1.50.

The Truman Annex also provides access, along a fenced pathway through the operating naval base, to the **Fort Zachary Taylor State Historical Site**, the construction of which, begun in 1845, took 21 years to finish, mostly due to yellow fever epidemics in the area. Used to block Confederate shipping during the Civil War, it was a state-of-the-art facility upon completion, with plumbing flushed by the tides and a desalination plant which made the seawater drinkable. However, over ensuing decades, the fort simply disappeared under sand and weeds. In 1947 it was turned over to the Navy, and subsequent excavation work has gradually revealed old armaments of weapons and ammunition from the Civil War – in fact, the most extensive collection of Civil War cannons in the US. The fort became a national landmark in 1973 and opened to the public as a park in 1985. It's hard to comprehend the full importance without joining the 45-minute **guided tour** (daily at noon & 2pm) which is included with the price of admission – details at the front gate.

Due to a recent renovation project, only certain sections are open to the public, and the fort's museum is also closed, its exhibits having been temporarily moved to the East Martello Tower (see p.261). In any event, most locals pass by the fort on the way to one of Key West's best beaches, the **Fort Zachary Taylor Beach**, with picnic facilities and shady palms that provide a nice alternative to the crowded sunset celebrations at Mallory Square. This beach is still largely undiscovered by tourists as they tend to congregate at the more popular Smathers Beach, and on extremely hot days when the seaweed and coral are drying on the beach, the potent sulfuric fumes can be a bit much.

WHITEHEAD STREET AND BAHAMA VILLAGE

Lengthy **Whitehead Street** continues down from Key West's Old Town, turning into a quiet strip that is home to a handful of attractions, most notably Ernest Hemingway's old Key West residence. Shopfronts in the area are modest, sidewalks are shaded by palms and banyan trees, and the residential feel to the neighborhood reveals a more down-to-earth side of Key West.

West of Whitehead Street, a grid of small byways constitutes **Bahama Village**, an engaging area refreshingly devoid of tourists and glossy restoration jobs. Most of the squat, slightly shabby homes – some of them once small cigar factories – are occupied by people of Bahamian and Afro-Cuban descent. Not only does this area have some of the best ethnic eateries around, but it also holds onto a very authentic Caribbean feel. Residents remain a tight-knit community, most of them working on the docks or the ships in Key West, and on Sundays you'll see the streets teem with residents dressed to the nines on their way to church. Sadly, tour trains are now running close by, and property developers have plans to bring Bahama Village up to speed with touristy areas to the east.

A more modern attraction here is the community swimming pool at the corner of Catherine and Thomas streets (daily 11am–5.45pm; free; ©292-8248), an Olympic-size pool open to the public with fantastic ocean views.

The Lighthouse Museum

Map 8, E7. 938 Whitehead St. Daily 9.30am–5pm; adults $6, under 12s $2.

From most places on Whitehead you'll easily catch sight of the **Lighthouse Museum** simply because it *is* an 86-foot lighthouse – one of Florida's first, raised in 1847, and still functioning. There's a tiny collection of lighthouse junk and drawings at ground level, and it's possible (if tedious) to climb to the top of the tower, though the views of Key West are actually better from the top-floor bar of the *La Concha* hotel (see p.263). Most of the pictures taken here are not of the lighthouse but of the massive Chinese banyan tree at the base, but you can ogle the lighthouse's huge lens (installed in 1858): a twelve-foot high, headache-inducing honeycomb of glass.

The Hemingway House

Map 8, E6. 907 Whitehead St. Daily 9am–5pm; adults $6.50, children $4.

It may be the biggest tourist draw in Key West, but to the chagrin of Ernest Hemingway fans, guided tours of the **Hemingway House** deal more in fantasy than fact. Although Hemingway owned this large, vaguely Moorish-style house for thirty years, he lived in it for only ten, and the authenticity of the furnishings – a motley bunch of tables, chairs, and beds much gloated over by the guide – is hotly disputed by Hemingway's former secretary.

Already established as the nation's foremost hard-drinking, hunting- and fishing-obsessed writer, Hemingway bought the house in 1931, not with his own money but with an $8000 gift from the rich uncle of his then wife, Pauline. Originally one of the grander Key West homes, built for a wealthy nineteenth-century merchant, the dwelling was seriously run down by the time the Hemingways arrived. Hemingway soon remodeled the house, added a swimming pool, and filled the house with an entourage of servants and housekeepers.

Hemingway produced some of his most acclaimed work in the deer-head-dominated study, located in a separate building, which Hemingway entered by way of a home-made rope bridge. Here he penned the short stories *The Short Happy Life of Francis Macomber* and *The Snows of Kilimanjaro*; plus the novels *For Whom the Bell Tolls* and *To Have and Have Not*, which describes Key West life during the Depression.

To see inside the house (and the study) you have to join the half-hour **guided tour** (every ten minutes). Among the tour's highlights are a Venetian glass chandelier in the dining room, pictures of the author's four wives, and a lovely ceramic cat sculpted by Picasso for Hemingway. Hemingway's studio is a spartan affair, with a quarry-tiled floor and deer heads that look onto his old Royal typewriter. In the garden, a water trough for the cats is supposedly a urinal from *Sloppy Joe's* (now called **Captain Tony's**, see p.269), where the big man downed many a pint. When Hemingway divorced Pauline in 1940, he boxed up his manuscripts and moved them to a back room at *Sloppy Joe's* before heading off to a house in Cuba with his new wife, journalist Martha Gellhorn.

WHITEHEAD STREET AND BAHAMA VILLAGE

After the tour you're free to roam at leisure and play with some of the fifty-odd cats skulking around the property. The story that these are descendants from a feline family that lived here in Hemingway's day is yet another dubious claim: the large colony of inbred cats once described by Hemingway was at his home in Cuba.

Audubon House and Tropical Gardens

Map 8, B3. 205 Whitehead St. Daily 9.30am–5pm; adults $7.50, children 6–12 $3.50.

At the corner of Greene and Whitehead streets stands the **Audubon House and Tropical Gardens**, the first of Key West's elegant Victorian properties to get a thorough renovation – so successful that it encouraged a host of others to follow suit and sent housing prices in the area soaring. The Audubon House takes its name from a man who actually had little to do with the place – famed ornithologist John James Audubon who visited Key West for a few weeks in 1832. Almost all of his time here was spent scrambling around the mangrove swamps (now protected as the Thomas Riggs Wildlife Refuge, see p.261) looking for the bird life he later portrayed in his highly regarded *Birds of America* portfolio. But Audubon's link to the house goes no further than the lithographs that decorate the walls and staircase. Original Audubon prints, hand-colored under his instruction, are for sale here at a few hundred to a few thousand dollars.

The man who actually owned the three-story home was a wrecker named John Geiger. In addition to twelve children of their own, Geiger and his wife took in many others from shipwrecks and broken marriages – their presence reflected in the large, well-worn children's room. Self-guided **tours** through the house require the visitor to wear a personal stereo system, which broadcasts the ghostly voices of Mrs Geiger and the children chatting at you about how life was back in their day.

CAROLINE AND GREENE STREETS AND INLAND

At the northern end of Duval Street turn right onto **Caroline** or **Greene Street**, and you'll come across numerous examples of late-1800s "**conch houses**," built in a mix-and-match style that fuses elements of Victorian, Colonial, and tropical architecture. The houses were raised on coral slabs, and rounded off with playful "gingerbread" wood trimming. To accommodate Key West's growing population the houses were erected quickly and cheaply and were seldom painted, though you will see many bright colors, evincing their recent transformation from ordinary dwellings to hundred-thousand-dollar winter homes. None of these houses is really open for visitation as they are mostly private residences so you'll have to enjoy them from the outside, but there are a few more **historic buildings** on the streets that you can visit, including the home of Key West's original millionaire, William Curry.

Curry Mansion

Map 8, D4. 511 Caroline St. Daily 10am–5pm; adults $5, under 12s $1.

In strong contrast to the tiny conch houses, the grand three-story **Curry Mansion**, now a guesthouse (see p.263) and museum, was once the abode of William Curry, Florida's first millionaire. Inside, amid a riot of Tiffany glass and sensational bird's-eye maple paneling, is a heady stash of strange and stylish fittings that include an antique Chinese toilet bowl and a lamp designed by Frank Lloyd Wright.

The museum is also the present-day home of Al and Edith Amsterdam, who are gracious hosts when they are not in their grand upstate New York estate. Much of the memorabilia and photographs on display are from their younger days, including a Westley Richards gun that belonged to Hemingway and was given to Mrs Amsterdam by one of the author's wives. Clamber up into the attic and you'll be rewarded with a fairy-tale assortment of antique furniture, including a wildly patterned, sequin-covered bed. Climbing even higher to the beautiful **Widows Walk** (a walkway around the rooftop where sailors' wives looked for signs of their husbands' return) affords terrific views over the town. Other highlights of the house include the still-used 1940 Doverlift elevator and the eighteenth-century furnishings of the music room.

Heritage House Museum

Map 8, E6. 410 Caroline St. Daily 10am–5pm; tours $6, under 12s free.

Across from the Curry Mansion, the **Heritage House Museum** is a prime example of Key West's Colonial-style architecture and dates back to the 1830s. The home has been in the same family for seven generations and the present owner, Jean Porter, lives in an annex of the house. Jean's mother, Jessie Porter, who died in 1979, was the great-granddaughter of William Curry (see previous page), and Miss Jessie, as she was known, was at the hub of Key West's efforts to preserve this historic section of town. Miss Jessie was also friends with such luminaries as Tallulah Bankhead, along with other famous celebs like Tennessee Williams, Gloria Swanson, and Thornton Wilder; their photographs are mounted in the hallway amidst the house's original furnishings and antiques. Robert Frost also came here and lived in a cottage in the garden – recordings of Frost reading his poetry are played among the lush foliage upon request. You can wander around the garden, but the cottage itself is out of bounds.

Land's End Village

Map 8, E3–F3.

Between Williams and Margaret streets, the dockside area has been spruced up into a shopping and eating strip called **Land's End Village**, with a couple of enjoyable bars (see p.269). One with more than drinking to offer is *Turtle Kraals*, in business as a turtle cannery until the 1970s, when harvesting turtles became illegal. There are tanks of pre-cooked sea life inside the restaurant (but no turtles) and, just along the short pier, a grim gathering of the gory machines which were once used to slice and mince green turtles – captured off the Nicaraguan coast – into a delicacy known as "Granday's Fine Green Turtle Soup." Apart from pleasure cruisers and shrimping boats along the docks, you might catch a fleeting glimpse of a naval hydrofoil – vessels of unbelievable speed employed on anti-drug-running missions from their base a mile or so along the coast.

Key West Cemetery

Map 8, G5. Corner of Angela and Frances streets. Open daily sunrise–6pm; free.

Leaving the waterfront and heading inland along Margaret Street for five blocks will take you to the **Key West Cemetery**, which dates back to 1847 and whose residents are buried in vaults above ground (a high water table and solid coral rock prevents the traditional six-feet-under interment). Despite the lack of celebrity stiffs, the many witty inscriptions ("I told you I was sick") suggest that the island's relaxed attitude toward life also extends to death. Most visitors wander around on their own or with the excellent *Walking and Biking Tour of Key West* book put out by local historian and preservationist Sharon Wells, which can be found in any local bookshop or the Chamber of Commerce in Mallory Square. She conducts private tours by appointment (©294-8310), which take in the grave of an E. Lariz, whose stone reads "devoted fan of singer Julio Iglésias," and the resting place of one Thomas Romer, a Bahamian born in 1789. He died 108 years later and was "a good citizen for 65 of them." Look out also for the fenced grave of Dr Joseph Otto; included on the plot is the grave of his pet deer, Elphina, and three of his Yorkshire terriers, one of which is described as being "a challenge to love."

A fifteen-minute walk east from the cemetery will lead you to the modest clapboard house kept by playwright **Tennessee Williams**, at 1431 Duncan St. Unlike his more flamboyant counterparts, Williams – Key West's longest-residing literary notable, made famous by his steamy evocations of Deep South life in novels such as *A Streetcar Named Desire* and *Cat on a Hot Tin Roof* – kept a low profile during his 34 years here. His two-story Bahamian home, to which he added a swimming pool and writing studio, though little else, is unfortunately not open to the public, but still worth passing by to view an excellent example of the island's classic conch architecture.

THE MARTELLO TOWERS AND SOUTH ROOSEVELT BOULEVARD

There's not much more to Key West for visitors beyond its compact Old Town. Most of the eastern section of the island – encircled by the north and south sections of Roosevelt Boulevard – is residential, but Key West's **longest beach** is located here, and there are several minor points of botanical, natural, and historical interest.

The first of these, the **West Martello Tower** at the southern end of White Street (Wed–Sun 9.30am–3.30pm; free), is one of two Civil War lookout points that complemented Fort Zachary Taylor, on the western edge of town. Little of historical value remains, and the tower now holds an attractive and fragrant tropical garden. Northeast from the tower, Atlantic Avenue soon joins up with **South Roosevelt Boulevard**, which skirts on one side the lengthy but slender **Smathers Beach** – the weekend hangout of choice for Key West's most toned physiques and a haunt of windsurfers and parasailors – and on the other the forlorn salt ponds of the **Thomas Riggs Wildlife Refuge**. From a platform raised above the refuge's mangrove entanglements, you should be able to spot a variety of wading birds prowling the grass beds for crab and shrimp. Save for the roar of planes in and out of the nearby airport, the refuge is a quiet and tranquil place; to gain admission you have to phone the Audubon House (©294-2116; see p.256) to learn the combination of the locked gate.

East Martello Museum and Gallery

3501 S Roosevelt Blvd. Daily 9.30am–5.30pm; adults $6, children 7–12 $3.

Just beyond the airport, the **East Martello Museum and Gallery** was another Civil War lookout post, and the solid, vaulted casements now store a fascinating assemblage on local history, plus the wild junk-sculptures of legendary Key Largo scrap dealer Stanley Papio and the Key West scenes created in wood by a Cuban-primitive artist called Mario Sanchez. There are also displays on local writers and memorabilia from films shot in Key West, like Sydney Pollack's *Havana*.

ACCOMMODATION

Key West is well known for its profusion of relatively inexpensive guesthouses, a number of which are exclusively gay (for our listing of those, see "Gay and lesbian Key West," p.273) and almost all of which are located around the Old Town. If you're looking to **camp**, try the modern sites at *Boyd's Campground*, 6401 Maloney Ave (✆294-1465), which is actually situated on Stock Island, just east of Key West before you cross the bridge from the Lower Keys. An explanation of accommodation codes is given on p.88.

Angelina Guest House
Map 8, D6. 302 Angela St ✆294-4480.
Once a notorious bordello, the *Angelina* has now been restored with a lovely wraparound veranda – perfect for people-watching right in the heart of Bahama Village. ②–③.

Bananas Foster
Map 8, D4. 537 Caroline St ✆294-9061 or 1-800/653-4888.
One of the best values in Key West for location, cost, and atmosphere. The attentive owners keep immaculate care of the seven themed rooms, whose motifs run everywhere from Victorian Honeymoon to Under the Sea. Small spa pool and hearty breakfasts. ④–⑥.

Blue Parrot Inn
Map 8, E5. 916 Elizabeth St ✆1-800/231-BIRD; fax 296-5697.
Centrally located historic-district spot, where the friendly owners serve excellent breakfasts by the pool and manicured courtyard garden. Rooms are on the small side; all with private baths. No children. ⑤.

Caribbean House
Map 8, D6. 226 Petronia St ✆1-800/543-4518; fax 296-9840.
A simple, large house with a maze of connecting hallways and plain but cozy rooms. Don't be discouraged by the seemingly run-down exterior – it's very safe, ideally situated in Bahama Village, and within walking distance of all major sights. ⑤-⑦.

La Concha Holiday Inn

Map 8, D6. 430 Duval St ✆1-800/745-2191 or 296-2991.
Now a link in the *Holiday Inn* chain, this colorful hotel first
opened in 1925 and has been refurbished to retain some of its
Twenties style. A big plus for most guests is the large swimming
pool. ⑤–⑥.

Crocodile & Mermaid

Map 8, F6. 729 Truman Ave ✆294-1894 or 1-800/773-1894; fax
295-4093.
A gem of a house with stunning interior decor. Fabulous gardens, a pool, and wine served each evening make for a deeply
relaxing stay. No children under 16. ⑤–⑥.

Curry Mansion Inn

Map 8, D4. 511 Caroline St ✆294-5349 or 1-800/253-3466; fax 294-
4093.
Pricey but worth it for a night in this landmark Victorian
home (see p.257). A perk – use of the pool and showers all day
after check-out. ④–⑦.

Duval House

Map 8, E6. 815 Duval St ✆294-1666; fax 292-1701.
The lower-priced rooms are excellent value, and a bit more
gets you a four-poster bed and a balcony overlooking the
grounds. One of the few places with ample parking. ④–⑥.

Eden House

1015 Fleming St ✆1-800/533-KEYS; fax 294-1221.
One of Key West's most relaxing hideaways, with charming
rooms (all with private baths) that surround a large pool and
hot tub, and are tucked behind trees along a wooden boardwalk. There are hammocks and porch swings throughout
the grounds; free parking, too. Big reductions off-season.
④–⑥.

ACCOMMODATION

263

Jabour's Trailer Court

Map 8, E4. 223 Elizabeth St ℂ294-5723.

Close to the Duval St scene – a safe and economical way to sleep in Key West. ①–②.

Key Lime Inn

Map 8, F7. 725 Truman Ave ℂ294-5229 or 1-800/549-4430; fax 294-9623.

A delightful selection of completely remodeled tiny cottages and poolside cabanas, just steps away from Duval Street. If they don't have availability, try their sister guesthouse, the *Merlinn Inn*. ⑤.

Key West Hostel

Map 8, F8. 718 South St ℂ296-5719.

Key West's only youth hostel with both dorm and private rooms. Though dorm beds go for $18 ($22 non-members), the cramped private rooms are dingy and bland – you'd be better off splurging for one of the guesthouses which offer more security, atmosphere, and cleaner accommodation. Bike rentals available. ①–② depending on bunk or private-room accommodation.

Marrero's Guest Mansion

Map 8, D5. 410 Fleming St ℂ294-6977 or 1-800/459-6212; fax 292-9030.

Supposedly haunted guesthouse whose late former owner, Mrs Marrero, rates guests' character by swaying the chandelier in the foyer. Centrally located, recently remodeled, and with outdoor hot tub and pool. No children. ④–⑤.

Pilot House

Map 8, D4. 414 Simonton St ℂ294-8719; fax 294-9298.

Sharing the same owners as *New Orleans House*, this guesthouse has contemporary suites in a classic, though over-renovated, Victorian house. The house was once owned by Joseph Otto, a prominent Prussian surgeon, who happens to have the craziest

ACCOMMODATION

grave in Key West Cemetery (see p.259). Great pool, break-fasts, and a peaceful, convenient location. ⑤-⑥.

Simonton Court
Map 8, D4. 320 Simonton St ℂ1-800/944-2687; fax 293-8446.
A renovated cigar factory with a wide selection of rooms and some well-equipped cottages dot this historic compound. No children. ④–⑥.

Tropical Inn
Map 8, D5. 812 Duval St ℂ294-9977; fax 292-1656.
Large, airy rooms in a charming restored "conch" house at the center of the action. Most of the rooms sleep three, all have mini-fridges, and the more expensive ones have balconies. Ask about the neighboring cottages with hot tubs and kitchens. ④–⑥.

Wicker Guesthouse
Map 8, D5. 913 Duval St ℂ296-4275 or 1-800/880-4275.
One of the least expensive guesthouses in Key West, actually comprising four restored "conch" houses. Most rooms have their own kitchenettes, though the cheaper rooms lack TVs and air-conditioning (but have ceiling fans). There's a communal jacuzzi and a heated pool; fine breakfasts are served in the garden. ③–④.

EATING

Food stalls and restaurants are in abundance throughout Key West, from low-budget **Cuban** cafés and sandwich shops to chicer venues that can be quite pricey indeed. As far as local cuisine goes, **seafood** is the thing, found nearly everywhere, and there are a few specialties to be on the lookout for too, like **conch fritters** and **key lime pie**. Price category explanations are on p.104.

EATING

A&B Lobster House
Map 8, D3. 700 Front St ℂ294-2536. Moderate–Expensive.
Overlooking the town's harbor, there could hardly be a more
scenic setting for indulging in fresh seafood or sampling the
offerings of the raw bar.

Alice's On Duval
Map 8, F8. 1125 Duval St ℂ292-4888. Moderate.
Located in the *La-Tè-Da* hotel, this place has great conch fritters and an eclectic menu that ranges from passionfruit salad to
rack of lamb. Mostly fills up with an attractive gay crowd.

Blue Heaven Café
Map 8, D6. Corner of Thomas and Petronia sts ℂ296-0867.
Cheap.
Although at first glance the appeal of sitting in this dirt yard in
Bahama Village might be a turn off, you shouldn't pass this one
up. Long a favorite with locals, the home-cookin' menu is
absolutely superb, with strong Bahamian flavors that stick to
your ribs.

BO's Fish Wagon
Map 8, D3. 801 Caroline St ℂ294-9272. Cheap.
This ramshackle contraption draped in fishing nets and lobster
buoys is a must for the freshest and cheapest seafood in town –
try the fish'n'chips and legendary conch fritters.

Café des Artistes
Map 8, E6. 1007 Simonton St ℂ294-7100. Expensive.
Fine tropical-French cuisine, using the freshest local seafood,
lobster, and steak.

Café Marquesa
Map 8, D4. 600 Fleming St ℂ292-1244. Moderate.
Attractive small café offering an imaginative new American-
style vegetarian-based menu at moderate prices.

Camille's

Map 8, D5. 703 Duval St ©296-4811. Cheap.

Laid-back lunches and dinners, but renowned for its delicious breakfasts. Try a brunch of shrimp cakes, blueberry pancakes, or French toast with mango coconut cream sauce for $6.

Caribe Soul

Map 8, E3. 425 Grinnell St ©296-0094. Moderate.

Bold Caribbean flavors are imparted to an assortment of fresh vegetables and meats. Sweet potato muffins, fried green apples, and crabcakes are among the well-executed treats; the shrimp eggs benedict is a must for breakfast.

Dining In The Raw

Map 8, G6. 800 Olivia St ©295-2600. Moderate.

There isn't much room to sit, but the exquisite vegetarian (mostly vegan) dishes can be prepared for take-out. Desserts include couscous banana cake and raw sweet potato pie.

El Siboney

Map 8, E8. 900 Catherine St ©296-4184. Cheap.

Absolutely the best Cuban food on the island, well-guarded by the locals and very hard to find since there's no sign. Heaps of yellow rice and pork, sweet fried plantains, and much more.

Half Shell Raw Bar

Map 8, E3. 231 Margaret St, at Lands End Village ©294-7496. Inexpensive.

Extremely laid-back spot in a former shrimp packing building, with the menu hand-written on blackboards. Ultra-fresh seafood – the oyster po'boy sandwich is excellent.

Kelly's

Map 8, D4. 301 Whitehead St ©293-8484. Inexpensive–Moderate.

Actress Kelly McGillis of *Top Gun* fame owns this excellent

EATING

restaurant, which has an on-site microbrewery, two levels of leafy, outdoor dining areas, and a fairly eclectic menu. The key lime pie comes with a delicious twist – a dense, crushed Oreo base.

Mangia, Mangia
Map 8, G4. 900 Southard St ⓒ294-2469. Inexpensive–Moderate. Away from the crowds of Duval, this restaurant makes every piece of pasta fresh – and you can watch them do it through their front window.

Mobster Lobster
Map 8, D5. 618 Duval St ⓒ294-1055. Moderate. A narrow passageway from Duval Street leads you to an open patio dining area with a giant banyan tree in the middle. The menu is heavy on Florida lobster and surf-and-turf dishes, as well as seafood pastas, salads, and chowders. Try the blackened tuna bites or coconut fried shrimp.

Seven Fish Restaurant
Map 8, E6. 632 Olivia St ⓒ296-2777. Moderate. Not cheap, but not hyped for the tourist market either. The food, primarily fish, is excellent and very fresh.

BARS, LIVE MUSIC, AND CLUBS

The anything-goes nature of the island is best exemplified in its many rough-and-ready **bars**, most of which are again along Duval Street, or just off it. Many of these have good **live music** on offer, too. Key West doesn't fare as well with **clubs**, though there are a few lively ones to be sure.

Bull & Whistle Bar
Map 8, D4. 427 Caroline St at Duval St ⓒ296-4545.

Loud and rowdy corner bar, with local musicians jamming each night. Check the list on the door to see who's playing or just turn up to drink.

Captain Tony's Saloon
Map 8, C3–C4. 428 Greene St ℂ294-1838.
Captain Tony himself frequents this dark watering hole, wall-papered in business cards, photos, and ladies' lingerie. If this scares you off then you're missing one of the liveliest, no-frills bars on the island. This rustic saloon, once known as the original *Sloppy Joe's* (see p.273), a noted hangout of Ernest Hemingway, is host to excellent rock bands at the bar's backstage and acoustic performances near its open-air entrance.

Conch Seafood Republic
Map 8, E3. 631 Greene St, Key West Bight ℂ294-4403.
Prime waterfront location, with some eighty varieties of rums, and nightly live music (except Mondays).

Finnegan's Wake
Map 8, F3. 320 Grinnell St ℂ293-0222.
Enjoyable Irish pub, with lots of Guinness and lots of men drinking it.

Full Moon Saloon
Map 8, F7. 1200 Simonton St ℂ294-9090.
Laid-back bar which offers live music – be it blues, jazz, reggae, or rap. Thurs–Sat until 4am.

Green Parrot Bar
Map 8, D5. 601 Whitehead St ℂ294-6133.
This has been a Key West landmark since 1890, for its reper-toire of local characters (including a ghost), its laid-back

Key West festivals

Winter

Early January. *Key West Literary Seminar*.
Four-day celebration of the island's literary famous four –
Tennessee Williams, Ernest Hemingway, Robert Frost, and
Thornton Wilder; well-known authors show up for discussions
and readings, and you can take walking tours of Hemingway's
and Williams' residences (℗1-888/293-9291).

Early February. *Key West Old Island Days Arts Festival*.
Cultural heritage celebration, showcasing artwork by local and
international artisans. Booths are set up along Whitehead
Street between Eaton and Green streets (℗294-12410).

Spring

April 23. *Conch Republic Independence Celebration*.
This festival commemorates the mock-secession of Key West
from the rest of the US when they protested a US Border
Patrol roadblock of US Hwy-1 in 1982. Celebration takes place
in Mallory Square (℗296-0213).

Summer

July 19–23. *Hemingway Days Festival*.
Island-wide celebrations of the writer's ten-year residence in
Key West, as well as his birthday on July 21st. Among the
more popular activities is the "Papa" Hemingway Look-Alike
Contest at *Sloppy Joe's* (see p.273). Fees are charged for cer-
tain events (℗294-4440).

Early September. *Women Fest*.
Lesbian-oriented series of events that features street fairs, a
film festival, and a gala Saturday night party (℗296-2491).

Mid-September. *Florida Keys Poker Run*.
Close to 20,000 Harley-Davidson riders hop on their hogs in Miami and make their way to Key West, playing poker at various islands along the way. The journey culminates in the closure of Duval Street, where riders park their motorcycles and hit the bars (©294-3032).

Fall

First two weeks of October. *Key West Theater Festival*.
Ten-day festival revolving around the works of up-and-coming playwrights (©292-3725 or 1-800/741-6945).

Last week of October. *Fantasy Fest*.
The best reason to be in Key West in the off-season may be this ten-day extravaganza, where you'll see outrageous costumes and masks being donned at lavish balls, a Masquerade March through Old Town, the Pretenders in Paradise costume contest, and a Caribbean-themed Goombay celebration. The last night a parade is held, with outlandish floats that poke fun at current fads and events. Book your accommodation well in advance (©296-1817).

Early November. *Cuban-American Heritage Festival*.
Key West's early Cuban influence is celebrated through historic tours, fishing tournaments, domino and dance competitions, and cigar-rolling exhibitions (©294-7618).

Early December. *Lighted Boat Parade*.
Every kind of boat imaginable is decorated in lights for the holiday season and paraded through the waters, starting at the *Schooner Wharf Bar* and running up past the *Hilton Resort and Marina*. Best viewing spots are in Mallory Square – get there early to claim your spot.

attitude and its affections for all things conch-related. Pool tables, dartboard, pinball machine, and an eclectic jukebox, with music from rockabilly to zydeco.

Havana Docks
Map 8, C3. *Pier House Hotel*, 1 Duval St ℂ296-4600.
An upscale bar offering unparalleled patio views of the sunset and the lilting strains of a tropical island band. Inside, there's more live music, usually jazz or Latin, Wed through Sat.

Hog's Breath Saloon
Map 8, C3. 400 Front St ℂ296-4222.
Very popular and hyped tourist spot, this is a place to drink yourself silly and then buy a T-shirt to prove it.

Louie's Backyard
Map 8, G9. 700 Waddell St ℂ294-1061.
Far from Duval Street, this is a classy and sophisticated hang-out. Its outdoor bar, "The Afterdeck," is literally right on the water and has a fantastic view. Open until 2am.

Margaritaville
Map 8, D4. 500 Duval St ℂ292-1435.
Owner Jimmy Buffett – a Florida legend for his rock ballads extolling a laid-back life in the sun – occasionally pops in to join the live bands that play here nightly, but you're more likely to be overwhelmed by the loud parrot shirts and paraphernalia sold here than the music. For true parrotheads only.

Rumrunners
Map 8, D4. 218 Duval St ℂ294-1017.
A multilevel entertainment complex that includes several venues catering to those interested in live classic rock. The complex also boasts indoor and outdoor dance areas and an open-air bar upstairs – good for spying on the crowds

strolling Duval Street. DJs spin everything from pop to reggae.

Sloppy Joe's

Map 8, D4. 201 Duval St ℂ294-5717.

Despite the memorabilia on the walls and the hordes of tourists, this bar – with decent live music nightly – is not the original haunt of Ernest Hemingway; for the real thing, go to *Captain Tony's Saloon*, listed on p.269.

Wax

Map 8, D5. 422 Applerouth Lane (no phone).

A gigantic, outrageous, and very welcoming dance venue that attracts a mixed clientele. High-energy music from 8pm through 4am on multilevel floors.

GAY AND LESBIAN KEY WEST

Key West is an incredibly **gay-friendly** community, its scene very open and somewhat outrageous, with plenty of outlets and resources for gay visitors. The Gay & Lesbian Community Center, 1075 Duval St (ℂ292-3223), is the best informational source, with pamphlets and brochures galore. They can make accommodation reservations and suggestions on where to go and what to see. Several free weekly newspapers (available at the center or gay-run guesthouses) are geared specifically toward the community like *Celebrate!Key West*, *Gay West*, and *Southern Exposure* – the latter two catering specifically to gay men.

Hotels and guesthouses

Atlantic Shores Resort

Map 8, F8. 510 South St ℂ296-2491 or 1-800/526-3559.

This Art Deco resort is hugely in vogue with the gay crowd. Lively atmosphere, not much sleeping going on. Wild tea-dance extravaganzas on Sundays, at which a sizable portion go nude. If you're not staying at the hotel, there's a $3 fee for a lounge chair and a towel. ③–⑦.

Attitudes
Map 8, D5. 410 Fleming St ℂ1-800/459-6212; fax 292-9030.
Formerly known as *Colors*, this beautifully restored nineteenth-century house has huge, lovely rooms, and a hallway covered with tobacco-leaf dyed papier mache. ⑤–⑥.

Big Ruby's
Map 8, E6. 409 Appelrouth Lane ℂ296-2323 or 1-800/477-7829; fax 296-0281.
Peaceful yet vibrant and social, this guesthouse offers enormous Sunday brunches, free drinks throughout the day, and enticingly designed rooms. Book in advance. The $300 a night penthouse suite is exceptional. ⑤–⑥.

Curry House
Map 8, D4. 806 Fleming St ℂ294-6777 or 1-800/633-7439; fax 294-5322.
The oldest all-male gay guesthouse in the area. Clean, well-liked, and comfortable. ④–⑥.

La Terraza de Marti
Map 8, F8. 1125 Duval St ℂ296-6706 or 1-877/528-3320.
Better known locally as "La-Te-Da," this pastel-interior house is at the center of gay social life. All sixteen guest rooms have private baths (some with jacuzzis) and fabulous French doors that lead to the garden and pool. While very popular with gays, the clientele is mixed. The tree-studded complex includes several bars and discos including a piano bar, drag queen revues, and a gay tea dance on Sundays. Prices drop by half out of season. ⑤–⑥.

New Orleans House

Map 8, D5. 724 Duval St ℂ294-8719 or 1-800/648-3780; fax 294-9298.

Spacious, clean rooms with full kitchens at this centrally located guesthouse. Ask for a room at the back to avoid the noise. Huge discounts out of season. ⑤.

Rainbow House

Map 8, E8. 525 United St ℂ292-1450 or 1-800/749-6696.

The lone lesbian-only guesthouse on the island, this attractive former cigar factory serves breakfast and has a pool and hot tub. ⑤–⑥.

Bars and clubs

801 Bourbon Bar

Map 8, D5. 801 Duval St ℂ294-4737.

Gay cabaret bar with nightly review shows at 11pm. Its neighbor, the *Bourbon Street Pub* (724 Duval St, 296-1992), hosts an all-male revue on the weekends.

Donnie's Club

Map 8, D4. 422 Appelrouth Lane ℂ294-2655.

A small, neighborhood bar where the guesthouse staff come for a quiet drink and to shoot pool.

Epoch

Map 8, D5. 623 Duval St ℂ296-8521.

The island's largest DJ disco with a tropical outdoor bar, video bar, and loud beat-driven music. Fairly mixed crowd, mostly under 25.

La-Te-Da

Map 8, F8. 1125 Duval St ℂ294-8435.

The various bars and discos of this hotel complex have long been a favorite haunt of locals and visitors. Very friendly and more casually upscale than its neighbors.

One Saloon of Key West

Map 8, D4. 1 Appelrouth Lane ©296-8118.

A small, dark, former leather bar now full of youngish men watching blue videos, which are a secondary attraction to the real flesh strutting on the bars.

CONTEXTS

A brief history of Miami

Early natives and European settlement

Miami's earliest residents were Tequesta Indians who settled around the mouth of the Miami River some 10,000 years ago; they lived and farmed the land alone until joined by Seminoles, in the 1400s, and were soon after completely wiped out by European settlements.

The first European sighting of Florida is believed to have been made by John and Sebastian Cabot in 1498, when they set eyes on what is now called Cape Florida, on Key Biscayne in Miami. Despite this early progress, development of the area would remain woefully stagnant for some 350 years, even as the rest of Florida would be settled and fought over.

In 1513, **Juan Ponce de León**, a Spaniard previously employed as governor of Puerto Rico (a Spanish possession), sighted land during Pascua Florida, the Spanish Easter "Festival of the Flowers," and named what he saw **La Florida** – or "Land of Flowers." Ponce de León sailed on around the Florida Keys, naming them **Los Martires**, for their supposed resemblance to the bones of martyred men, and **Las Tortugas** (now the Dry Tortugas), for the turtles he saw around them.

Spanish and British occupation in Florida

Spain controlled Florida in the 1500s and made St Augustine the main settlement, though it was razed by a war at the end of the century, as the British began to establish their colonies along the Atlantic coast north of Florida. By the 1700s the British were making further forays south, and once the British captured the crucial Spanish possession of Havana, Spain willingly parted with Florida to get it back.

The 1783 Treaty of Paris, with which Britain recognized American independence, returned Florida to Spain, but the country was ill-equipped to capitalize. Spain was forced to sell land to US citizens, and the First Seminole War in 1814, along with Andrew Jackson's military forays into the state, sped the process of turning the territory to American control.

Spain formally ceded Florida to the US in 1819, in return for the US assuming the $5 million owed by the Spanish government to American settlers in land grants (a sum which was never repaid). The US settlers mostly coveted northern and central Florida for its rich land, and had little interest in the southern reaches.

The establishment of a city

Two years before the Second Seminole War ended in 1842, a trading post called **Fort Dallas** was established along the Miami River, marking the first permanent white settlement in the Miami area. At the end of the war, Colonel **William English** decided to stay in Fort Dallas and further develop the post, beginning an advertising campaign to sell plots of land to homesteaders. With Florida's entry into **statehood** on March 3, 1845, prospects for the city indeed looked bright, but ten years later, a **third Seminole War** broke out, lasting for three years, soon to be followed by the **Civil War**, both of which delayed any real development, other than the building of a post office and a few other structures.

In 1870, **William Brickell**, a successful entrepreneur from Ohio, took up where English left off and continued Fort Dallas's development by building a grand home and expanding the trading post further in along the river. A year later, a fellow Ohioan, **Ephraim Sturtevant**, purchased land along Biscayne Bay and began to dredge the area between what is now downtown Miami and **Coconut Grove** to make it suitable to build on. Sturtevant's daughter, **Julia Tuttle**, visited the town in 1875; realizing its immense potential, she began to purchase acres of land along the river.

Just a few miles down the road, Coconut Grove was in the midst of establishing its own identity, helped along by folks such as Ralph Middleton Munroe, an eccentric sea captain famed for his yacht designs, who encouraged others to invest and build there, including Charles and Isabella Peacock, business owners who came over from England and erected south Florida's first hotel in the Grove, the *Bay View House*, in 1882. The first post office, school, and yacht club soon followed.

The railroad moves in

Despite the inroads made by the various real estate magnates of the late 1800s, Miami still had little contact with the outside world. This would change with a deal between **Henry Flagler**, railroad magnate who had made his fortune through his partnership with John D. Rockefeller and his Standard Oil company, and Julia Tuttle. In the apocryphal story, Flagler was resistant to extend his existing railroad from Palm Beach south to Miami, until Julia Tuttle sent him a package full of fresh orange blossoms on the heels of the 1894-95 winter "Big Freeze," which had destroyed most citrus crops in northern Florida. Thinking that such a tropical climate would attract northern vacationers, Flagler began to revise his plans, and agreed to the extension in exchange for land from Tuttle and the Brickells.

In 1896 Flagler's railroad pulled into the still-sleepy trading post; soon after, Flagler would begin his relentless building projects, which included the posh *Royal Palm Hotel* on the banks of the river, and the dredging of a channel for the **Port of Miami** (today called "Government Cut"), connecting Biscayne Bay to the Atlantic Ocean. Miami became an official city the same year as the railroad's arrival, and was named for what was believed to be the Tequesta word for "sweet water."

The link between Miami and the beach

The development of Miami's mainland would soon be superseded by a piece of land that was mere swamp only decades before. In 1882, **John Collins** had bought a fetid strip of property directly east of downtown Miami, in the hopes of turning it into a fruit and vegetable plantation. The only problem was that the land was in effect an off-shore island, three miles east of Miami proper with nothing connecting it to the mainland. Collins set out to construct a rudimentary bridge but ran out of money halfway through.

His vision was carried out some thirty years later by **Carl Fisher**, millionaire and Indianapolis racetrack designer, who saw a lucrative goldmine in Collins' island and agreed to finance the project in exchange for two hundred acres of oceanfront property. Fisher constructed Miami's first causeway in 1913, a more durable structure than Collins', and **Miami Beach** was born, incorporated into the city of Miami two years later.

World War I and the Great Depression

World War I gave Miami an economic shot in the arm, as the military arrived to police the coastline and develop sea-warfare projects, and the small city boomed as a destination for the wealthy. Long before multinational banks dominated Brickell Avenue in downtown, the leafy road was home to sprawling mansions on the water and was referred to as "**Millionaire's Row**." Among the many great buildings to be constructed was **Villa Vizcaya**, work on which lasted from 1914 to 1916, employing a whopping ten percent of the city's workforce at the time.

When Prohibition was introduced in 1919, the many secluded inlets in southern Florida became secure landing sites for spirits from the Caribbean. The illicit booze flowed in the thriving resort of Miami Beach, a picture-postcard piece of beach landscaping replacing what had been a barely habitable mangrove island. Drink was not the only illegal pleasure pursued in the nightclubs: gambling and prostitution were also rife and were soon to attract the attention of big-time gangsters such as **Al Capone**, who used to host many "meetings" in the tower suite of the *Biltmore Hotel* in Coral Gables.

The lightning-paced creation of Miami Beach was no isolated incident. Throughout the city, new communities appeared almost overnight, and Miami's population soared to 30,000 by 1920. Developer **George Merrick** inherited a huge plantation from his father in 1910 and began drawing up plans for a perfect utopia community he termed "City Beautiful." In 1921 Merrick started pitching his idea to potential investors and by 1925 his corporation had raked in a staggering $150 million. **Coral Gables** would soon become a reality, full of Mediterranean-style architecture and decorative touches, and littered with Spanish names for its streets and plazas.

The land boom, however, was a tenuous proposition, and while millions of dollars technically changed hands each week during its peak year of 1925, thanks to the frenzy of real estate speculation and land development, little hard cash actually moved. Most deals were paper transactions with buyers paying a small deposit into a bank. The inflation inherent in the system finally went out of control in 1926, and banks – and, subsequently, large corporations – went bust. A hurricane devastated Miami and south Florida that same year, destroying 5000 homes, flooding downtown Miami, and virtually obliterating Miami Beach, followed by another in 1928. With the Florida land boom well and

WORLD WAR I AND THE GREAT DEPRESSION

truly over, the Wall Street Crash in 1929 made times even harder and destroyed millionaires like Henry Flagler and George Merrick.

The Art Deco District beginnings and World War II

With Miami in the economic throes of the Depression, Roosevelt's New Deal and the Florida citrus industry saved Miami from total bankruptcy and allowed the city to begin a slow recovery.

Miami Beach was actually the main beneficiary of this recovery, with hundreds of hotels, residences, and other buildings thrown up in the mid to late 1930s, to keep up with a once-again thriving tourist industry. Many of these structures took on the modern look of **Art Deco**, led by the designs of archictects L. Murray Dixon and Henry Hohauser.

Chapter 3, "Miami Beach," contains details and history of the Art Deco movement and its impact on Miami architecture and design.

Elsewhere in Miami, the **Pan American Airways** airline opened on Dinner Key in Coconut Grove, connecting Miami to 32 Central and South American countries and making it the main base of business and trade between America and Latin America. Any further private construction would be halted by the breakout of World War II in 1939, as extra materials went to the war effort. The military, however, helped pave roads, clear land, and dig wells, and many soldiers who were stationed here returned after the war.

The 1950s and 1960s: Cuban immigration and racial tensions

Tourism was Miami's major economic staple in the postwar years, and the population age soon began an upward shift, as retirees, notably a large Jewish contingent from the US Northeast, became enticed by the climate and came to settle in Miami Beach, earning it the unflattering nickname of "God's Waiting Room." But not everyone was welcome on the beach. Despite a federal Supreme Court ruling in favor of desegregation, blacks continued to be banned from Miami Beach after dark and were subject to discrimination in many city restaurants, hotels, schools, and businesses. Things did not get too much better during the 1960s, and the intolerable conditions that blacks had to live in led in part to the first **Liberty City riot**, in August 1968, just the first of several violent uprisings in Miami's depressed areas.

Miami's **ethnic makeup** was in any case to dramatically change with the 1959 Cuban Revolution. When Castro came to power and took hold of tobacco and other big business for the government, the stage was set for a mass exodus from the nearby island. Many of the immigrants who came over the next five years were members of Cuba's elite, tossed out because of the potential threat they posed.

US-Cuban relations during this period were strained at best; the US began their embargo of Cuba after Castro nationalized the economy, and in 1961, created a fiasco at the **Bay of Pigs**, when CIA-trained Cuban exiles, who were invading Cuba, were doomed to failure when President Kennedy refused to lend air support to help the operation. During the following year's **missile crisis**, a tense game of cat and mouse between the US and the USSR over Soviet missile bases on the island, world war was only narrowly avoided; afterwards, Miami became the base of the US government's covert anti-Castro operations. In 1965 the US Government organized so-called "**Freedom Flights**," which brought more than 300,000 Cubans to Miami over the next eight years. Most of these immigrants, and their predecessors, settled west of downtown Miami in an area soon to be known as Little Havana.

Originally the US embraced the Cubans, establishing a Cuban Refugee Center in Miami and passing a landmark law, the **Cuban American Adjustment Act** (1966), which gave permanent residence to any Cuban who lived in the US for one year – a special law which no other immigrant group has ever received. This would in the future cause tension in Miami between Cubans and Haitians, another group with a large number of exiles seeking refuge in the city.

More history on Cuban exiles in Little Havana and their impact on Miami can be found on p.46.

The 1970s: economic decline and architectural preservation

The 1970s continued the serious economic decline begun the decade before, as the beach lost much of its cachet and the city struggled to deal with the waves of Cuban immigration. With the loss of tourism along the beach many businesses went bust, and it seemed that the Art Deco buildings in Miami Beach would be the next to go, especially with the supposed need for modernization and new development.

Such movement was halted starting in 1976, when hotel-owner Barbara Baer Capitman took her obsession with the Art Deco style one step further. With the help of her son, Leonard Horowitz, and others, she founded the **Miami Design Preservation League**, which worked to protect the bulldozing of the Deco structures and was able to designate a 24-block area in Miami Beach as part of the National Register of Historic Places. The area, often known as the Art Deco district, is pretty much synonymous with South Beach, its preserved buildings part-and-parcel of Miami's modern-day image.

The 1980s: *Miami Vice* and drug culture

Though the 1980s got off to an inauspicious start, with another **Liberty City Riot** (see p.285) and continued racial unrest, the decade saw Miami Beach again becoming the hot place to be, helped in part by the revitalization of the Art Deco hotels and by the success of the television show *Miami Vice*, which lured fashion photographers to the sands for all sort of photo shoots and runway shows. The series became closely aligned with the city's image, which was a bit of a double-edged sword; while setting trends in music, fashion, and design, it also played up Miami's role as a city full of drug runners and underground crime.

Indeed, Miami's proximity to various Latin and South American countries with large drug production operations perfectly positioned the city as a gateway for drug smuggling and money laundering; estimates suggest that at least a quarter of the cocaine entering the US arrives through Florida alone. The inherent violence of the drug trade, along with lax Florida gun laws that have made gun shops nearly as popular as sunglass stands in the city, helped Miami earn the unflattering designation as the "murder capital of the US" in the late 1980s, a label it has largely shaken off, though some incidents of violence against tourists in the 1990s resullied its reputation. In 1993 Governor Lawton Chiles responded by creating the **Task Force on Tourist Safety**, which improved the visibility of road signs, added new tourist information centers at key arrival points, and made rental cars harder to pick out.

While these social problems were ongoing, much money was being made by US-Latin American trade, both legal and contraband, and being poured into the coffers of a burgeoning **banking** industry, which set up shop in gleaming high towers just south of downtown.

Hurricane Andrew

In August 1992, natural disaster struck Miami again, as **Hurricane Andrew** brought winds of 168mph tearing through the city's southern regions (blowing down the radar of the National Hurricane Center in the process); it ripped roofs off homes, gutted supermarkets, and left many without power, living in ruins, or just downright homeless.

The hurricane's damage had lasting power; indeed, signs of its handiwork are still apparent in the form of abandoned homes and destroyed businesses (the Deering Estate along Old Cutler Road in Miami has barely recovered, and still retains an eerie graveyard of stripped trees standing in memorial). In response, many parks have replaced uprooted trees with species endemic to Florida, which are much more likely to survive future hurricanes. At the Fairchild Tropical Garden in Miami, you can see a particularly strange remnant of the disaster – a gigantic tree lying prone on its side, toppled by the hurricane but continuing to grow.

Contemporary Miami and the future

The struggles of Miami's past threaten to remain the struggles of Miami's future. **Racial issues** have long been vexed in Miami and show no real signs of abating, despite attempts by the city to promote its multiculturalism and diversity. Black–white relations are often strained, and many Anglo-Americans are rueful of the powerful positions attained by Cubans who have steadily worked their way up the system since the Sixties. At the other end of the spectrum, large-scale immigration – legal and otherwise – into south Florida from the poor and unstable countries of Latin America and the Caribbean has put considerable pressure on the state's social services (such as they are), and played into the hands of right-wingers, who favor strict measures to curtail the influx.

The influence of **Cuban exiles** is a potboiler as well. In 1996, in an attempt to appease right-wing elements of that community, Clinton agreed to accept the Helms-Burton law threatening sanctions on foreign businesses with interests in Cuba, which infuriated the governments of Canada, Britain, Mexico, and other important US allies and trading partners. Anytime some volatile issue comes up, whether it's the idea of reinstituting US-Cuba flights or sending refugees back to the island, the threat of vocal dissent, even violence, looms.

But Miami is largely well positioned for the new century and its challenges. Its economy experienced a late-1990s boom, like many American cities; tourists still come in droves to enjoy baking on the beach; and the city remains a crucial base for business between the Americas. And as long as the city can keep the focus on its sunny side, rather than its seamy side, none of these look set to change anytime soon.

Books

Miami's mark on the literary world is certainly not earth-shattering, but many writers have been moved enough by its history, idyllic image, or its spot at the junction of two clashing worlds to bring it to life with some vibrancy. A specialty of local writers is spinning a **crime story**, and folks like Elmore Leonard and Carl Hiaasen have made careers out of the wacky characters that populate places like South Beach and Coconut Grove. Publishers listed are US only.

History

Edward N. Akin *Flagler: Rockefeller Partner & Florida Baron* (Florida Atlantic University Press). Solid biography of the man whose Standard Oil fortune helped build Florida's first hotels and railroads.

Manuel Baerga *Inside the Miami Drug Cartel* (Wine Press). A detailed account of fortunes being won and lost in the city's drug underworld, with first-hand narratives of how the syndicate operates.

Dorothy and Thomas Hoobler *The Cuban American Family Album* (Oxford University Press). A mini-history book with compelling first-person interviews and accounts of families before and after the Cuban Revolution, and their difficult emigration to Miami and other US cities. Dramatic photographs and even some family recipes.

Marsha Bellavance Johnson *Tennessee Williams in Miami and Key West: A Guide* (Computer). A slender book detailing the playwright's life in south Florida and the places he haunted.

John M. Kirk *José Marti: Mentor of the Cuban Nation* (University Press of Florida). A look at José Marti, the most powerful reactionary figure in Cuban resistance history.

Howard Kleinberg *Miami Beach – A History* (Centennial Press). A wonderful collage of colorful archival photos and text on Miami Beach's humble beginnings and present Art Deco District, by a former editor-in-chief of the city's dominant newspaper from long ago, *The Miami News*.

Helen Muir *The Biltmore, Beacon for Miami* (Valiant Press). A behind-the-scenes glimpse at Miami's most famous hotel and its incredible role in the city's history (ranging from a war hospital to a gambling haunt).

Alejandro Portes *City on the Edge: The Transformation of Miami* (University of California). An in-depth account of ethnic minorities in Miami and resultant race relations.

Natural history

Joan Gill Blank *Key Biscayne: A History of Miami's Tropical Island and the Cape Florida Lighthouse* (Pineapple Press). Paperback volume covering the beginnings of Key Biscayne and the important role the lighthouse played in local water commerce.

Mark Derr *Some Kind of Paradise* (University Press of Florida). A cautionary history of Florida's penchant to mishandle its environmental assets, from spongers off the reefs to Miami's ruthless hotel contractors.

Donald C. Gaby *An Historical Guide to the Miami River and its Tributaries* (Historical Museum of Southern Florida). The river as water source and spur for development of the city, from early Tequesta settlements on.

Bill Pranty *A Birder's Guide to Florida* (American Birding Association). Detailed accounts of when and where to find Florida's birds, including maps and seasonal charts. Aimed at the expert but still good for the novice bird-watcher.

Travel impressions

T. D. Allman *Miami: City of the Future* (Grove/Atlantic o/p). Excellent, incisive look at modern Miami, which gets a bit bogged down when going further back than *Miami Vice*.

Edna Buchanan *The Corpse had a Familiar Face* (Random House). Sometimes sharp, often sensationalist account of the author's years spent pounding the crime beat for the *Miami Herald* – five thousand corpses and gore galore.

Joan Didion *Miami* (Vintage Books). A riveting though ultimately unsatisfying voyage around the impenetrably complex and wildly passionate exile politics of Cuban Miami.

Norman Mailer *Miami and the Siege of Chicago* (World Publications Inc). A rabid study of the American political conventions of 1968, the first part frothing over the Republican Party's shenanigans at Miami Beach when Nixon beat Reagan for the presidential ticket.

David Rieff *Going to Miami: Exiles, Tourists, and Refugees in the New America* (Penguin). An exploration of Miami through the minds of its conservative Cubans, its struggling black and Haitian communities, and its resentful Anglos – but with too many sexist musings to be credible.

Alexander Stuart *Life on Mars* (Transworld Publishers Limited o/p). "Paradise with a lobotomy" is how a friend of the author described Florida. This is an often amusing series of snapshots of both the empty lives led by the beautiful people of South Beach and the redneck "white trash" of upstate.

John Williams *Into the Badlands: Travels through urban America* (HarperCollins). The author's trek across the US to interview the country's best crime writers begins in Miami, "the city that coke built," its compelling strangeness all too briefly reveled in.

Architecture and photography

Barbara Baer Capitman *Deco Delights* (Dutton). A tour of Miami Beach's Art Deco buildings by the woman who championed their preservation.

Laura Cerwinske *Miami: Hot & Cool* (Three Rivers Press). Coffee-table tome with text on high-style south Florida living and glowing and color pics of Miami's beautiful homes and gardens. Her book *Tropical Deco: The Architecture & Design of Old Miami Beach* also delivers a wealth of architectural detail.

Gary Monroe *Life in South Beach* (Forest & T o/p). A slim volume of monochrome photos showing Miami Beach's South Beach before the restoration of the Art Deco District and the arrival of globetrotting trendies.

Arva Moore Parks *Miami Then & Now* (Centennial Press). A small paperback with black-and-white comparison photos side by side of what certain areas of the city looked like from as far back as 1880 to today. An interesting look at how development can dramatically affect the landscape.

Nicholas Patricios *Building Marvelous Miami* (University Press of Florida). A detailed account of how Miami moved from a poor trading post to a wealthy financial center; includes 250 photos documenting the city's architectural development.

Bill Wisser *South Beach: America's Riviera, Miami Beach, Florida* (Arcade). A comprehensive pictorial view of the Art Deco buildings in South Beach.

Fiction

Pat Booth *Miami* (Ballantine). It had to happen: bestselling author uses the glitz-and-glamour of Miami's South Beach as a backdrop to a pot-boiling tale of seduction and desire.

Edna Buchanan *Nobody Lives Forever* (Kensington Publishing Corp). Tense, psycho-killer thriller played out on the mean streets of Miami.

Marjory Stoneman Douglas *A River in Flood* (University Press of Florida). A collection of short stories (first published separately in the *Saturday Evening Post* in the Twenties and Thirties) that reflects on the many facets of Florida life: from hurricanes to cock

FICTION

fights. Today, nearly 110, Marjory Stoneman Douglas is the grand dame of Florida writers.

Stanley Elkin *Mrs Ted Bliss* (Hyperion). A newly widowed Miami Beacher finds herself mixed up with a drug lord and a Hebrew-speaking American Indian, in this amusing novel by the underrated late author.

Carl Hiaasen *Double Whammy* (Warner Books). Ferociously funny fishing thriller that brings together a classic collection of warped but believable Florida characters; among them a hermit-like ex-state governor, a cynical Cuban cop, and a corrupt TV preacher. By the same author, *Skin Tight* explores the perils of unskilled plastic surgery in a Miami crawling with mutant hitmen, bought politicians, and police on gangsters' payrolls. Hiaasen also helped write *Naked Came the Manatee* (Putnam), a serial novel actually done by a consortium of local writers, including Dave Barry and Edna Buchanan; it's a riotous, if slightly uneven tale full of local color.

Hialeah Jackson *The Alligator's Farewell* (Dell). A fast-paced detective novel set in Miami and the Keys – a private agency investigates an apparent suicide at a nuclear facility which leads to a wild trail of drugs, jewel thieves, gambling, and a strange assortment of reptiles.

David Leddick *My Worst Date* (St Martin's Press). Gay coming-of-age novel set in South Beach that rings true.

Elmore Leonard *Stick*; *La Brava* (William Morrow & Co). The pick of this highly recommended author's Florida-set thrillers, respectively detailing the rise of an opportunist through the money, sex, and drugs of Latino Miami; and a low-life on the seedy South Beach before the preservation of the Art Deco District.

Theodore Pratt *The Barefoot Mailman* (Florida Classics). A Forties account of the long-distance postman who kept the far-flung

FICTION

294

settlements of pioneer-period Florida in mail by hiking the many miles of beach between them.

John Sayles *Los Gusanos* (Harper Perennial). Absorbing, if long-winded novel set around the lives of Cuban exiles in Miami – written by a cult film director.

Ana Veciana Suarez *The Chin Kiss King* (Plume). A poignant look at three female generations in a Cuban-American family, living under one roof and trying to cope with tragedy, one another, and the modern city of Miami.

Charles Willeford *Miami Blues* (St Martin's Press). The best-known (also see "Film," p.298) but not the best of a highly recommended series starring Hoke Mosely, a cool and calculating, but very human, Miami cop. Superior titles in the series are *The Way We Die Now*, *Kiss Your Ass Goodbye*, and *Sideswipe*.

Cook books

Sue Mullin *Nuevo Cubano Cooking* (Chartwell Books). Easy-to-follow instructions and mouthwatering photographs of recipes fusing traditional Cuban cooking with nouvelle cuisine.

Steven Raichleu *Miami Spice* (Workman). Latin American and Caribbean cooking meets Florida and the "Deep South," resulting in some of the tastiest dishes in America. Clear recipes and interesting background information.

Caroline Stuart *The Food of Miami: Authentic Recipes from South Florida and the Keys* (Periplus World Food Cookbooks). Written by a Florida native, with recipes from some of Miami's top restaurants and hints on preparing local specialties.

Miami on film

Miami's location – and reputation for having a glamorous surface and a seedy underbelly – has made it a prime setting for Hollywood films. Most have to do with some form of escapism, whether that means a slick action flick, a riveting cop thriller, or just some libidinous teens coming to South Beach to take part in Spring Break-like activities. The following list of films, with director and year given, is by no means comprehensive but picks out the best – or at least most notable – of the bunch.

Ace Ventura, Pet Detective (Tom Shadyac, 1994). The film that launched Jim Carrey's thousand faces. Carrey stars as a bequiffed investigator on a quest to recover Snowflake, the Miami Dolphins' kidnapped mascot, on the eve of the Super Bowl.

The Bellboy (Jerry Lewis, 1960). This film was shot almost entirely within Miami Beach's ultra-kitsch pleasure palace *The Fontainebleau* (the same hotel where James Bond sunbathes in the beginning of 1964's *Goldfinger*). Jerry Lewis, in his debut as writer-director, plays Stanley, the bellhop from hell, and cameos as vacationing movie star "Jerry Lewis."

The Birdcage (Mike Nichols, 1996). Nichols' Miami remake of *La Cage Aux Folles* makes playful use of South Beach's gay scene, portraying the rejuvenated Art Deco playground as a bright paradise of pecs, thongs, and drag queens. Impresario Armand (Robin Williams) and reigning Birdcage diva Albert (Nathan Lane) are happily cohabitating until Armand's son brings his ultra-conservative future in-laws to dinner.

Black Sunday (John Frankenheimer, 1976). Palestinian terrorists, with the aid of disgruntled Vietnam vet Bruce Dern, plan to wipe out 80,000 football fans, including the President, in the Orange Bowl on Super Bowl Sunday. Though the first half of the movie

unfolds in Beirut and LA, the heart-stopping climax results in
some fine aerial views of Miami.

Blood and Wine (Bob Rafelson, 1997). Jack Nicholson plays a dodgy
Miami wine dealer with access to the cellars of Southern Florida's
rich and famous. He enlists a wheezy expat safe-breaker (Michael
Caine) and a feisty Cuban nanny (Jennifer Lopez) in his scheme to
snag a million-dollar necklace. When the jewels end up in the
hands of his jilted wife (Judy Davis) and perpetually pissed-off
stepson (Stephen Dorff) the action heads south to the Florida Keys.

The Cocoanuts (Joseph Santley & Robert Florey, 1929). Set during
Florida's real estate boom, the Marx Brothers' first film stars
Groucho as an impecunious hotel proprietor attempting to keep
his business afloat by auctioning off land (with the usual
interference from Chico and Harpo) in Cocoanut Grove, "the Palm
Beach of tomorrow." Groucho expounds on Florida's climate
while standing in what is really a sand-filled studio lot.

Get Shorty (Barry Sonnenfeld, 1995). John Travolta stars in this
black comedy about a Miami loan shark who flies to Los Angeles
to collect a debt and ends up making films. The movie is based
on Elmore Leonard's book of the same name, and only features
the city for a short time in the beginning.

The Heartbreak Kid (Elaine May, 1972). An underrated comic
masterpiece written by Neil Simon, in which Charles Grodin
marries a nice Jewish girl, and then, on the honeymoon drive
down to Miami, starts to regret it. His doubts are compounded
when goddess Cybil Shephard starts flirting with him on the
beach while his sunburnt bride lies in bed.

A Hole in the Head (Frank Capra, 1959). Frank Sinatra plays an
irresponsible Miami Beach hotel owner who has dreams of
striking it rich by turning South Beach into "Disneyland." The
breezy opening titles are pulled on airborne banners across the
Miami Beach skyline.

FILM

Illtown (Nick Gomez, 1995). Tony Danza stars as a gay mob boss, and a gaggle of familiar indie stars (Michael Rapaport, Adam Trese, Lili Taylor, and Kevin Corrigan) play an unlikely bunch of Miami drug dealers.

Miami Blues (George Armitage, 1990). Adapted from Charles Willeford's fiction, this quirky crime story about a home-loving psychopath (Alec Baldwin), the naive hooker he shacks up with (Jennifer Jason Leigh), and the burnt-out homicide detective who's on their trail (Fred Ward), is set in a seedy back-street Miami that glitters with terrific characters, gritty performances, and delicious offbeat details.

Miami Rhapsody (David Frankel, 1995). Sarah Jessica Parker (kvetching like a female Woody Allen) weighs commitment against the marital dissatisfaction and compulsive infidelity of her extended family in an otherwise picture-perfect Miami.

Moon Over Miami (Walter Lang, 1941). Gold-digging, Texas-hamburger-stand waitress Betty Grable takes her sister and aunt to Miami, "where rich men are as plentiful as grapefruit, and millionaires hang from every palm tree." Grable has little trouble snagging herself a couple of ripe ones in this colorful, sappy musical comedy. On-location shooting took place in Winter Haven and Ocala, a few hundred miles north of Miami.

Salesman (The Maysles Brothers, 1968). The second half of this brilliant and moving documentary follows four Bible salesman to Opa-Locka on the outskirts of Miami. It's not a tale of beaches and luxury hotels, but rather low-rent apartments, cheap motels, and the quiet desperation of four men trying to sell overpriced illustrated Bibles door-to-door.

Scarface (Brian De Palma, 1983). Small-time Cuban thug Tony Montana arrives in Miami during the 1980 Mariel boatlift and murders, bullies, and snorts his way to the top of his profession, becoming Miami's most powerful drug lord. One of the great

FILM

Florida movies, De Palma's seductive and shocking paean to excess and the perversion of the American Dream stars Al Pacino in a legendary, go-for-broke performance.

Some Like It Hot (Billy Wilder, 1959). Wilder's classic farce starts in 1929 in Chicago. Jazz musicians Tony Curtis and Jack Lemmon escape retribution for witnessing the St Valentine's Day massacre by disguising themselves as women and joining an all-girl jazz band on a train to Miami. Though *Some Like it Hot* could be a candidate for the best film ever set in Miami, it was actually shot at the *Hotel del Coronado* in San Diego.

The Specialist (Luis Llosa, 1994). Sharon Stone seeks revenge on Miami mobsters who wiped out her family and hires ex-CIA expert Sylvester Stallone to carry out her plan. Rather formulaic, but there are incredible views of the city throughout including cinematic scenes along the MacArthur Causeway with the cruise ships and skyline behind them, and numerous shots of the *Clay Hotel*.

Striptease (Andrew Bergman, 1996). Demi Moore shows off her new assets in this so-called comedy when financial difficulties arise from the strain of being a single mom and raising a kid. She turns to stripping in a sleazy Miami club and earns her money the hard way.

There's Something About Mary (The Farrelly Brothers, 1998). Years after a heinous pre-prom disaster (involving an unruly zipper), Rhode Island geek Ben Stiller tracks down Mary, the eponymous object of his affection, to her new home in Miami. Once there he finds he's not the only one suffering from obsessive tendencies. A hysterical, gross-out masterpiece.

Tony Rome (Gordon Douglas, 1967). Wise-cracking, hard-living private eye Frank Sinatra tangles with pushers, strippers, gold diggers, and self-made millionaires on the wild side of Miami (the town his love interest Jill St John calls "Twenty miles of beach looking for a city"). The film is a run-of-the-mill detective yarn, but Frank was entertaining enough to warrant a sequel: *Lady in Cement*.

True Lies (James Cameron, 1994). Blockbuster action flick with Arnold Schwarzenegger as a CIA surveillance agent, Jamie Lee Curtis his unsuspecting wife, and Tom Arnold his partner along for comic relief. The scene where they blow up the bridge is an old causeway in Miami Beach that is now a dive site and can be viewed underwater.

INDEX

Rough Guides
on the Web

www.travel.roughguides.com

We keep getting bigger and better! The Rough Guide to Travel Online
now covers more than 14,000 searchable locations. You're just a click
away from access to the most in-depth travel content, weekly
destination features, online reservation services, and an outspoken
community of fellow travelers. Whether you're looking for ideas for
your next holiday or you know exactly where you're going, join us online.

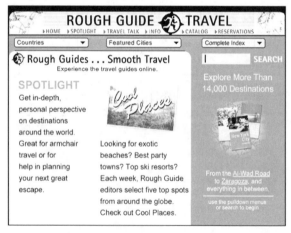

You can also find us on Yahoo!® Travel (http://travel.yahoo.com) and
Microsoft Expedia® UK (http://www.expediauk.com).

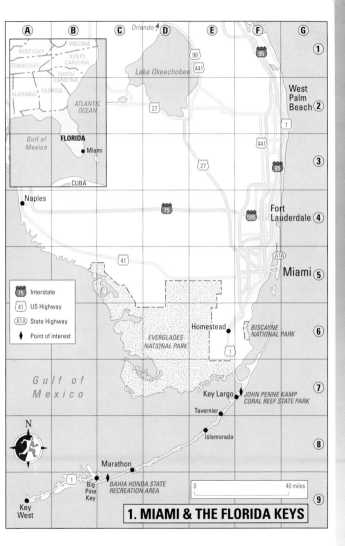

1. MIAMI & THE FLORIDA KEYS

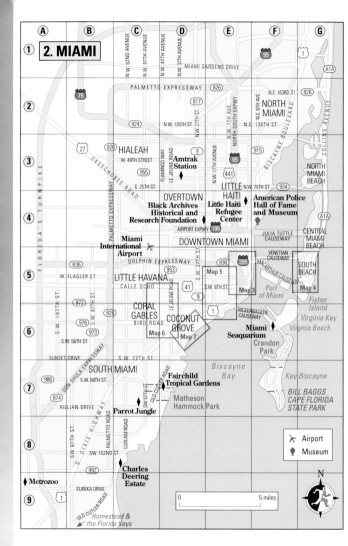

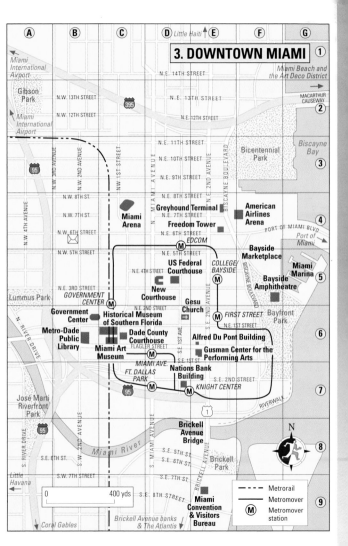

3. DOWNTOWN MIAMI

Little Haiti

Miami Beach and
the Art Deco District

Miami
International
Airport

Gibson
Park

N.E. 14TH STREET

MACARTHUR
CAUSEWAY

N.W. 13TH STREET

N.E. 13TH STREET

2

395

N.E. 12TH STREET

Miami
International
Airport

N.E. 11TH STREET

Biscayne
Bay

95

N.E. 10TH STREET

Bicentennial
Park

3

N.E. 9TH STREET

N.W. 8TH ST.

N.E. 8TH STREET

N.W. 7TH STREET

Greyhound Terminal

American
Airlines
Arena

Miami
Arena

N.E. 7TH STREET

N.W. 6TH STREET

Freedom Tower

PORT OF MIAMI BLVD.

4

N.E. 6TH STREET

Port of
Miami

N.W. 5TH STREET

EDCOM

N.E. 5TH STREET

Bayside
Marketplace

Lummus Park

N.E. 3RD STREET

N.E. 4TH STREET

US Federal
Courthouse

COLLEGE/
BAYSIDE

Miami
Marina

5

GOVERNMENT
CENTER

New
Courthouse

Gesu
Church

Bayside
Amphitheatre

Government
Center

Historical Museum
of Southern Florida

N.E. 2ND STREET

FIRST STREET

Bayfront
Park

Metro-Dade
Public
Library

Dade County
Courthouse

N.E. 1ST STREET

6

FLAGLER STREET

Alfred Du Pont Building

Miami Art
Museum

MIAMI AVE.

Gusman Center for the
Performing Arts

FT. DALLAS
PARK

S.E. 1ST ST.

Nations Bank
Building

95

S.E. 2ND STREET

José Martí
Riverfront
Park

KNIGHT CENTER

7

RIVERWALK

95

1

Brickell
Avenue
Bridge

N

8

Miami River

S.E. 5TH ST.

Brickell
Park

Little
Havana

S.E. 6TH ST.

0   400 yds

S.E. 7TH STREET

Coral Gables

S.E. 8TH STREET

Brickell Avenue banks
& The Atlantis

Miami
Convention
& Visitors
Bureau

9

- - - - Metrorail
──── Metromover
Ⓜ Metromover
station

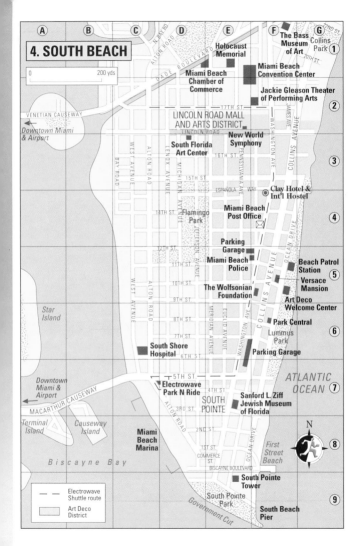

4. SOUTH BEACH

0 ——————— 200 yds

(A) (B) (C) (D) (E) (F) (G)

ALTON ROAD
DADE BOULEVARD
BAY RD
72ND ST.
20TH ST.

The Bass Museum of Art — (1)
Collins Park — (1)

Holocaust Memorial

Miami Beach Chamber of Commerce

Miami Beach Convention Center

Jackie Gleason Theater of Performing Arts — (2)

VENETIAN CAUSEWAY

Downtown Miami & Airport

17TH ST.

LINCOLN ROAD MALL AND ARTS DISTRICT
LINCOLN ROAD

New World Symphony

South Florida Art Center

WEST AVENUE
BAY ROAD
ALTON ROAD
LENOX AVENUE
MICHIGAN AVENUE
16TH ST.
PENNSYLVANIA AVE.
WASHINGTON AVENUE
JAMES AVE.
COLLINS AVENUE

— (3)

15TH ST.

ESPAÑOLA WAY

Clay Hotel & Int'l Hostel

Flamingo Park

Miami Beach Post Office

14TH ST.
JEFFERSON AVENUE
MERIDIAN AVENUE
OCEAN DRIVE

— (4)

Parking Garage

Miami Beach Police

12TH ST.
11TH ST.

Beach Patrol Station — (5)

Versace Mansion

The Wolfsonian Foundation

10TH ST.
9TH ST.
EUCLID AVENUE
COLLINS AVENUE

Art Deco Welcome Center

Park Central

8TH ST.

Lummus Park

7TH ST.

Parking Garage — (6)

Star Island

South Shore Hospital

6TH ST.
5TH ST.

ATLANTIC OCEAN — (7)

Downtown Miami & Airport

MACARTHUR CAUSEWAY

Electrowave Park N Ride

4TH ST.

SOUTH POINTE

3RD ST.

Sanford L. Ziff Jewish Museum of Florida

Terminal Island

Causeway Island

2ND ST.

Miami Beach Marina

1ST ST.
COMMERCE ST.
BISCAYNE BOULEVARD

N

First Street Beach — (8)

Biscayne Bay

South Pointe Tower

South Pointe Park

Government Cut

South Beach Pier — (9)

— — — Electrowave Shuttle route

▭ Art Deco District

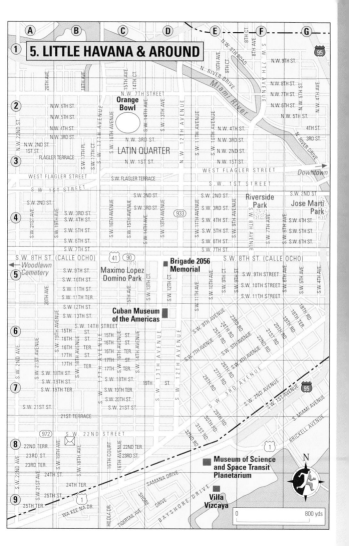

5. LITTLE HAVANA & AROUND

Orange Bowl

LATIN QUARTER

Miami River

Downtown

Riverside Park

Jose Marti Park

Woodlawn Cemetery

Maximo Lopez Domino Park

Brigade 2056 Memorial

Cuban Museum of the Americas

Museum of Science and Space Transit Planetarium

Villa Vizcaya

0   800 yds

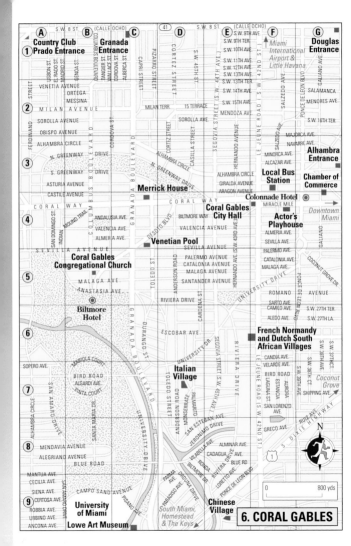

6. CORAL GABLES

S.W. 8TH ST. (CALLE OCHO) · 41 · S.W. 8TH ST. (CALLE OCHO)

A **B** **C** **D** **E** **F** **G**

(1) Country Club Prado Entrance — Granada Entrance — Douglas Entrance

Miami International Airport & Little Havana

S.W. 9TH AVE.
S.W. 10TH AVE.
S.W. 11TH AVE.
S.W. 12TH AVE.
S.W. 13TH AVE.
S.W. 14TH AVE.
S.W. 15TH AVE.

LISBON ST. · EL PRADO ST. · MADRID ST. · GENOA ST. · ZAMORA ST. · TANGIER ST. · WALLACE ST. · CORDOVA ST. · ALBERCA ST. · CAPRI STREET · PIZARRO STREET · CORTEZ STREET · S.W. 43RD AVE. · SEGOVIA STREET (S.W. 44TH AVE.) · HERNANDO AVENUE · LE JEUNE ROAD (S.W. 42ND ST.) · SALZEDO AVE. · PONCE DE LEON BLVD · GALIANO AVE.

COLUMBUS BOULEVARD

VENETIA AVENUE
ORTEGA
MESSINA
SALAMANCA
MENORES AVE.

(2) MILAN AVENUE — MILAN TERR. — 15 TERRACE — S.W. 16TH TER.

FERDINAND STREET

SOROLLA AVENUE — SOROLLA AVE.
OBISPO AVENUE
ALHAMBRA CIRCLE — ALHAMBRA CIRCLE

MAJORCA AVE.
NAVARRE AVE.
MINORCA AVE.
ALCAZAR AVE.

Alhambra Entrance

(3) N. GREENWAY — N. GREENWAY DRIVE — ALHAMBRA CIRCLE — GIRALDA AVENUE — ARAGON AVENUE

S. GREENWAY
ASTURIA AVENUE

Local Bus Station

Chamber of Commerce

CASTILE AVENUE

Merrick House

Colonnade Hotel

(4) CORAL WAY — CORAL WAY — MIRACLE MILE

Coral Gables City Hall

Downtown Miami

SAN DOMINGO ST. · INDIAN MOUND TRAIL · BILTMORE WAY

ANDALUSIA AVE.
VALENCIA AVE.
ALMERIA AVE.

GRANADA BOULEVARD · DESOTO BLVD · CASILLA STREET · CORTEZ STREET

Actor's Playhouse

ALMERIA AVE.
SEVILLA AVE.
PALERMO AVE.

GALIANO

(5) SEVILLA AVENUE — SEVILLA AVENUE

Venetian Pool

Coral Gables Congregational Church

MALAGA AVE.
ANASTASIA AVE.

PALERMO AVENUE
CATALONIA AVENUE — CATALONIA AVE.
MALAGA AVENUE — MALAGA AVE.
SANTANDER AVENUE

ANDERSON ROAD · IS DE TOLEDO ST · CARDENAS ST. · HERNANDO (S.W. 40TH AVE.)

RIVIERA DRIVE

ROMANO AVENUE
SARTO AVE.
CAMILO AVE. — S.W. 27TH TER.
ALEDO AVE. — S.W. 27TH LA.

PONCE DE LEON BLVD · COCONUT GROVE DR · UNIVERSITY DRIVE

(6) **Biltmore Hotel**

ESCOBAR AVE.

French Normandy and Dutch South African Villages

GRANADA ST. · DURANGO ST. · UNIVERSITY DR. · SEGOVIA STREET (S.W. 45TH AVE.) · RIVIERA DRIVE

CANDIA AVE.
VELARDE AVE.
BIRD ROAD
ESTANZA
AURORA
SAN LORENZO AVE.

Coconut Grove

S.W. 37TH CT. · S.W. 38TH AVE. · S.W. 36TH CT. · S.W. 39TH AVE. · SHIPPING AVE.

(7) SOPERO AVE.

MARQUILA COURT
BIRD ROAD
ALGARDI AVE.
PINTA COURT

Italian Village

SAN AMARO DRIVE · SANTA MARIA DR. · ANDERSON ROAD · TOLEDO STREET · MONSERRATE · PALMARITO · SAN ESTEBAN DR · LE JEUNE ROAD (S. W. 42ND ST.)

GRECO AVE.

ROUTE 1 · S. DIXIE HIGHWAY

N

(8) MENDAVIA AVENUE
ALEGRIANO AVENUE
BLUE ROAD

JERONIMO DRIVE
ALMINAR AVE.
VILABELLA AVE.
CADAGUA AVE.
RONDA — BLUE RD.
RIVIERA DRIVE

ALHAMBRA CIRCLE

(9) MANTUA AVE.
CECILIA AVE.
SIENA AVE.
CERTOSA AVE.
ROBBIA AVE.
URBINO AVE.
ANCONA AVE.

ALGARDI AVE. · SAN AMARO DRIVE · CAMPO SAND AVENUE · PISANO ST.

University of Miami

Lowe Art Museum

PARMA AVE. · ROBBIA AVE. · PARADISO AVE. · ORDUNA DRIVE · RONDA · RIVIERA DRIVE · BLUE RD. · LORETTO AVE. · PONCE DE LEON BLVD

Chinese Village

South Miami, Homestead & The Keys

0 — 800 yds

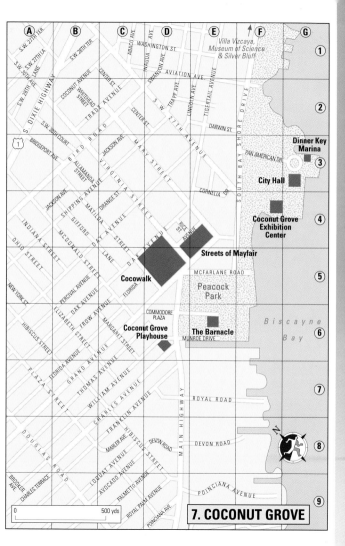

7. COCONUT GROVE

Map Labels

Columns (top): A · B · C · D · E · F · G
Rows (right): 1 · 2 · 3 · 4 · 5 · 6 · 7 · 8 · 9

Villa Vizcaya, Museum of Science & Silver Bluff

Dinner Key Marina

City Hall

Coconut Grove Exhibition Center

Streets of Mayfair

Cocowalk

Peacock Park

Biscayne Bay

Coconut Grove Playhouse

The Barnacle

Streets
S.W. 27TH TER.
S.W. 27TH LA
S.W. 27TH LANE
S.W. 30TH AVE
S.W. 28TH ST
S.W. 28TH TER.
ABACO AVE
WASHINGTON ST.
INAGUA AVE
CENTER ST
COCONUT AVENUE
WHITEHEAD STREET
TRADE AVENUE
SWANSON AVE
AVIATION AVE
TRAPP AVE
LINCOLN AVE
TIGERTAIL AVENUE
SOUTH BAY SHORE DRIVE
S. DIXIE HIGHWAY
S.W. 30TH COURT
BRIDGEPORT AVE
BIRD ROAD
JACKSON AVE
VIRGINIA STREET
MARY STREET
S.W. 27TH AVENUE
CENTER ST
DARWIN ST.
PAN AMERICAN DR.
CORNELIA DR.
ALLAMANDA STREET
SHIPPING AVENUE
MATILDA STREET
ORANGE ST
GIFFORD LANE
McDONALD STREET
DAY AVENUE
OAK AVENUE
RICE ST.
AVENUE
INDIANA STREET
OHIO STREET
NEW YORK ST.
PERCIVAL AVENUE
OAK AVENUE
FLORIDA
ELIZABETH STREET
FROW AVENUE
MARGARET STREET
COMMODORE PLAZA
McFARLANE ROAD
HIBISCUS STREET
PLAZA STREET
FLORIDA AVENUE
GRAND AVENUE
THOMAS AVENUE
WILLIAM AVENUE
CHARLES AVENUE
MUNROE DRIVE
MAIN HIGHWAY
ROYAL ROAD
DOUGLAS ROAD
FRANKLIN AVENUE
HIBISCUS STREET
DEVON ROAD
MARLER AVE
BROOKER AVE.
CHARLES TERRACE
LOQUAT AVENUE
AVOCADO AVENUE
PALMETTO AVENUE
ROYAL PALM AVENUE
POINCIANA AVE.
POINCIANA AVENUE

0 _____ 500 yds

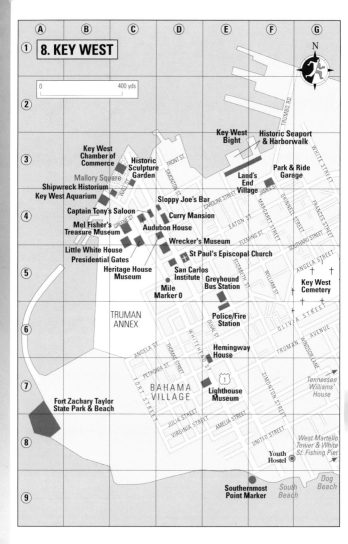

8. KEY WEST

N

0   400 yds

Key West Chamber of Commerce
Historic Sculpture Garden
Key West Bight
Historic Seaport & Harborwalk
Mallory Square
Shipwreck Historium
Key West Aquarium
Land's End Village
Park & Ride Garage
Sloppy Joe's Bar
Captain Tony's Saloon
Curry Mansion
Mel Fisher's Treasure Museum
Audubon House
Wrecker's Museum
Little White House
St Paul's Episcopal Church
Presidential Gates
Heritage House Museum
San Carlos Institute
Greyhound Bus Station
Key West Cemetery
Mile Marker 0
Police/Fire Station
TRUMAN ANNEX
Hemingway House
BAHAMA VILLAGE
Lighthouse Museum
Tennessee Williams' House
Fort Zachary Taylor State Park & Beach
Youth Hostel
West Martello Tower & White St. Fishing Pier
Southernmost Point Marker
South Beach
Dog Beach

FRONT ST.
SIMONTON ST.
TRUMBO RD.
WHITE STREET
JAMES ST.
MARGARET STREET
GRINNELL STREET
FRANCES STREET
CAROLINE STREET
EATON ST.
FLEMING ST.
SOUTHARD STREET
ANGELA STREET
WILLIAM ST.
ELIZABETH ST.
OLIVIA STREET
TRUMAN AVENUE
ANGELA ST.
THOMAS STREET
WHITEHEAD ST.
DUVAL ST.
PETRONIA STREET
FORT STREET
SIMONTON STREET
WINDSOR LANE
JULIA STREET
VIRGINIA STREET
AMELIA STREET
UNITED STREET